GUIDE TO
Economic
Indicators

SECOND EDITION

GUIDE TO
Economic
Indicators

SECOND EDITION

NORMAN FRUMKIN

M.E. Sharpe
Armonk, New York
London, England

Library of Congress Cataloging-in Publication Data

Frumkin, Norman.
Guide to economic indicators / by Norman Frumkin—2nd ed.
p. cm.
Includes bibliographical references and index.
ISBN 1-56324-243-5—ISBN 1-56324-244-3 (pbk.)
1. Economic indicators—United States.
2. Business cycles—United States—Statistics.
3. United States—Economic conditions—Statistics.
I. Title.
HC103.F9 1994
330.973'0021—dc19
94-4400
CIP

Printed in the United States of America

The paper used in this publication meets the minimum requirements of
American National Standard for Information Sciences—
Permanence of Paper for Printed Library Materials,
ANSI Z 39.48-1984.

♾

BB (c)   10   9   8   7   6   5   4   3   2   1
BB (p)   10   9   8   7   6   5   4   3   2   1

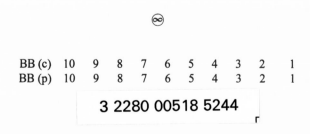

To Sarah, Jacob, and Samuel

In memory of
Anne Frances Frumkin and Joseph Harry Frumkin

CONTENTS

ILLUSTRATIONS

Tables

Figures

PREFACE

Guide to Economic Indicators is a reference book that provides basic information on the nature of over sixty statistical measures of the performance of the American economy. It is meant for economists and for those with no special training in economics.

This second edition updates the explanations of the indicators and the data themselves to reflect their characteristics as of 1994. It also expands the coverage to include several new indicators and new introductory topics. The new indicators are:

- Retail sales
- Corporate profits
- Collective bargaining settlements
- Home sales
- Business firm formation and growth
- Growth cycles
- Experimental recession indexes
- Business optimism indexes
- Purchasing managers' index
- Federal funds interest rates
- Nasdaq and AMEX stock market price indexes

The new introductory topics are the calculation of growth

rates, the use of graphics in presenting economic data, and distinctions between items defined as goods, services, and structures.

Richard Bartel, editor of *Challenge*, suggested a second edition to reflect the evolving nature of the indicators. I appreciate his continuing interest in my work.

Edward Steinberg reviewed all of the new material and several modifications to the existing text. His incisive comments raised the level of the discussion and clarified the exposition. David Hirschberg called my attention to the new data on business firm formation and growth and provided the initial writeup for that section. As a result of a discussion with Steven Rurka on the credibility of economic statistics produced by the federal government, I have included a section on the integrity of economic indicators below in this preface. Others whom I thank for reviewing particular sections are: Alvin Bauman, Robert Bretz, Glenn Crellin, Jerry Donahoe, Joseph Duncan, Sarah Frumkin, Joseph Gilvary, Gary Katz, Bradford Leigh, Jean Maltz, Ronald Piencykoski, Fritz Scheuren, James Spellman, James Stock, Theodore Torda, Jack Triplett, Mark Watson, Othmar Winkler, and Paul Zarrett. While their contibututions helped considerably, I am responsible for the book. The staff of M. E. Sharpe expertly converted the manuscript into the book: Christine Florie was the project editor; Bessie Blum was the copyeditor; Nancy Connick was the typesetter.

Maintaining the Integrity of Economic Indicators

Economic indicators are more than "statistics." They are the factual base for public policies and actions that affect the economic well-being of all Americans. It is essential for the vitality of a democracy that these data be impeccably objective, that they be prepared with the highest professional standards, and that they have no hint of political interference. Only with such integrity will the people have confidence in the data.

The indicators are produced mainly by agencies in the executive branch of the U.S. government, such as the Bureau of the

Census, Bureau of Labor Statistics, Bureau of Economic Analysis, National Agricultural Statistics Service, and the Internal Revenue Service. From the 1970s to the early 1990s, there have been occasional allegations that the indicators were politicized by "cooking" the preparation of the statistics to make the president who is in office at the time look better. On further examination, these allegations of tampering with the data were shown to be unfounded. Although this is comforting, it still leaves the possibility of future tainting, which must be guarded against. While some data may be more vulnerable to "cooking" than others— for example, the estimation of the gross domestic product is based on more statistical judgments that conceivably could be shaded than is the unemployment rate, which is based on household survey information—the possibility of tampering exists with all data.

One institutional device for insulating statistical agencies from political pressure is for the head of the agency to be appointed by the president and confirmed by the Senate, as is done for the director of the census, commissioner of labor statistics, and commissioner of internal revenue. This may give the agency heads the appearance, if not the reality, of heightened stature for resisting pressures from their political superiors, which in these cases are the secretary of commerce, secretary of labor, and secretary of the treasury. Senate confirmation probably has greater weight when it is specified for a period of time that does not coincide with the presidential term, as is the case of the four-year term for the commissioner of labor statistics. At the same time, a career civil service employee probably has more independence than a political official. Thus, to the extent that an agency head who is confirmed by the Senate in reality becomes a political official, the "independence effect" of the confirmation is diminished. There obviously are no tidy answers.

A second institutional device that may lessen political interference with the data is the Office of Management and Budget's directive, which requires statistical agencies of the federal government to limit access to their facilities where the data for major economic indicators are being prepared preceding the day when they are released to the public (referred to as a "lockup"). During the lockup, which may last several days, only certain employees of the statistical agency have access to the data. The lockup was originally instituted to prevent leaks of unpublished data that give recipients of leaks an unfair advantage in financial markets, but it could have a secondary benefit of fending off attempts to interfere with the data preparation. On the other hand, the argument can be made that if many people know a number ahead of time, a political appointee could not have that number changed without causing a scandal; if, however, only a few people know the number, the political appointee could conceivably use some leverage (for example, the threat of funding cuts) to get them to change the number. Again, there are no tidy answers.

On balance, I believe the above mechanisms of Senate confirmation of statistical agency heads and of limiting access to the data preparation through the lockup procedure lessen the chances that economic indicators can be compromised. But no system is foolproof when there is a determination to violate it. Thus, these and future measures to protect the integrity of data will reduce, but not eliminate, attempts to contaminate the data for political gain. Therefore, it is essential that the press and analysts be vigilant in safeguarding the integrity of the numbers and sound the alarm when they believe the data may be suspect. This is added insurance for maintaining accurate information, which is a bulwark of a free society.

References

Office of Management and Budget, Executive Office of the President. 1985. "Statistical Policy Directive No. 3: Compilation, Release, and Evaluation of Principal Federal Economic Indicators." *Federal Register*. September 25.

Duncan, Joseph W. 1993. "Integrity in Official Statistics." *Business Economics*. July.

Johnson, Bruce, and Lori Rectanus. 1993. "The Integrity of

Federal Statistics: A Case Study from the GAO Perspective." *Business Economics*. July.

Carson, Carol S. 1993. "Assuring Integrity for Federal Statistics: Focus on GDP." *Business Economics*. July.

Norwood, Janet L. 1993. "Perception or Reality: Can We Trust Federal Statistics." *Business Economics*. July.

GUIDE TO
Economic
Indicators

SECOND EDITION

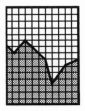

1
INTRODUCTION

This book provides concise descriptions of over sixty economic indicators developed primarily by U.S. government agencies but also by private organizations. The indicators reflect the overall dimensions of the domestic and international aspects of the American economy as well as particular segments of it.

This introduction briefly describes how the indicators are used to track the economy and provides background material on using economic indicators, including how to interpret changes in them and how to evaluate their accuracy and presentation. The introduction concludes by explaining how the information in this book is arranged.

Interpreting Business Cycles
with Economic Indicators

The economy continually operates in recurring phases of rising and falling activity, which are referred to as business cycles. Economic indicators are used to measure overall economic activity for classifying it as rising (expansion) or falling (recession), as well as to determine the cyclical turning points of these expansions and recessions. The actual and technical determination of expansions and recessions is made by a committee of economists under the auspices of the National Bureau of Economic Research

(NBER), a private nonprofit economic research organization. The dating of business cycles by this nongovernmental organization is adopted by the U.S. government as the official periods of expansion and recession. It is accepted by a wide range of economists and politicians, regardless of their differing views regarding economic analysis and policy formulation.

The NBER committee does not rely on a specific formula. The committee bases its decision on judgments about the overall direction in which the preponderance of the indicators are moving. For example, a recession is often but not always indicated when the real gross domestic product (GDP in constant dollars, which abstracts from rising or falling prices) declines for two successive quarters. Sometimes several indicators move contrary to the GDP trend. One of the challenges of economic analysis is to assess the import of such variations.

Most analysis of economic indicators, then, is concerned with changes in the indicators over time—the cyclical fluctuations between expansion and growth and recession and decline. While the absolute volume or level of economic activity is of some interest, movements from one period to the next are more important for tracking the economy. The indicators often show change in terms of percent or as index numbers, making relative comparisons over long time periods easier. It is customary to think in terms of one year in assessing economic performance. Over the period of a year, of course, some changes simply reflect natural seasonal variations. Thus, to interpret indicators effectively, an analyst must understand index numbers, annualized and annual movements, and seasonality. In addition, because those indicators that are measured in dollars (such as the gross domestic product or wage earnings) are affected by increases and decreases in prices, the analyst must understand the measurement of indicators in constant dollars that abstract from these price changes. It also is important for the analyst to understand how alternative methods of calculating growth rates and charting economic data graphically lead to different perceptions of economic performance.

Index Numbers

Economic data represent the myriad of transactions between buyers and sellers in consumer, industrial, labor, and financial markets involving both private parties and governments. In order to analyze this vast amount of detail, the transactions are summarized into groups and overall totals. One method of summarizing is through index numbers, which are a convenient way of quickly assessing the direction and level of changes in economic activity. Index numbers are typically associated with indicators of industrial production and prices, although they are also used for many other economic activities.

An index number starts with a base period, usually a single year or the average of a few consecutive years. The base period is typically (but not always) defined as equivalent to 100, and all levels of activity of the indicator before and after the base period are represented as percentage differences from the base. For example, using the base of 100, an index of 95 means that the indicator for that period (month, quarter, or year) is 5 percent below the base period, and an index of 128 means that the indicator is 28 percent above the base period. The formula for calculating the percent change between two periods is:

$$\frac{\text{Period 2}}{\text{Period 1}} - 1.0 \times 100.$$

Thus, in the example,

$$\frac{128}{95} = 1.347 - 1.0 = 0.347 \times 100 = 34.7\%.$$

Assuming 95 is the period 1 index and 128 is the period 2 index, the percent change between the two periods is 34.7.

The base period is typically selected according to the availability of detailed survey data. It also is desirable that the period be one during which the economy is relatively balanced, neither one that is booming with high inflation nor one that is depressed with high unemployment. However, this criterion is secondary. The availability of the required data dominates the determination of the base period.

There are two typical ways (but these are not the only ones) of using the base period as a point of departure in constructing the index. One is to assume that the relative importance of each item in the index (referred to as weights) is unchanged over time, and the only factor resulting in a change in the index is the movement of the components over time—for example, production for a production index or prices for a price index. The other is to assume that changes in the importance of one item to another in the index do occur, as one existing item is substituted for another or replaced by a new product because of changing prices and tastes and new technologies. In this case, changes in the index result from the effects of substitution and new products, as well as from the movement of the basic production or price character- istic of the index.

These differing methodologies affect the movements of pro- duction and price indexes over time. Both involve the quantity and price components of the value of each item in the index. For production indexes, when the relative price of each item is held constant from the base period, a higher rate of growth in produc- tion (or lower rate of production decline) typically appears over time compared with when the relative importance of each item reflects the current period price. This occurs because a new prod- uct with high growth rates often has a high price when intro- duced, and the price subsequently declines as output expands. For price indexes, the effect of maintaining the same relative quantity of each item in the index over time tends to show a higher rate of price increase (or lower rate of price decline) than when each item in the index represents the actual items bought in each period as a result of buyers switching to lower-priced sub- stitutes and new products (after the new product price declines).

Preference for using either methodology depends on the analytic use intended for the index. For example, when the focus is on measuring price change for purchasing the same items over time, a price index based on constant weights is used; but when the focus is on measuring price change for the actual items purchased, a current-weighted price index is used. It is sometimes difficult to determine which one more accurately reflects actual economic behavior. When two indexes are available for the same activity based on the alternative methodologies, changes over time may be considered as a range bounded by the lower and upper limits rather than as a single figure.

Annualized and Annual Movements

Three measures are related to annual trends: the seasonally adjusted annual rate, annual change, and December-to December or fourth-quarter-to fourth quarter change.

The *seasonally adjusted annual rate* (SAAR) reflects what the yearly movement of the indicator would be if the same rate of change (adjusted for seasonal variations) were to continue for the next eleven months (monthly indicator) or for the next three quarters (quarterly indicator). This figure represents the same rate of change for the current month or quarter compounded over the rest of the year. The SAAR provides a quick view of how a very short-term movement compares with a twelve-month period. It also facilitates comparisons of growth rates for periods of differing lengths. However, it is important to recognize that SAAR figures assume a constant rate of change for comparative purposes only—they are not meant to forecast what is expected to occur.

Annual change figures compare the average level of the indicator in one year with the average level of the next year. These averages are computed from data for the twelve months or four quarters of the indicator and, thus, help to compensate for the effects of unusually high or low activity periods when analyzing short periods during the year.

December-to-December or *fourth-quarter-to-fourth quarter change* figures focus on economic change from the end of one calendar year to the end of the next calendar year. This kind of data is often used in economic reports at the beginning of the calendar year to predict the coming twelve months. It provides a more current assessment of the most recent and coming twelve-month periods that the above annual change figures. However, any single period during the year may have abnormally high or low rates of economic growth or inflation. Because these data are not averaged over an annual period, they can provide a distorted view of annual change.

Seasonality

There are many factors—such as changes in the weather, holidays, school vacations, yearly automobile model changes, annual tax returns, and so forth—that cause normal seasonal up and down movements in economic activity during the year. If not taken into account, these fluctuations could distort real trends in the economy. (See Figure 1.1, which charts retail sales during 1992 in both seasonally adjusted and unadjusted numbers.) For example, Christmas buying can make the economy look prosperous in December when, in fact, Christmas shopping is below average. Or the normal summer shutdown of auto assembly plants for the new model year can make the economy look dormant in the summer when, in fact, fewer plants have shut down than is typical. To prevent seasonal variations from distorting the economic picture, most economic data are seasonally adjusted.

Seasonal adjustment attempts to eliminate movements in economic indicators caused by such factors as increased sales in November and December due to Christmas shopping, decreased construction work in winter because of cold weather, and the large number of students looking for work in summer months. The adjustments are based on experience in previous years and capture typical movements that are expected from the average experience. Because they cannot indicate special circumstances in particular time periods, however, aberrations should be watched for in analyzing current trends.

Figure 1.1 **Seasonal Patterns of Retail Sales: 1992**

Millions of dollars

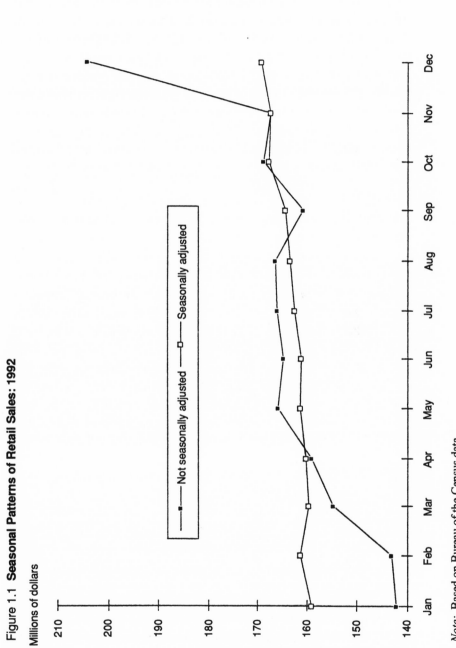

Note: Based on Bureau of the Census data.

For those indicators that are not seasonally adjusted, comparing trends of several consecutive months with the same months of the previous year is an indirect technique of seasonal adjustment that helps determine when the indicator is actually rising or falling. However, this method cannot identity cyclical turning points on a current basis because it focuses on year-to-year monthly change and does not provide a seasonally adjusted view of current movements in their own right.

It is beyond the scope of this book to detail the various statistical techniques of making seasonal adjustments or to analyze whether any particular indicator should be seasonally adjusted. However, the source publications of monthly or quarterly indicators and this book note whether, in fact, each indicator is seasonally adjusted or not.

Current Dollars versus Constant Dollars

Many economic indicators are measured in current and constant dollars. Current dollars include the combined effect of changes in quantity and price over time, and, thus, represent the *dollar value* of economic activity. For example, the value of retail sales shoes includes the number of pairs of shoes multiplied by their unit prices. Constant dollars only include the effect of changes in quantity over time, which is the *physical volume* of economic activity. Constant dollar figures, which are stated in prices of a particular base period such as 1987 dollars, are not affected by increases or decreases in prices. Because constant dollars are based on what the value would be if prices were the same as in the base period, they are a measure of quantity.

Constant dollar figures are difficult to relate to as actual figures because of price changes since the base period. For example, in the 1990s it is difficult to think of average weekly earnings in 1987 dollars. However, for some analyses, such as rates of economic growth or changes in workers' purchasing power, a measure of quantity (in constant dollars) rather than a measure of value (in current dollars) is the relevant figure. For example, it is far more meaningful to compare the change in weekly wages measured in constant dollars than in current dollars because of the effect of inflation on purchasing power. Thus, while wages in current dollars may have risen from one period to the next, wages in constant dollars may have declined because prices of goods and services that workers buy rose more than wages and, consequently, workers' purchasing power (or real income) declined.

Evaluating the Accuracy of Economic Indicators

There are many kinds of questions that can be raised about the accuracy of economic indicators. Conceptual issues, such as whether the indicators measure what they purport—for example, if the unemployment rate truly represents the proportion of people out of work or if the consumer price index truly represents inflation to the consumer—are beyond the scope of this book. More practical considerations, such as how closely the underlying data represent the definitions of the indicator, are also incapable of being measured. Such errors clearly do exist because secondary data are used as source information for constructing economic indicators. For example, data based on income tax returns that were originally developed for assessing the economic effects of existing income tax laws and of proposed changes in tax laws, are used for estimating certain components of the gross domestic product and for obtaining information on small firms for the economic censuses. Even though some data sources may not exactly correspond to the definitional concepts of certain indicators, secondary sources are used in constructing economic indicators to hold down the costs of data collection and to limit the reporting burden on the public.

There are two fairly simple ways to evaluate the accuracy of economic indicators, however. The effect of data errors and the relative accuracy of an indicator can be estimated by taking into account the extent of revisions to the preliminary data and, in the case of indicators based on surveys, the sampling reliability of the surveys. Quantitative measures of the effect of these errors have been developed in some cases.

Error due to revision reflects changes in the figures from when they are initially provided to the later, more accurate information. The size of revision error is based on the past experience of these changes. For example, two-thirds of the revisions between the advance and latest estimates of real gross domestic product have been within a range of –1.3 to 2.2 percentage points. Thus, based on a 67 percent confidence, it is likely that an advance quarterly estimate of real GDP growth at an annual rate of 2.0 percent will be revised within a range of 0.7 to 4.2 percent. Raising the confidence level to 90 percent increases the likely revision to a range of –0.6 to 5.5.

Error due to sampling results from the likelihood that data obtained from a sample of a population differ from what they would be if the entire population were surveyed. Estimates of sampling error are developed from mathematical formulas of probability, and there is a predetermined direct relationship between error size and its chances of occurring. For example, the sampling error for housing starts based on a 67 percent confidence is plus or minus 3 percent. Thus at a confidence of 67 percent, it is likely that a monthly figure of housing starts at an annual rate of 1.5 million units ranges within 1.455 and 1.545 million if all starts were surveyed. Raising the confidence level to 95 percent doubles the sampling error to a range of 1.41 to 1.59 million.

When such estimates are available, it is important to take them into account. However, whether estimates of error are available or not, it is clear in all cases that any single number provided by an indicator cannot always exactly represent reality. Because of the various sources of error inherent in economic data, in general, an indicator should be considered as representing a range rather than an actual figure. Analysis of the specific or related data, as well as estimates of the size of revisions or sampling errors available, can suggest whether actual measurements fall closer to upper or lower bounds of that range.

Revisions

Economic indicators are developed from data gathered in surveys of households, businesses, and governments, and from tax and regulatory reports submitted to the federal and state governments. The indicators are available weekly, monthly, quarterly, or annually, depending on the data series. Because policy makers in the administration, Congress, and Federal Reserve Board want the indicators as soon as possible following the month or quarter to which they refer, the figures are initially provided on a preliminary basis and are revised in subsequent months as more complete and accurate data are obtained. Revisions are sometimes substantial, and it is important that preliminary information be treated as tentative. The use of preliminary and revised information results from the tension between the need for both timely and accurate data. In analyzing current information, it is desirable to view the most recent data in the context of previous trends and to wait for the more accurate revised data to determine whether there has been a continuation or change from the trend.

Some sources provide a figure indicating the probable range of revisions. Typically, these are indicators developed from more than one data source, such as the gross domestic product and the industrial production index, or from surveys using nonprobability samples (see "Sampling Reliability" below).

In addition to revisions that are made on a current basis, more comprehensive revisions are made annually, every five years, or every ten years, depending on the indicator. These are referred to as "benchmark" revisions. For particular indicators, they result in a revision of all historical data as in the case of the gross domestic product; in other cases, application of the new definitions and data-estimating methodologies is limited to future figures of the indicator, as for the consumer price index. The decision about whether to revise historical data is based on consideration of several factors—the need to have a consistent series over time balanced against the lack or weakness of comparable data for earlier time periods, the theoretical question of whether to "rewrite history" by including factors that previously were not considered in economic analysis and policy making, and the additional costs for statistical programs to make the more extensive revisions. When the historical data are not revised, there is a break in the series where the previous data are not fully consistent with the new data. The inconsistencies in data should be recognized when analyzing long-term trends.

The benchmark in more accurate because it is based on data obtained from a larger sample of survey respondents including, in some cases, the universe of the whole population, such as the five-year economic censuses and the ten-year census of population. It is also more accurate because there is more time to check the validity of the reported survey data. Thus, the benchmark provides more complete and precise information for checking the accuracy of the indicator at particular points in time and for revising historical data and estimating current data.

Sampling Reliability

A survey is typically based on a sample of respondents from the universe of the entire population being surveyed. Many indicators are based on a probability sample survey, which represents all groups of the universe in proportion to the size of each group. However, it is unlikely that any single sample corresponds precisely to the distribution of the groups in the universe. Thus, a sampling error is calculated to indicate the possible range of error in the survey data. The unemployment rate is an example of an economic indicator for which a sampling error is provided.

If a sample does not fully represent the components of the universe in accordance with the relative importance of each component, the survey is not based on a probability sample. For indicators based on nonprobability samples, only revision error rates can be calculated. The survey of manufacturers' shipments, orders, and inventories is an example of an economic indicator for which a revision error, but not a sampling error, is provided.

However, even for probability samples, the present state of knowledge does not allow an estimate of the accuracy with which respondents answer survey questions. Error attributable to inaccurate answers is known as nonsampling or reporting error, and all survey data, including those obtained from the universe as well as from a sample, contain an unknown amount of such inaccuracy.

Presentation of Economic Data

The perception of economic trends is affected by how economic data are summarized and packaged. It is apparent from reading the newspapers that economists differ in their assessments of the economy although they base their assessments on the same data. This section highlights two aspects of data presentation that influence the perception of statistical changes over time: (1) calculating growth rates and (2) charting economic data graphically.

Calculating Growth Rates: Beginning and Ending Dates

The magnitude of change over a general time period is influenced by the economic conditions existing at particular beginning and ending dates for which the calculations are performed. Average rates of growth for approximately the same periods differ somewhat if the end points are changed slightly. This is illustrated in the case of the real gross domestic product during 1982–92 (fourth quarters). Table 1.1 shows two average annual growth rates over the period that vary with small changes in the initial year, one using 1982 and one using 1983. The growth rate of 2.9 percent for 1982–92 declines to 2.5 percent when calculated for 1983–92. The variation reflects different economic environments—1982:4 is the first quarter of a recovery from a recession and 1983:4 is 1 1/4 years into the recovery.

In calculating long-term growth rates, it is preferable to avoid using end years that represent different phases of the business cycle in order not to distort average rates of growth for the entire period. In the above example, the 1983–92 end years meet this criterion since they have both been rising in their recoveries from previous recessions for 1 1/4 and 1 3/4 years, respectively. By

Table 1.1

Real Gross Domestic Product
(billions of 1987 dollars, seasonally adjusted rate)

1982:4	3,759.6
1983:4	4,012.1
1984:4	4,194.2
1985:4	4,333.5
1986:4	4,427.1
1987:4	4,625.5
1988:4	4,779.7
1989:4	4,856.7
1990:4	4,833.8
1991:4	4,838.5
1992:4	4,990.8

Average annual change
1982:4–1992:4: 2.9%
1983:4–1992:4: 2.5%

contrast, the 1982–92 terminal years raise the growth rate because they start with a point that is only one quarter into the recovery and end with a point that has been rising for 1 3/4 years.

Charting Data Graphically: Arithmetic and Ratio Scales

Data are depicted visually on charts to convey the main points of the statistics, while requiring a minimum effort by the viewer. Use of such graphics is related to the adage that "a picture is worth a thousand words." Different types of scales are used on the axes of charts to highlight absolute or relative (percentage) changes in the data: arithmetic scales are used to illustrate absolute changes and ratio scales are used to illustrate relative changes. These are different measures, and the viewer of graphic data should know which type of scale is used on the chart.

Arithmetic scales have the same distance (for example, as measured in inches) between two points when the absolute difference between one set of numeric values is the same as the difference between another set of numeric values, regardless of the size of the numbers. Thus, on an arithmetic scale, the distance between 10 and 100 is the same as the distance between 100 and 190. The absolute difference in both cases is 90. On an arithmetic scale, if the absolute differences from point to point are the same all along the line (for example, each point is ten units higher than the previous point), then the slope of the line is the same between all points. When the absolute differences between two sets of two points are not the same, the slope of the line changes accordingly by becoming more or less steep.

By contrast, ratio (or logarithmic) scales have equal distances when the ratio between one set of two numbers is the same as the ratio between another set of two numbers, regardless of the size of the numbers. For example, on a ratio scale, the distance between 10 and 100 is the same as the distance between 100 and 1,000, since the ratio difference is ten to one in both cases. Thus, on a ratio scale, the slope of the line between 10 and 100 is the same as the slope between 100 and 1,000. When the ratios between two sets of two points are not the same, the slope of the line also changes by becoming more or less steep.

Conventionally, time is shown on the horizontal (x) axis and data values are shown on the (y) axis of a chart. Time — weeks, months, years, and so on — is always on an arithmetic scale because there is no reason to vary distances for periods of the same time segments. On the other hand, data values are shown on an arithmetic scale when the analysis emphasizes absolute change, but on a ratio scale when relative change is the primary interest. Because a ratio scale is based on logarithms of the data, a chart in which the horizontal time axis is an arithmetic scale and the vertical axis of the data is a ratio scale is also called a semilogarithmic (or semilog) chart.

Figures 1.2a and 1.2b illustrate the difference between arithmetic and ratio scales. They are both plotted from merchandise exports (excluding military sales) data from 1960 to 1992; exports rose from $20 billion in 1960 to $440 billion in 1992. Although they present the same data, the two graphs are not comparable. The year-to-year changes in Figure 1.2a represent

18

Figure 1.2a **Merchandise Exports: Arithmetic Scale**

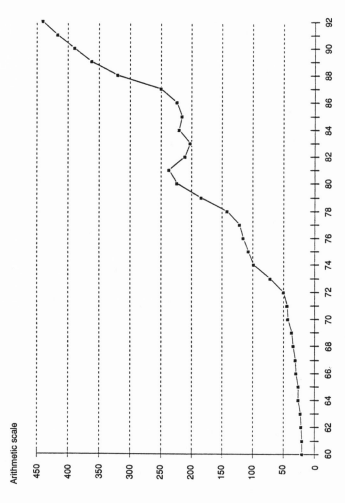

Arithmetic scale

Note: Slope of line indicates yearly absolute changes. Periods with same slope have the same dollar change.

Figure 1.2b **Merchandise Exports: Ratio Scale**

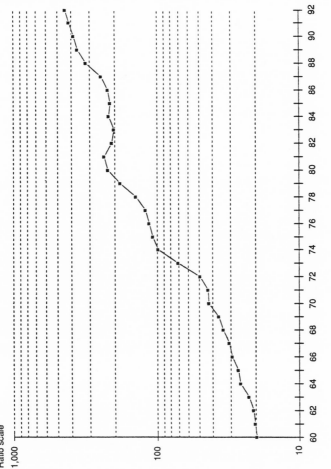

Note: Slope of line indicates yearly relative changes. Periods with the same slope have the same percentage change.

the absolute change, while the year-to-year changes in Figure 1.2b represent the relative change.

Distinctions among "Goods," "Services," and "Structures"

Economic output produced in various industries is classified as goods, services, or structures. In some cases the definition is obvious, although the distinctions are sometimes ambiguous. The various industries are coded by number in the Standard Industrial Classification system.

Goods are three-dimensional products as well as liquid and gas products that may be transported from one location to another. All goods except gases are materials that have a mass. Gases are invisible but they may be stored in a container. Goods are commodities that are produced in the agriculture, mining, and manufacturing industries.

Services are outputs produced in all of the nongoods industries except construction. While service industries interact with goods industries, services are characterized by something other than goods. Personal, business, finance, insurance, real estate, and professional services industries may facilitate, enhance, or otherwise affect goods production, but they do not directly produce goods. Electric and gas utilities, transportation, and wholesale and retail trade services industries are more closely associated with goods products. They are not defined as goods industries, however, for the following reasons: a kilowatt of electric power is energy that travels through wires; truck, rail, air, ship, and pipeline transportation industries move the goods that are produced in agricultural, mineral, and manufacturing industries; and wholesale and retail trade industries distribute and market goods that are produced in agricultural, mineral, and manufacturing industries. In addition, the term "services" in the *gross domestic product* and in the *balance of payments* includes wage payments to foreign workers who commute across the border from their home country.

Structures are residential, commercial, school, hospital, and other buildings, as well as nonbuilding facilities such as roads, bridges, dams, and power plants. Structures are produced in the construction industries. While structures are three-dimensional products, they are not classified as goods because they are built as an integral part of the land and consequently are not moved from place to place.

The three-way classification is governed by the primary activity of the enterprise producing the item or the primary mode of production, rather than by the ultimate use of the item. For example, a bakery that makes bread and sells it to stores for sale to the public is classified as a manufacturing industry, while a bakery that makes bread on the same premises as the store that sells it to the public is classified as a retail trade industry. To take another example, mobile homes are made in factories and thus are classified as manufacturing industry products; although a mobile home is subsequently attached to the ground when it is bought for housing, it nevertheless is defined as a manufactured product rather than as a structure.

Using This Book

The more than sixty indicators described in this book are grouped under forty-eight generic categories. For example, several types of interest rates are grouped under the interest rate category. The book presents the indicators in alphabetic order so that readers may quickly locate a particular indicator. However, for analytical purposes, it is helpful to know how the indicators interrelate in describing the economy. Below, the indicators are grouped under common topics to help those with interest in a particular segment of the economy.

Topical Grouping of the Indicators

ECONOMIC GROWTH

Gross Domestic Product

CONSUMER SPENDING

Retail Sales
Personal Income and Saving
Consumer Attitude Indexes

INVESTMENT

Plant and Equipment Expenditures
Corporate Profits
Business Optimism Indexes

LABOR

Unemployment
Employment
Help-Wanted Advertising Index
Average Weekly Hours
Average Weekly Earnings
Productivity
Unit Labor Costs
Employment Cost Index
Collective Bargaining Settlements

PRICES

Inflation
GDP Price Measures
Consumer Price Index
Producer Price Indexes
Import and Export Price Indexes
CRB Futures Price Index

PRODUCTION

Industrial Production Index
Capacity Utilization
Manufacturers' Orders
Inventory-Sales Ratios

HOUSING

Housing Starts
Home Sales

FINANCE

Money Supply
Flow of Funds
Bank Loans: Commercial and Industrial
Consumer Installment Credit
Interest Rates
Stock Market Price Indexes and Dividend Yields

GOVERNMENT

Government Budgets and Debt

INTERNATIONAL

Balance of Trade: U. S. Merchandise Exports and Imports
Balance of Payments: U. S. International Economic Transactions
International Investment Position of the United States
Value of the Dollar

CYCLICAL INDICATORS

Leading, Coincident, and Lagging Indexes
Experimental Recession Indexes
Growth Cycles
Purchasing Managers' Index

ECONOMIC WELL-BEING

Distribution of Income
Poverty
Business Firm Formation and Growth
Business Failures
Farm Parity Ratio

Format

The following is used for the description of each indicator:

Introductory Statement. Capsule summary of what the indicator represents.

Where and When Available. Primary and secondary publication sources for obtaining the indicator and publication dates for the preliminary and revised information.

Content. Definition of the indicator and the scope of its coverage.

Methodology. Data and estimating techniques used in constructing the indicator.

Accuracy. Range of sampling or revision error in the indicator.

Relevance. Significance of the indicator for economic analysis and policymaking.

Recent Trends. Behavior of the indicator during 1980−92.

Historical Data. Annual data for the indicator from 1980 to 1992. They are based on statistics available in the fall of 1993.

References from Primary Data Source. Publications of the organization that provides the indicator that describes the items above.

To facilitate cross-referencing, indicators covered in this book are italicized whenever they are mentioned in sections other than those in which they are the primary focus.

Statistical Sources

Most of the indicators in this book are produced and published by federal government agencies. In the dissemination of economic statistics, there is a distinction between primary and secondary data. The term "primary data" refers to economic indicators published in journals or reports by the organization that produces the figures, while "secondary data" refers to indicators published by organizations other than the producer of the figures. The following monthly journals, which include both primary and secondary data, are the main vehicles for publishing the indicators: the *Survey of Current Business* of the Bureau of Economic Analysis in the U.S. Department of Commerce; the *Monthly Labor Review* and *Employment and Earnings* of the Bureau of Labor Statistics in the U.S. Department of Labor; and the *Federal Reserve Bulletin* of the Federal Reserve Board. A handy secondary publication is the monthly *Economic Indicators*, which is prepared by the U.S. Council of Economic Advisers for the Joint Economic Committee of Congress. These publications are cited as primary or secondary sources of the indicators under the "Where and When Available" category. They are sold by the U.S. Government Printing Office. The appendix tables of the annual *Economic Report of the President* are the most convenient source for historical data; single copies are available free from the Executive Office of the President.

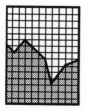

2
AVERAGE WEEKLY EARNINGS

Average weekly earnings represent the money income of workers in private nonagricultural industries. Because wages and salaries reflect the composition of employment in high-paying and low-paying industries and occupations, the figures are affected by changes in the composition of these employment characteristics.

Where and When Available

Data on average weekly earnings of workers are provided monthly by the Bureau of Labor Statistics in the U.S. Department of Labor. The data are published in a press release and in two monthly BLS journals, the *Monthly Labor Review* and *Employment and Earnings*. Secondary sources include *Economic Indicators* and the *Survey of Current Business*.

The figures are available on the third Friday after the week containing the twelfth of the month (which falls on the first or second Friday of the month) following the month to which they refer. On the day the monthly numbers are published, the commissioner of labor statistics reports on recent employment and unemployment trends to the Joint Economic Committee of Congress. Preliminary data are provided for the immediately preceding month; these are revised in the subsequent two months. Annual revisions are made in June of the following year.

Content

Average weekly earnings data cover the wages and salaries of production workers in manufacturing industries, as well as the wages, salaries, and commissions of nonsupervisory workers in other private nonagricultural industries. Earnings include wages for time at work and for paid vacations, sick leave, holidays, and overtime (whether or not a premium is paid for overtime). Bonuses, retroactive payments, tips, and in-kind payments such as free rent and meals are excluded, as are health, retirement, and other noncash fringe benefits, as well as the employer share of social security taxes. Earnings are excluded for office and sales workers in manufacturing and for supervisors and executives in all industries.

The data are provided in current dollars and in constant (1982) dollars.

The average weekly earnings figures are seasonally adjusted.

Methodology

The data for weekly earnings are obtained from the survey of employer payrolls used to measure *employment*. The methodology of the survey is described in that section. There is no independent benchmark figure for weekly earnings; the figures are revised every June with the annual employment benchmark to reflect revisions in the distribution of employment among industries. Average weekly earnings are derived by multiplying *average weekly hours* by average hourly earnings. Average hourly earnings are estimated by dividing payrolls by hours for production and nonsupervisory employees during the pay period. The constant dollar figures are calculated by dividing actual earnings by the *consumer price index* for urban wage earners and clerical workers.

Accuracy

There are no estimates of sampling or revision error for average weekly earnings.

Table 2.1

Average Weekly Earnings in Private Nonagricultural Industries

	Current dollars	1982 dollars	Percent change from preceding year	
			Current dollars	1982 dollars
1980	$235.10	$274.65	6.9%	5.8%
1981	255.20	270.63	8.5	−1.5
1982	267.26	267.26	4.7	−1.2
1983	280.70	272.52	5.0	2.0
1984	292.86	274.73	4.3	0.8
1985	299.09	271.16	2.1	−1.3
1986	304.85	271.94	1.9	0.3
1987	312.50	269.16	2.5	−1.0
1988	322.02	266.79	3.0	−0.9
1989	334.24	264.22	3.8	−1.0
1990	345.35	259.47	3.3	−1.8
1991	353.98	255.40	2.5	−1.6
1992	363.95	255.22	2.8	−0.1

Relevance

Average weekly earnings data are based on job-related earnings of workers of modest income. Currently, this working population of civilian family households and unrelated individuals accounts for approximately one-third of the noninstitutional population (people outside of jails, old-age homes, long-term medical care, and other sheltered housing). The earnings figures are relevant for several reasons. First, they provide a measure of consumer purchasing power as indicated by changes in wage earnings for an important segment of the spending public. Second, because they gauge the economic well-being of workers, their trends may track the direction of future wage demands. Finally, comparisons of wages in different industries help to indicate the types of jobs being created.

Recent Trends

Average weekly earnings in constant dollars declined during 1980–92 in general (Table 2.1). Real earnings declined in ten of the thirteen years over the period.

Reference from Primary Data Source

Bureau of Labor Statistics, U.S. Department of Labor. 1992. *BLS Handbook of Methods*. Chapter 2. September.

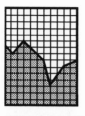

3
AVERAGE WEEKLY HOURS

Average weekly hours represent the length of the work week in private nonagricultural industries. The figures are affected by changes in both the industrial and occupational composition of employment.

Where and When Available

Data on average weekly hours in the workplace are provided monthly by the Bureau of Labor Statistics in the U.S. Department of Labor. The data are published in a press release and two monthly BLS journals, the *Monthly Labor Review* and *Employment and Earnings*. Secondary sources include *Economic Indicators* and the *Survey of Current Business*.

The figures are available on the third Friday after the week containing the twelfth of the month (which falls on the first or second Friday of the month) following the month to which they refer. On the day the monthly numbers are released, the commissioner of labor statistics reports on recent employment and unemployment trends to the Joint Economic Committee of Congress. Preliminary data are provided for the immediately preceding month; these are revised in the subsequent two months. Annual revisions are made in June of the following year.

Content

Average weekly hours measure time on the job, including straight-time and overtime hours (whether or not a premium is paid for overtime), for the average of full-time and part-time workers. The inclusion of paid absences from work means that hours are counted on the basis of "hours paid for" rather than "hours worked." The hours information includes production workers in manufacturing industries and nonsupervisory workers in other industries. Hours are excluded for office and sales workers in manufacturing and for executives in all industries.

Separate data on overtime hours are provided for manufacturing industries. These are defined to include worktime for which premium pay is received beyond straight-time workday or workweek. Holiday hours are included only if premium wages are paid. Hours associated with incentive pay for shift differentials such as night or weekend work, hazardous conditions, or similar situations are excluded. Because these separate data on overtime are limited to work for premium pay, they differ from the overtime included in average weekly hours, which includes *all* overtime even if no premium pay is involved.

The average weekly hours figures are seasonally adjusted.

Methodology

The data for hours are obtained from the survey of employer payrolls used to measure *employment*. The methodology of the survey is described in that section. There is no independent benchmark figure for weekly hours; they are revised every June with the annual employment benchmark because of revisions in the composition of employment among industries. Weekly hours are derived by dividing total hours paid for by the number of employees during the pay period. These are adjusted for pay periods that are longer than one week so that they represent a seven-day period. Separate data are collected on the survey form for overtime hours.

Table 3.1

Average Weekly Hours in Private Nonagricultural Industries

	All private nonagricultural industries	Manufacturing industries	Overtime in manufacturing industries
1980	35.3	39.7	2.8
1981	35.2	39.8	2.8
1982	34.8	38.9	2.3
1983	35.0	40.1	3.0
1984	35.2	40.7	3.4
1985	34.9	40.5	3.3
1986	34.8	40.7	3.4
1987	34.8	41.0	3.7
1988	34.7	41.1	3.9
1989	34.6	41.0	3.8
1990	34.5	40.8	3.6
1991	34.3	40.7	3.6
1992	34.4	41.0	3.8

Accuracy

Although the hours are not based on a probability sample, an estimate of errors due to sampling has been developed assuming a random sample. This indicates that the relative error is plus or minus 0.1 percent.

Relevance

Average weekly hours are a sensitive barometer of labor demand. Employers generally prefer to increase or decrease hours worked before hiring or laying off workers in response to movements in *retail sales, corporate profits, manufacturers' orders, inventory–sales ratios,* or planned production schedules. This is particularly true when the changes in the demand for labor are small or are expected to be temporary. Weekly hours in manufacturing is a component of the leading index of *leading, coincident, and lagging indexes.* The monthly volatility of weekly hours makes discerning a short-term trend difficult. Movements over several months should be assessed when analyzing trends.

Recent Trends

Average weekly hours in all private nonagricultural industries declined by close to one hour, from the early 1980s to the early 1990s (Table 3.1). Weekly hours rose by over one hour in manufacturing industries, and overtime in manufacturing industries increased by one hour over the same time period.

Reference from Primary Data Source

Bureau of Labor Statistics, U.S. Department of Labor, 1992. *BLS Handbook of Methods*. Chapter 2. September.

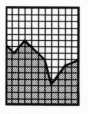

4
BALANCE OF PAYMENTS:
U.S. INTERNATIONAL
ECONOMIC TRANSACTIONS

The balance of payments accounts are the most comprehensive measure of U.S. international economic transactions with other countries. The transactions include exports and imports of goods and services, income receipts and payments on foreign investments, transfer payments such as pensions and government grants, and changes in U.S. and foreign holdings of financial assets and liabilities associated with international monetary reserves, loans, investments, and securities transactions. The various "balances" focus on the difference between exports and imports and international flows of transfer payments, but exclude financial assets and liabilities. When exports exceed imports, the balance is in surplus, and when imports exceed exports, the balance is in deficit. A surplus balance is sometimes referred to as "favorable" and a deficit as "unfavorable."

Where and When Available

The Bureau of Economic Analysis in the U.S. Department of Commerce provides quarterly measures of the balance of payments. They are published in a press release and in BEA's monthly journal, the *Survey of Current Business*. Secondary sources include *Economic Indicators* and the *Federal Reserve Bulletin*.

The figures are available seventy-five days after the quarter to which they refer. They are initially revised in the succeeding quarter and then subsequently in June of the following year as part of the annual revisions. The annual revisions also change the figures for several of the preceding years. Constant dollar measures for certain components of the balance of payments are published as part of the *gross domestic product.*

Content

Conceptually, the balance of payments is composed of two broad components. One is foreign trade in goods and services plus unilateral transfers. The other is the money and capital flows necessary to finance trade, transfers, and grants. The two components are definitionally equivalent but do not match statistically because of inadequacies in the data. The difference caused by these data problems is noted as the "statistical discrepancy."

Balance of payments data are provided for total U.S. transactions with all nations and separate transactions with particular nations and regions of the world. The United States includes the fifty states and the District of Columbia, Puerto Rico (except transactions between the states and Puerto Rico), and the Virgin Islands.

The balance of payments figures are in current dollars. They are converted to constant dollars for the *gross domestic product.*

Several elements comprise the foreign trade, transfer, and grant categories of the balance of payments. *Exports and imports of goods, services, and income* encompass merchandise trade in the *balance of trade* plus the following: transfers under the foreign military sales program; defense purchases; passenger and freight transportation between the United States and other countries provided by American and foreign companies; other services provided by Americans and foreigners, such as insurance, telecommunications, construction, and engineering; income from royalties and license fees; and dividend and interest income paid by Americans and foreigners on foreign investments.

Unilateral transfers are transactions between U.S. residents and residents of foreign countries in which goods, services, or financial assets are transferred and nothing of economic value is received in return. Examples include U.S. government military and nonmilitary grants for which no payment is expected or where the payment terms are agreed to at a future time after the transfer occurs; private and government pension payments to American workers living in foreign countries and by other nations to foreign workers living in the United states; and gifts sent abroad by individuals and nonprofit organizations.

Increases or decreases in U.S. assets abroad and foreign assets in the United States measure the means of financing the above foreign trade in goods and services, unilateral transfers, and military grants. The main elements of *U.S. assets abroad* are as follows. *U.S. government official reserve assets* include the U.S. gold stock, special drawing rights and reserve position in the International Monetary Fund, and U.S. Treasury and Federal Reserve holdings of foreign currencies. *Other government assets* include loans to foreign nations and to U.S. private parties for investment abroad, capital contributions to international organizations except the IMF, and U.S. holdings of foreign currencies and other short-term assets associated with foreign aid programs and financial operations such as guarantee programs of the Export-Import Bank. *U.S. private assets* include direct investment abroad (ownership of at least 10 percent of foreign companies) by U.S. private parties, U.S. private holdings of foreign bonds and stocks, and U.S. bank and nonbank loans to foreigners.

The main elements of *Foreign assets in the United States* are as follows. *Foreign official assets* are investments by foreign governments in U.S. government securities, U.S. government liabilities for foreign deposits in advance of delivery of foreign military sales items, and foreign government holdings of U.S. corporate debt and equity securities and of state and local government securities. *Other foreign assets* are direct investment in the United States (ownership of at least 10 percent of American companies) by foreign private parties; private foreign holdings of U.S. Treasury securities, state and local government securities, and corporate debt and equity securities; and loans to Americans by foreign banks and nonbanks.

The indicator provides five separate balances of exports minus imports: (1) merchandise trade; (2) goods and services; (3) investment income; (4) goods, services, and income; and (5) balance on current account (goods, services, income, and all unilateral transfers). Balances are not calculated for changes in financial assets and liabilities because meaningful distinctions are difficult to make for such categories as short-term and long-term capital.

The balance of payments figures are seasonally adjusted.

Methodology

Information for the balance of payments figures comes from several sources. Data for merchandise exports and imports are based mainly on Census Bureau surveys (see *balance of trade*). The main sources for the components are: BEA surveys of incoming and outgoing foreign direct investment; U.S. Travel and Tourism Administration surveys of average international traveler expenditures and U.S. Immigration and Naturalization Service data on the number of travelers; BEA surveys of international operations of U.S. and foreign ship operators and airlines; Census Bureau data on the tonnage of merchandise exports and imports; Treasury Department surveys (conducted by the Federal Reserve Bank of New York) of international assets and liabilities of U.S. banks and nonbank companies; and reports by the Department of Defense on foreign military sales and the Department of Agriculture on foreign aid shipments of food.

The quarterly figures are based on reported data for most items and estimates for those for which reported data are available either annually or less frequently. They are revised every June when more complete information is available. These revisions change some of the components for the past three to five years.

The constant dollar figures for certain components of the balance of payments, which are published as part of the *gross domestic product*, are derived by deflating the current dollar figures by the *import and export price indexes*, the defense and gross domestic product implicit price deflators from the *GDP price measures*, and foreign consumer price indexes (adjusted for changes in the *value of the dollar*).

The statistical discrepancy is defined as the accounting difference between the sum of credits and debits in the balance of payments. Credits are exports of goods, services, income, unilateral transfers to the United States, capital inflows or a decrease in U.S. assets, decrease in U.S. official assets, and increase in foreign official assets in the United States. Debits are imports of goods, services, and income, unilateral transfers to foreigners, capital outflows or increase in U.S. assets, increase in U.S. official reserve assets, and decrease in foreign official assets in the United States. A discrepancy results from the fact that data for the various components are developed independently and, consequently, are not fully consistent in coverage, definition, timing, and accuracy. The discrepancy is a net figure in which overstatement of one data element is offset by understatement of another data element. When the discrepancy is positive, it signifies unrecorded funds entering the United States; a negative discrepancy indicates unrecorded funds leaving the United States.

Accuracy

There are no estimates of sampling or revision error in the balance of payments figures. Since offsetting errors among the data elements may reduce the statistical discrepancy, that figure provides an overall minimum magnitude of the net inconsistencies in the various data sources.

Relevance

The balance of payments reflects U.S. participation in world markets overall. It points up the relative importance of international product markets to our economy and indicates those markets that are gaining or losing ground. It also highlights shifts in international investment, including the effect on interest flows and dividend flows entering and leaving the United States. The extent to which the United States consumes and produces for world markets affects the *gross domestic product*.

The impact of international transactions, including their financing, affects the *value of the dollar* and American competitiveness. When Americans spend and invest more money abroad than foreigners spend and invest in the United States, the value of the dollar tends to decrease; greater spending and investment by foreigners in the United States tends to raise the dollar.

A large balance of payments deficit limits the flexibility of the Federal Reserve Board in conducting monetary policy (see *balance of trade*). Large deficits also create a growing foreign debt that raises interest payments to foreigners and thereby reduces the standard of living for Americans.

Recent Trends

The patterns of international transaction in goods, services, and income changed direction during 1980–92 (Table 4.1). Imports rose faster than exports from 1980 to 1987, while exports rose faster than imports from 1988 to 1992. This led to a decline in the deficit of the balance of payments from $144 billion in 1987 to $35 billion in 1992.

Trends in U.S. assets abroad and foreign assets in the United States also varied over the period. U.S. asset outflows exceeded foreign asset inflows during 1980–82, but foreign asset inflows exceeded U.S. asset outflows during 1983–92. The differential of foreign asset inflows peaked in 1987 at $169 billion, and was $79 billion in 1992.

The statistical discrepancy ranged from minus $15 billion to $41 billion. The discrepancy was positive in nine of the thirteen years over 1980–92, which indicated that, on a net basis, the statistical reporting system most often underestimated funds entering the United States.

Table 4.1

Balance of Payments: U.S. International Economic Transactions
(billions of dollars)

	Exports of goods, services, and income	Imports of goods, services, and income	Unilateral transfers (excess of flows abroad over flows to U.S. = minus)	U.S. assets abroad (increase in capital outflow = minus)	Foreign assets in the U.S. (increase in capital inflow = plus)
1980	344.4	−333.8	−8.4	−87.0	58.1
1981	380.9	−364.2	−11.7	−114.1	83.0
1982	361.4	−355.8	−17.1	−122.3	92.4
1983	350.8	−377.5	−17.7	−58.7	83.4
1984	389.9	−469.7	−20.6	−29.7	102.0
1985	378.3	−479.2	−23.0	−34.7	131.0
1986	397.0	−523.0	−24.2	−91.3	223.2
1987	443.2	−587.4	−23.1	−61.3	230.0
1988	552.5	−654.7	−25.0	−91.4	219.5
1989	633.9	−709.4	−26.1	−129.3	213.6
1990	688.8	−746.8	−33.8	−44.1	105.2
1991	708.5	−723.4	6.6	−60.0	83.4
1992	730.5	−764.0	−32.9	−51.0	129.6

	Statistical discrepancy	Balance on merchandise trade	Balance on goods, services, and income
1980	25.4	−25.5	10.7
1981	25.0	−28.0	16.7
1982	41.4	−36.5	5.6
1983	19.8	−67.1	−26.7
1984	28.0	−112.5	−79.7
1985	27.6	−122.2	−100.9
1986	18.3	−145.1	−126.0
1987	−1.4	−159.6	−144.3
1988	−0.9	−127.0	−102.2
1989	17.4	−115.2	−75.5
1990	30.8	−109.0	−58.0
1991	−15.1	−73.8	−14.9
1992	−12.2	−96.1	−33.5

Reference from Primary Data Source

Bureau of Economic Analysis, U.S. Department of Commerce. 1990. *The Balance of Payments of the United States: Concepts, Data Sources, and Estimating Procedures*. May.

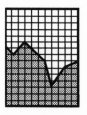

5
BALANCE OF TRADE:
U.S. MERCHANDISE EXPORTS
AND IMPORTS

The balance of trade represents foreign trade in merchandise. Merchandise is goods as distinct from services (see introductory section on *distinctions among goods, services, and structures*). The "balance" represents the difference between exports and imports. When exports exceed imports, the balance is in surplus, and when imports exceed exports, the balance is in deficit. A surplus is sometimes referred to as a favorable and a deficit as an unfavorable balance. (International transactions in services and investments are included in the *balance of payments*.)

Where and When Available

Two agencies provide balance of trade figures. The Bureau of the Census in the U.S. Department of Commerce provides monthly figures, and the Bureau of Economic Analysis in the U.S. Department of Commerce provides monthly and quarterly figures. The date from the two agencies are based on different definitions. The Census data are published in a press release and supplement and in *Exports, General Imports, and Imports for Consumption, SITC Rev. 3 Commodity by Country*. Secondary sources include *Economic Indicators*, the *Survey of Current Business*, and the *Federal Reserve Bulletin*. The BEA data are published in a press release and in BEA's monthly journal, the *Survey of Current*

Business. Constant dollar figures are published as part of the *gross domestic product.* Secondary sources include *Economic Indicators* and the *Federal Reserve Bulletin.*

The Census figures are available forty-five days after the month to which they refer. They are initially revised the following month and subsequently in quarterly and annual reports. The BEA figures are available seventy-five days after the quarter to which they refer. They are initially revised in the succeeding month and quarter and subsequently in June of the following year as part of the annual *balance of payments* revisions.

Content

Merchandise export and import data are provided for U.S. total foreign trade with all nations, plus detail for trade with particular nations and regions of the world as well as for individual commodities. U.S. trade includes that of the fifty states and the District of Columbia, Puerto Rico, and the Virgin Islands. The trade figures exclude shipments between the United States and the Commonwealth of Puerto Rico, the Virgin Islands, and other U.S. possessions; however, supplementary figures are provided on U.S. export and import trade with Puerto Rico, U.S. exports to the Virgin Islands, and imports from Guam, American Samoa, and the Northern Mariana Islands.

The Census and BEA data are provided in current and constant dollars. The BEA constant dollar measure is prepared as part of the *gross domestic product.*

Exports cover domestically produced goods plus imported items that subsequently are exported without substantial physical change to the imported item (referred to as a re-export). Exports are valued at the dollar price at the U.S. port of export. This includes inland transportation, insurance, and other costs to deliver the merchandise alongside the ship or plane, but it excludes overseas transportation, insurance, and other charges beyond the U.S. port (referred to as f.a.s., free alongside ship). The month of exportation is the month that the shipment leaves the United States.

Imports cover goods for immediate consumption plus those stored in Customs bonded warehouses and in U.S. Foreign Trade Zones. They are valued in two ways. One is the Customs value, which is essentially equivalent to the f.a.s. price at the foreign port of export (see exports above). The other is the Customs/f.a.s. value plus overseas transportation, insurance, and other charges in delivering the merchandise to the United States (referred to as c.i.f. cost-insurance-freight). Both measures exclude U.S. import duties. The month of importation is the month when the Customs Bureau releases the merchandise to the importer. Census presents separate figures using both the f.a.s. and the c.i.f. valuations and BEA only uses the Customs/f.a.s. valuation.

The main distinction between the Census and the BEA figures is that BEA adjusts the Census measures to conform to the *balance of payments* concepts. This results in three primary differences: (1) foreign military sales and U.S. military agencies' purchases from abroad identified in the Census documents are excluded by BEA but included elsewhere in the balance of payments accounts; (2) inland truck and rail freight costs to the Canadian border for exports to and imports from Canada are excluded by Census and included by BEA; and (3) the Census figures only include nonmonetary gold that is shipped across international borders, while BEA figures also include nonmonetary gold that changes ownership through book entries without being shipped across international borders. Nonmonetary gold represents all trade in gold in which at least one of the parties to the transaction is a private party; it excludes gold movements between governments, central banks, and international monetary institutions. Monetary gold represents gold movements between the U.S. treasury or the Federal Reserve Board acting for the Treasury and foreign governments or their central banks and the International Monetary Fund.

The balance of trade figures are seasonally adjusted.

Methodology

The basic data on merchandise exports and imports are developed from surveys conducted by the Census Bureau. They are adjusted by the BEA to reflect the balance of payments measures.

Bureau of the Census

The export statistics are derived mainly from mandatory information supplied by commercial exporters to the Customs Bureau, which provides the data to the Census Bureau. Customs checks the accuracy of these exports requiring licenses from the State Department for military items and from the Commerce Department for nonmilitary strategic materials. These figures are supplemented by data from some exporters who report their shipments directly to the Census. In addition, the Department of Defense reports military aid shipments data to Census. Export data for shipments over $2,500 are compiled form the universe (100 percent sample) of all such reports. These account for 96.5 percent of all exports. Shipments under $2,501 are estimated from factors based on ratios of low-valued exports to total exports in past periods. (The threshold dollar exemption for low-valued exports from reporting requirements is raised from time to time, most recently in January 1987.)

The import statistics derived from mandatory information supplied by importers to the Customs Bureau, which reviews the documents for accuracy and provides the corrected data to Census. Import data for shipments over $1,250 are compiled from the universe (100 percent sample) of all such reports. These account for 98.5 percent of all imports. Shipments under $1,251 are estimated from factors based on ratios of low-valued imports to total imports for past periods. The threshold dollar exemption, exempting low-valued imports from reporting requirements, is raised from time to time, most recently in January 1990.

Bureau of Economic Analysis

The statistical adjustments made to conform the Census data to the balance of payments measures are based on separate information obtained from a variety of sources, such as the Department of Defense for military exports, Census data for U.S. inland freight and Census and BEA reconciliations with Statistics Canada for inland freight costs for Canadian foreign trade, and the Federal Reserve Board for nonmonetary gold trade.

The constant dollar measures are derived mainly by deflating the current dollar figures by the *import and export price indexes.* These are supplemented for petroleum imports by the Census Bureau unit value indexes, which are imprecise measures of foreign traded goods, and by the *producer price indexes* for transportation equipment and computers.

Accuracy

There are no estimates of sampling or revision error in the balance of trade figures. Since practically all of the Census data are based on surveys of the universe of exporters and importers, any sampling error for low-valued shipments would be insignificant. The monthly trade statistics are highly volatile from month to month.

Relevance

The balance of trade impacts the *gross domestic product, employment, inflation,* and the *value of the dollar.* It also has long-term implications for U.S. independence in managing our economy and for our standard of living. Export and import levels are influenced by economic growth at home and abroad and by the competitive position of American products in international markets and foreign goods in U.S. markets.

A surplus in the trade balance or a reduction in the trade deficit stimulates economic growth and job expansion, while a deficit or reduction in the surplus restrains economic growth and employment. This occurs because exports are produced in the United States and thus generate American production and employment, while American spending for imports stimulates production and employment abroad.

Over the long run, imports tend to hold down inflation because imports compete with American goods. Imports also moderate inflation during temporary shortages of domestic goods by providing a supplementary supply. Shortages may occur when drought or frost reduces food harvests; when an unexpected surge occurs in consumption; or when sudden bottlenecks appear in the production of lumber, paper, or other products for which domestic supply cannot be expanded readily.

A large balance of trade deficit limits the flexibility of the Federal Reserve Board in conducting monetary policy for managing the economy. The deficit is financed by borrowing from domestic lenders or from abroad. Borrowing from domestic lenders to finance the deficit could lead to higher *interest rates*, unless accommodated by an increase in the *money supply*, which in turn may raise the rate of *inflation*. Borrowing from abroad can lead to a rise in the *value of the dollar*: the influx of foreign funds into the United States bids up the dollar compared to other currencies, which worsens the deficit by making exports more expensive and imports cheaper.

A continuing large deficit financed from abroad creates growing foreign debt. Over the long run, this results in greater amounts of money paid in interest as payments to foreigners. Consequently, U.S. incomes and the U.S. standard of living are reduced.

Recent Trends

The merchandise trade balances showed a marked change in direction during 1980–92, although it was always in a deficit position during the period (Table 5.1). The deficit increased sharply during most of the 1980s, and peaked at $152–160 billion in 1987,

Table 5.1

Balance of Trade: U.S. Merchandise Exports and Imports
(billions of dollars)

	Census trade, f.a.s.			BEA balance of payments, f.a.s		
	Exports	Imports (f.a.s.)	Balance	Exports	Imports (f.a.s.)	Balance
1980	225.6	245.3	−19.7	224.3	249.8	−25.5
1981	238.7	261.0	−22.3	237.0	265.1	−28.0
1982	216.4	244.0	−27.5	211.2	247.6	−36.5
1983	205.6	258.0	−52.4	201.8	268.9	−67.1
1984	224.0	330.7	−106.7	219.9	332.4	−112.5
1985	218.8	336.5	−117.7	215.9	338.1	−122.2
1986	227.2	365.4	−138.3	223.3	368.4	−145.1
1987	254.1	406.2	−152.1	250.2	409.8	−159.6
1988	322.4	441.0	−118.5	320.2	447.2	−127.0
1989	363.8	473.2	−109.4	362.1	477.4	−115.2
1990	393.6	495.3	−101.7	389.3	498.3	−109.0
1991	421.7	488.5	−66.7	416.9	490.7	−73.8
1992	448.2	532.7	−84.5	440.1	536.3	−96.1

	Census trade, c.i.f.		
	Exports	Imports (c.i.f.)	Balance
1985	218.8	352.5	−133.6
1986	227.2	382.3	−155.1
1987	254.1	424.4	−170.3
1988	322.4	459.5	−137.1
1989	363.8	493.2	−129.4
1990	393.6	517.0	−123.4
1991	421.7	508.4	−86.6
1992	448.2	554.0	−105.9

depending on the definition. It subsequently declined to $85−96 billion in 1992.

Generally, the deficit under the Census import f.a.s. definition is the lowest and that for the Census import c.i.f. definition is the highest, with the BEA balance of payments deficit measure between the two. In 1992, the deficits were: Census f.a.s. — $85 billion; BEA balance of payments — $96 billion; and Census c.i.f. — $106 billion.

References from Primary Data Sources

Bureau of Economic Analysis, U.S. Department of Commerce. 1990. *The Balance of Payments of the United States: Concepts, Data Sources, and Estimating Procedures.* May.

Bureau of the Census, U.S. Department of Commerce. Monthly. *Exports, General Imports, and Imports for Consumption, SITC-Rev.3 Commodity by Country.*

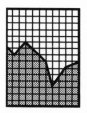

6
BANK LOANS: COMMERCIAL
AND INDUSTRIAL

Commercial and industrial bank loans are loans made by commercial banks to individuals, partnerships, and corporations for nonfarm business use. They also include bank loans made to investors for financial acquisitions such as company takeovers. The indicator thus focuses on loans made to income-generating business activity as distinct from household consumer use.

Where and When Available

Commercial and industrial bank loan data are provided weekly and monthly by the Federal Reserve Board. They are published in three statistical releases and in the *Federal Reserve Bulletin*, the FRB's monthly journal. Secondary sources include *Economic Indicators* and the *Survey of Current Business*.

The weekly figures are available every Friday for the week ending Wednesday of the previous week. The monthly figures are available the fourth Friday of the month after the month to which they refer. The measures are revised on a continuing basis with the receipt of more accurate data.

Content

Commercial and industrial bank loans represent loans outstanding. Therefore, they include existing loans from the previous period and new loans, minus those repaid during the period. Secured and unsecured loans are included. In addition to traditional loans extended to borrowers, the data include nonfinancial commercial paper (negotiable notes sold by nonfinancial businesses) and bankers acceptances (bills for which banks pledge their credit on behalf of their customers). Bank loans, excluding paper and banker acceptances, are provided separately for borrowers whose primary address is the United States (including Puerto Rico and U.S. territories) from those with foreign addresses.

The data exclude loans to farmers, securities and real estate firms, other banks, companies that mainly extend business or personal credit, commercial paper of financial institutions bought by banks, and loans secured by real estate. No figures are available on the distribution of short-term and long-term loans.

The bank loan figures are seasonally adjusted.

Methodology

The bank loan data are obtained from weekly reports of a sample of Federal Reserve member and nonmember banks, both large and small, and from quarterly reports for banks not reporting weekly. Data on commercial paper and bankers acceptances are based on weekly reports of large banks. The weekly and monthly figures for all commercial banks include estimates for banks not reporting weekly. Estimates for the nonweekly reporting banks are based on relationships developed from the quarterly reports of all banks, those reporting weekly and those reporting quarterly. The bank loan figures are benchmarked to the quarterly reports four times a year.

Accuracy

Estimates of revisions to the bank loan figures are encompassed within a larger statistical category of "bank credit," which includes commercial and industrial and other bank loans plus U.S. government and other securities owned by banks. Revisions for this much broader category are within plus or minus 0.5 percent-

Table 6.1

Bank Loans: Commercial and Industrial

	Loans outstanding (billions of dollars)	Annual percent change
	December	Dec. to Dec.
1980	325.7	11.8%
1981	355.4	9.1
1982	392.5	10.4
1983	414.2	5.5
1984	473.2	14.2
1985	500.2	5.7
1986	536.7	7.3
1987	566.4	5.5
1988	605.3	6.9
1989	638.4	5.5
1990	642.6	0.7
1991	617.0	−4.0
1992	597.6	−3.1

age point of the annual growth rate of bank credit. The commercial and industrial bank loan component probably has a larger revision error, although the actual range is not known.

Relevance

The bank loan data provide a clue to business's willingness to go into debt. For analytical purposes, the monthly change and the monthly level are viewed differently. A rapid increase in bank loans suggests an optimistic outlook for business prospects, while a slow rate of loan expansion indicates a cautious business outlook.

By contrast, the simple existence of debt is a burden to business because of the principal and interest payments. Thus, existing debt becomes a depressant to further borrowing. The monthly level of existing commercial and industrial loans (in constant dollars) is a component of the lagging index of the *leading, coincident, and lagging indexes*.

Recent Trends

Bank loans to commercial and industrial borrowers had three distinct patterns during 1980–92 (Table 6.1). They rose rapidly in 1980 – 84, with annual increases averaging 10 percent. The annual increases declined to an average rate of 6 percent in 1985 – 89. There was a further sharp drop in 1990 – 92, with loans actually declining in 1991 and 1992 by 4 and 3 percent, respectively.

Reference from Federal Reserve System

Samansky, Arthur W. 1981. *Statfacts: Understanding Federal Reserve Statistical Reports.* Federal Reserve Bank of New York. November.

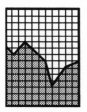

7
BUSINESS FAILURES

Business failures represent the number of companies that go out of business because of money owed to creditors. They include businesses that are closed due to court proceedings such as bankruptcy, foreclosure, and attachment or receivership, as well as those that were voluntarily closed either through compromises with creditors or leaving unpaid debts. Failures exclude businesses that are closed due to causes such as lack of capital, inadequate profits, poor health or retirement of the owner, and change of name or location.

Where and When Available

Business failures measures are provided weekly, monthly, and quarterly by The Dun & Bradstreet Corporation. The figures are published in press releases and in the annual *Business Failure Record.*

The figures are available five days after the week to which they refer and two weeks after the month or quarter to which they refer. They are revised in subsequent weeks and months, and the annual revised figures are published in March of the following year.

Content

Business failures count the number of corporations and unincorporated businesses going out of business where a loss to creditors is involved. Information is provided on the dollar liabilities and age of the failed companies, causes of the failures, and the rate of failures (failures per 10,000 ongoing businesses). Additional detail on failures is provided by industry and by state.

The dollar liabilities reflect the debt at the time of the failure (the day the company closes operations). Liabilities include all accounts and notes payable and all obligations, whether or not secured, known to be held by banks, officers, affiliated companies, supplying companies, and governments. Liabilities exclude publicly held bonds sold on securities exchanges. Assets are not used to offset liabilities in the data.

The business failure figures are not seasonally adjusted.

Methodology

Business failures data are obtained by Dun & Bradstreet reporters through checks of court records for bankruptcies, foreclosures, receivership, attachment, and so forth. Data for noncourt failures are obtained from local credit management groups and boards of trade, sales notices in newspapers, sheriff and auction sales, and personal contacts resulting from this monitoring. The figures are based on the universe count of all failures — samples are not used.

The failures data differ from the bankruptcy statistics of the Administrative Office of the U.S. Courts mainly because court figures are based on case numbers. In court proceedings, each partner is assigned a case number in contrast to the D & B grouping of all partners as one business failure. In addition, the D & B business failure data exclude some bankruptcies designated by the courts as business bankruptcies. The D & B assessments of court data find some court-designated business bankruptcies to be personal bankruptcies and find that some cases listed by the courts as a business were never actually in business.

The failure rate is calculated by dividing the number of failures by the number of firms that D & B classifies in its data base of all existing firms; this figure is then multiplied by 10,000 to obtain a rate of failure per 10,000 firms (the rate is expressed per 10,000 firms to ensure that the relatively small number of failures in relation to all firms is a whole number). The data base excludes firms that are organized as a tax shelter, fledgling businesses that hope to become a going concern, and enterprises that are, in fact, persons moonlighting on second jobs to provide small additions to family income. Thus, it is smaller than the number of taxable firms in Internal Revenue Service statistics.

The D & B failure data were revised in 1984 by adding the following industries to the coverage: agriculture; forestry and fishing; finance; insurance, and real estate; and all services. Therefore, data prior to 1984 are not comparable (particularly relative to the level of business failures) with the subsequent years.

Accuracy

Because the failures figures are based on a universe count of firms, there are no measures of sampling error. Also, there are no estimates of revision error.

Relevance

Business failures indicate the ability of businesses, particularly small businesses, to withstand financial setbacks. When failures increase or are at relatively high levels, people are likely to be pessimistic about undertaking new enterprises (*business firm formation and growth*). By contrast, when failures decline or are at low levels, a more conducive environment for small business is indicated.

Failures are related to business firm formation and growth in previous years as well as to external and internal factors affecting the economic well-being of firms. Because new businesses are risky ventures, an increasing number of new firms leads to an increasing number of failures. Failures also result from external causes beyond the control of management, such as a slowly growing or declining *gross domestic product* and high *interest rates*, as well as from factors specific to the company, such as

Table 7.1

Business Failures

	Number of firms (000)	Average liability per failure ($000)	Failure rate per 10,000 listed firms
1980	12	395	42
1981	17	414	61
1982	25	627	88
1983	31	513	110
1984*	52	562	107
1985	57	645	115
1986	62	726	120
1987	61	568	102
1988	57	693	98
1989	50	841	65
1990	61	924	74
1991	88	1,099	107
1992	97	972	110

Failures by age of business

	Total	3 years or less	4 to 5 years	6 to 10 years	Over 10 years
1991	100%	24.8	16.4	27.3	31.5
1992	100%	24.1	16.0	27.5	32.4

*Because of a change in methodology, the figures are not comparable with those before 1984.

incompetent or inexperienced management, competition in products and local markets, expenses, and debt.

Recent Trends

Business failures averaged 50,000–60,000 firms during 1984–90, and then rose to 88,000 and 97,000 firms in 1991 and 1992 (Table 7.1). Because of the addition of agricultural, financial, and service industry firms to the series in 1984, the data for 1980–83 are not comparable with the later years.

The failure rate, which is the number of failing firms per 10,000 listed firms, was typically 100–110 during 1984–92. The major exceptions were the sharp declines in 1989 and 1990. Average liabilities per failure rose substantially between 1984–88 and 1989–92. Three-fifths of the failures occurred in firms in existence for six or more years in 1991 and 1992.

Reference from Primary Data Source

The Dun & Bradstreet Corporation. Annual. *Business Failure Record.*

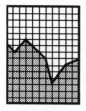

**8
BUSINESS FIRM FORMATION
AND GROWTH**

Business firm formation and growth data represent the number of firms starting in business that have employees and the number of existing firms that hire workers for the first time. The data comprise all employers that begin paying unemployment insurance taxes to state employment security agencies. The employers are primarily for-profit businesses plus a small number of not-for-profit, government, and international organizations. A separate series includes companies that take over existing businesses and file as a new company to pay unemployment insurance taxes for the first time. Information is not available separately for the number of new startup firms commencing business with employees or for the number of existing firms that hire workers for the first time.

Where and When Available

Business firm formation and growth data are provided quarterly by the Office of Advocacy in the U.S. Small Business Administration. The data are available quarterly from the Office of Advocacy in the report, "Current Gross Firm Turnover Rates." Annual data are published in *The State of Small Business: A Report of the President.*

The figures are published eight weeks after the quarter to which they refer. They are revised the following quarter.

Content

Firm "formation" refers to the startup of new firms that have employees and firm "growth" refers to the first hiring of employees by firms in which the owner initially was the only worker. This distinction is limited to very small businesses. When a small business starts in operation, it is included in the data only if the business has employees on the payroll. If a startup firm initially has no employees but subsequently hires one or more workers, it is included in the business firm formation and growth data when the first employees are reported to the state employment security agencies. In this case, the data reflect the growth of the firm, not its initial formation. In addition to the national total, business firm data are provided for all states and ten broad regions of the country.

The business firm formation and growth figures are on a company basis. A small amount of double counting of large firms results from intrastate and interstate aspects of the data. First, large companies having two or more divisions or subsidiaries within a state typically make one consolidated company payment of unemployment insurance taxes within the state. Double counting occurs in the exceptional cases when the divisions or subsidiaries pay their own unemployment taxes. This intrastate double counting is rare, although its extent is not known.

The second source of double counting occurs because large companies that operate in more than one state are counted separately in each state. A rough measure of this interstate double counting is 131,000 reports in 1990, about 2 percent of all companies with employees.

The firm formation and growth data are seasonally adjusted.

Methodology

The business firm formation and growth data are based on applications of firms to state employment security agencies to obtain an employer identification number (EIN). These data are collected from universe counts of all new applications for an EIN. The data are compiled by the Employment and Training Administration in the U.S. Department of Labor. The Department of Labor provides the state data to the Office of Advocacy of the Small Business Administration, which in turn edits the data, consolidates the state data to national totals and ten broad regions of the country, and disseminates the national and geographic information to the public.

Accuracy

There are no estimates of sampling error because the data are obtained from the universe of firms. There are no estimates of revision error.

Relevance

New and expanding businesses increase *employment* and *plant and equipment expenditures*. Startup firms with employees and existing firms that begin hiring workers reflect business confidence and willingness to take financial risks in pursuit of profits (see *business optimism indexes* and *corporate profits*).

Because business startups are risky ventures, an increasing number of startups leads to an increasing number of *business failures*. Some new ventures borrow money for initial investments and startup costs, and thus are sensitive to *interest rates* because of their dependence on *bank loans: commercial and industrial*.

In general, business startups and the initial hiring of employees by existing firms are associated with the dynamism and entrepreneurial spirit in the economy. Almost all are small businesses that respond to a new demand or are the source of new products and new production technologies, which sometimes result in patents for uniqueness of the invention.

Recent Trends

The number of new startup firms plus firms hiring workers for the first time rose from 596,000 in 1982 to 769,000 in 1990, and

Table 8.1

Business Firm Formation and Growth

	1 Startup and first-time hirng firms (000)	2 Business population (all existing firms with employees in the previous year) (000)	3 Startup and first-time hiring firms as a percentage of the business population (1)/(2) x 100
1982	596	4,664	12.8%
1983	633	4,738	13.4
1984	691	4,825	14.3
1985	715	4,995	14.3
1986	725	5,121	14.2
1987	748	5,207	14.4
1988	733	5,388	13.6
1989	745	5,504	13.5
1990	769	5,565	13.8
1991	726	5,636	12.9
1992	736	5,680	13.0

then receded to 726,000–736,000 in 1991–92 (Table 8.1). As a proportion of the business population (all existing firms with employees in the previous year), the startup and first-time hiring firms ranged from 12.8 percent to 14.4 percent over the eleven-year period. The share was largest during 1984–87 and smallest in 1982 and 1991–92. The business population is a continuing inventory of all firms that rises with the onset of startup and first-time hiring firms and declines when existing firms go out of business or report no employees for eight consecutive quarters. The continuous growth in the business population indicates that the annual additions outweigh the deductions, although the increments vary from year to year.

References from Primary Data Source

Executive Office of the President. 1992. *The State of Small Business: A Report of the President.* Pages 22–23.

Hirschberg, David A. 1994. "Formation of Business Firms: A New Series." *Monthly Labor Review.* Forthcoming.

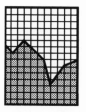

9
BUSINESS OPTIMISM INDEXES

Business optimism indexes represent the expectations of business executives regarding their company's sales, employment, prices, inventories, profits, new orders, and exports in the coming quarter as compared with the actual levels in the same quarter of the previous year. The indexes indicate the percentage of companies expecting an increase over year-earlier levels. Executives are more optimistic about short-run future prospects for their firms when the indexes increase and they are less optimistic about the short-run future when the indexes decrease.

Where and When Available

Business optimism indexes are prepared quarterly by The Dun & Bradstreet Corporation. The figures are published in the bi-monthly newsletter, *Dun & Bradstreet Looks at Business*, and in a press release. The data are available in March, June, September, and December about the fifteenth of the month, which is two weeks before the coming quarter: December for the January– March quarter, March for April–June, June for July–September, and September for October–December. The business optimism indexes are not revised.

In addition to U.S. business optimism indexes, optimism indexes are provided for other countries and regions of the world in these publications. The discussion in this section pertains to the U.S. optimism indexes, although the content and methodology are similar for the other indexes.

Content

Business optimism indexes provide expectations of company executives of directional movements in business activity for the coming quarter in all for-profit industries except agriculture and finance. The directional movements specify an "increase," "decrease," or "no change." The index reflects the percentage of companies anticipating an increase in activity in the coming quarter compared to the level of activity in the same quarter of the previous year. This differs from most economic indicators, which measure changes between consecutive periods, such as from month to month or quarter to quarter, and which give the magnitude as well as the direction of the change.

Separate business optimism indexes are prepared for sales, employment, prices, inventories, profits, new orders, and exports. In addition, component indexes are provided for broad industry categories and for geographic regions of the country.

The business optimism indexes are not seasonally adjusted. However, the indexes implicitly eliminate seasonal variation because they compare activity with the same season (that is, the same quarter) of the previous year. This is discussed further in the introduction under "Seasonality."

Methodology

The business optimism indexes are based on telephone surveys of a sample of company executives conducted every quarter by The Dun & Bradstreet Corporation. Approximately 2,000 companies are surveyed for the national indexes and 3,000 companies for the regional indexes. The sampled companies are selected randomly from the Dun & Bradstreet data base of existing firms (the data base is derived from the Dun & Bradstreet credit rating operation).

The survey obtains data on directional movements in comparison to the same quarter of the previous year for sales, employment, prices, inventories, profits, new orders, and exports. For example, in the survey conducted in November 1992, companies were asked with regard to sales: "How do you expect your firm's volume of sales in the first quarter of 1993 to compare with your firm's volume of sales in the first quarter of 1992?" The answer is "increase," "decrease," or "no change." For each of the seven categories of sales, prices, and so forth, an index is calculated by subtracting the percentage of survey respondents expecting a decrease from the percentage expecting an increase. The responses of all companies are weighted equally regardless of the size of the firm.

This type of index, which provides the direction but not the magnitude of the change, and which gives equal weight to all survey respondents, is a diffusion index (diffusion indexes are discussed further in the *Purchasing Managers' Index*).

Accuracy

There are no estimates of sampling or revision error for the business optimism indexes.

Relevance

Business optimism indexes reflect changes in executives' perceptions of business conditions for their own firms in the coming quarter. When viewed over periods of four or more quarters, they suggest trends in the psychology of executives, which in turn indicates whether they tend to be in an expansive, retrenching, or stay-the-course frame of mind. This affects company actions on *plant and equipment expenditures, employment, average weekly hours,* and *inventory*—sales ratios, because firms' planning horizons generally include the upcoming quarter about which the survey asks.

Since the optimism indexes are based on comparisons with the

Table 9.1

Business Optimism Indexes

	Sales	Employees	Prices	Inventories
1990:1	59	16	33	18
2	57	16	33	18
3	60	17	30	17
4	50	11	33	15
1991:1	36	8	35	10
2	36	10	24	7
3	48	11	23	9
4	46	9	21	8
1992:1	40	7	19	7
2	52	11	18	12
3	61	17	21	17
4	54	12	16	13

	Profits	New orders	Exports
1990:1	53	55	31
2	54	52	36
3	53	62	36
4	43	46	31
1991:1	34	39	33
2	36	44	29
3	47	50	39
4	40	51	26
1992:1	35	43	37
2	44	51	33
3	52	66	32
4	46	56	30

same quarter in the previous year, in economic analysis the indexes relate to the same year-earlier comparisons for other economic indicators. For example, the percentage change in the sales optimism index for the first quarter of 1993 corresponds to the percentage change in the *gross domestic product* from the first quarter of 1992 to the first quarter of 1993.

Recent Trends

During 1990–92, the seven business optimism indexes were generally similar to the cyclical movements of the period (Table 9.1).

This is characterized by the quarters immediately preceding the 1990–91 recession, the recession, and the recovery from the recession. The exception is exports, which are driven by demand in foreign countries and do not show a cyclical pattern.

The index levels are noticeably higher for sales, profits, and new orders than for employees, prices, inventories, and exports. The quarter-to-quarter movements are fairly volatile, with frequent substantial changes in direction.

References from Primary Data Source

Duncan, Joseph W. 1990. "The Dun & Bradstreet Survey of Business Expectations: An Historical Review." The Dun & Bradstreet Corporation. January.

Handler, Douglas P., and Tiziana Mohorovic. 1991. "An Overview of Dun & Bradstreet International Survey Methodologies and Results." The Dun & Bradstreet Corporation.

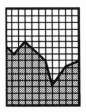

10
CAPACITY UTILIZATION

The capacity utilization rate (CUR) measures the proportion of plant and equipment used in production by the manufacturing, mining, electric and gas utilities industries. It covers the same industries as the *industrial production index*. When production rises faster than capacity, the CUR increases, but when production rises slower (or declines), the CUR decreases.

Where and When Available

The CUR is prepared monthly by the Federal Reserve Board. It is published in a press release and in the *Federal Reserve Bulletin,* the FRB's monthly journal. Secondary sources include *Economic Indicators.*

The figures are available in the middle of the month after the month to which they refer, the same day as the *industrial production index.* Preliminary data are provided for the preceding month; these are revised in the subsequent three months. Annual revisions are made in the fall.

Content

The CUR, expressed as a percent, is the ratio of the industrial production index to plant and equipment capacity. The formula is:

$$\text{CUR} = \frac{\text{Industrial Production Index}}{\text{Plant and Equipment Capacity}} \times 100.$$

Because the numerator is discussed in the section on the production index, this section explains the denominator, or capacity.

The capacity figure represents the economy's ability to produce goods and power assuming the existing plant and equipment facilities are used over the normal operating period for each industry—this ranges from a forty-hour workweek to continuous operations seven days a week. Capacity gradually increases over time as more plant and equipment investment is added each year than physical capital is scrapped. This long-term upward trend shows no cyclical fluctuation. In contrast, industrial production is a highly volatile indicator over the course of the business cycle. As a result, CUR movements mirror the volatile movements of the production index. Industries rarely operate at a CUR of 100 percent, and thus typically have unused or spare capacity available to expand production when demand increases.

The CUR figures are seasonally adjusted.

Methodology

Because the *industrial production index* is available monthly, the primary task for developing the CUR is to provide a measure of capacity. For most industries, direct measures of capacity, such as the number of items that can be produced if the industry is operating at a CUR of 100 percent, are not available. Consequently, indirect measures of capacity are widely used. These are typically derived from year-end surveys of capacity utilization conducted in manufacturing industries by the Census Bureau. Capacity is inferred from these year-end CUR survey data by dividing these figures by the industrial production index for each industry. The resultant capacity figures are modified to reflect supplementary information on direct measures of capacity and on the value of stock of existing capital facilities. The monthly trends between these year-end levels of capacity are obtained by connecting the year-end points by a straight trend line. Monthly movements of the current year are extrapolated according to the monthly trend of the previous year. Supplementary information on direct measures of capacity is obtained from industry sources for a small number of manufacturing industries. Capacity estimates in the mining and utilities are based on data from the Departments of Energy and the Interior and from industry sources.

Accuracy

The typical revision to monthly CUR movements between the preliminary estimate and the third monthly revision is 0.25 percentage point.

Relevance

The CUR is used as an indicator of future *plant and equipment expenditures*. Generally, the higher the CUR, the greater the tendency for plant and equipment shortages to exist, which in turns leads to additional investment. However, it is important to analyze the CUR together with trends on business profits (see *corporate profits*) for clues to future investment. There is no specific CUR level that indicates a shortage of capacity or signals additional investment. Although the difference between 100 percent utilization and the CUR theoretically represents the unused capacity that is available to increase production to meet an increased demand, in fact, CURs typically do not top the 90th percentile except for continuous processing industries such as paper, chemicals, or petroleum refining, or during wartime when mobilization is high and less efficient facilities are put into production.

The CUR is also used to assess future *inflation* in a direct relationship. However, statistical linkages between CUR and price movements are not strong.

Recent Trends

The CUR for manufacturing, mining, and utilities industries fluctuated during 1980–92, ranging from 75–76 percent in 1983–84

Table 10.1

Capacity Utilization (percent)

	Total	Manufacturing	Mining	Utilities
1980	82.1%	80.2%	94.0%	85.5%
1981	80.9	78.8	94.6	82.8
1982	75.0	72.8	86.5	79.5
1983	75.8	74.9	79.9	80.3
1984	81.1	80.4	84.4	82.5
1985	80.3	79.5	82.9	83.5
1986	79.2	79.1	78.2	80.2
1987	81.5	81.6	79.9	82.0
1988	83.7	83.6	84.4	94.1
1989	83.6	83.1	85.9	86.0
1990	82.1	81.1	89.1	86.0
1991	79.2	77.8	88.6	86.3
1992	79.8	78.8	86.8	85.3

to close to 84 percent in 1988−89. It was 79−80 percent in 1991 −92 (Table 10.1). The movements and levels of this overall CUR rate were similar to those for manufacturing industries; the most noticeable difference is that the manufacturing level was typically 0.5 to 1.0 percentage point lower than the total CUR for all industries.

Both the mining and utilities CURs were several percentage points higher than those for manufacturing. The mining industries typically had the highest CUR and also had the most volatile year-to-year movements. The utilities industries had the least volatile yearly movements, except for 1988 and 1989.

References from Primary Data Source

Board of Governors of the Federal Reserve System. 1978. *Federal Reserve Measures of Capacity and Capacity Utilization.*

Raddock, Richard D. 1993. "Industrial Production, Capacity, and Capacity Utilization Since 1987." *Federal Reserve Bulletin.* June.

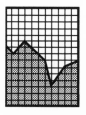

11
COLLECTIVE BARGAINING
SETTLEMENTS

Collective bargaining settlements are new contractual agreements between unions and management on money wages and fringe benefits. They represent changes in future years over the lifetime of the contract. The size of the settlement is measured over the future years of the contract at an annualized rate. Three measures of the change in settlements for a reference period are provided: (1) *wage-rate changes* in money wages of the new contract; (2) *compensation-rate changes* of money wages and fringe benefits that cumulate over the lifetime of the contract without regard for when the changes take effect; and (3) *compensation-cost changes* in money wages and fringe benefits that reflect when the changes take effect. In addition to data on settlements, data are presented on wage-rate changes under contracts in force during the reference period, including those resulting from settlements and those reached earlier and remaining in force.

Where and When Available

Measures of collective bargaining settlements are prepared quarterly for private industry and semiannually for state and local governments by the Bureau of Labor Statistics in the U.S. Department of Labor. The measures are published in press releases and in the monthly BLS journals, *Compensation and Working*

Conditions and *Monthly Labor Review.*

The private industry data are available about four weeks after the quarter to which they refer. The state and local government data are available semiannually in February and August. They are revised annually every March.

Content

Collective bargaining measures for private industry cover settlements for production workers in manufacturing industries and nonsupervisory workers in nonmanufacturing industries. Those for state and local governments cover all classes of workers, supervisory and nonsupervisory. The settlements data for money wages cover agreements for bargaining units of 1,000 workers or more, and the settlements data for compensation (money wages and fringe benefits) cover agreements for bargaining units of 5,000 workers or more.

Lump-sum payments are one-time payments that are not included in the future wage base. They are included only in the compensation-cost measures. Cost-of-living adjustments are included only in the wage-rate change data for all contracts in effect when the amount becomes known, based on actual movements of the *consumer price index, producer price indexes,* or other measures specified in the contract.

The annualized rate of change reflects the average rate of change on a twelve-month basis over the lifetime of the contract. In multiyear contracts, pay changes are often spread unevenly over the different years of the contract. The compensation-cost measure weights each element of the contract according to the time when it is in effect. For example, in a three-year contract, a pay increase that begins in the first year is weighted more than an increase that begins in the second year. By contrast, the other collective bargaining measures—wage rate and compensation rate—weight all pay changes equally regardless of when they go into effect.

The collective bargaining data are not seasonally adjusted.

Methodology

Data for the collective bargaining measures are obtained by the Bureau of Labor Statistics from surveys of companies, the file of union contracts maintained by BLS, the file of pension and insurance benefit payments maintained by the Department of Labor's Office of Labor—Management Standards, newspapers and magazines, and union, management, and trade publications. The lifetime of the contract runs from the beginning date to the termination date, except for contracts that are reopened before the termination date. If new agreements are reached in contract reopenings, the termination date of the settlement is the reopening date.

The rate of change of the settlement is the percentage change in the average rate from what it was just prior to the settlement to what it would be at the end of the contract. The average rate change for all settlements is the sum of the products of each settlement times the number of workers covered, divided by the number of workers under all settlements.

Accuracy

The revision error in the collective bargaining settlements data for annualized wage-rate changes in 77 percent of the estimates is zero change, in 21 percent of the estimates plus or minus 0.1 percentage point, and in 2 percent of the estimates plus or minus 0.2—0.4 percentage point.

Relevance

Collective bargaining settlements affect worker incomes *(average weekly earnings)* and employers' costs *(employment cost index)*. Although unions represent only 16 percent of all workers (12 percent in private industry and 37 percent in federal, state, and local governments), collective bargaining agreements also impact the pay of nonunion workers. This occurs because nonunion employers tend to meet at least part of the union increases

Table 11.1

Collective Bargaining Settlements
(annualized percentage rate of change)

	Wage-rate changes	
	Private industry	State and local governments
1980	7.1	NA
1981	7.9	NA
1982	3.6	NA
1983	2.8	NA
1984	2.4	5.1
1985	2.7	5.4
1986	1.8	5.7
1987	2.1	5.1
1988	2.4	5.3
1989	3.4	5.1
1990	3.2	5.0
1991	3.2	2.8
1992	3.0	2.1

Note: The data represent settlements reached in each year. The annualized rate is the average twelve-month rate for multiyear contracts. See text.
NA: Not available.

in order to compete for workers and to dissuade their workers from becoming unionized. Because they affect workers' incomes, collective bargaining settlements also affect the *distribution of income.*

Employee compensation accounts for approximately 60 percent of the *gross domestic product,* and thus is the largest single item in the cost of production. When employee compensation per hour increases more than *productivity,* the concomitant increase in *unit labor costs* tends to result in higher prices. By contrast, when productivity increases more than compensation per hour, the decline in unit labor costs tends to result in stable or lower prices.

Recent Trends

Wage-rate changes in private industry collective bargaining settlements declined sharply in the early 1980s, and continued at the much lower levels through 1992 (Table 11.1). From annual increases of approximately 7−8 percent in 1980 and 1981, they declined to 3.5 percent in 1982 and generally drifted lower during 1983−87 to around 2 percent. They rose slightly to the 3 percent level during 1988−92.

Wage-rate changes in state and local governments' collective bargaining settlements were slightly over 5 percent for most of the 1984−90 period (these data first became available in 1984). Subsequently, they declined sharply to 3 percent in 1991 and 2 percent in 1992.

Reference from Primary Data Source

Bureau of Labor Statistics, U. S. Department of Labor. 1992. *BLS Handbook of Methods.* Chapter 7. September.

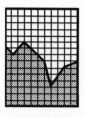

12
CONSUMER ATTITUDE INDEXES

Two organizations provide indicators of consumer attitudes. They focus on consumer perceptions of general business conditions and of their personal financial well-being, plus their attitudes toward purchasing big-ticket items that last a relatively long time — homes, cars, furniture, and major household appliances. This section covers the overall indicators of both organizations: (1) the "consumer confidence index" of The Conference Board, and (2) the "consumer sentiment index" of the University of Michigan. Both indexes measure similar phenomena but, because the methodologies differ and the concepts are not identical, there are periods when their movements differ. This section presents separate descriptions of the Conference Board and Michigan measures, summarizes the main differences between the two, and then analyzes the relevance and recent trends of both.

Consumer Confidence Index

The consumer confidence index (CCI) reflects consumers' attitudes toward the economy, local job markets, and their own financial condition.

Where and When Available

The CCI is provided monthly by the Consumer Research Center of The Conference Board. It is published in two Conference

Board monthly reports, the *Consumer Confidence Survey* and the *Economic Times*. Secondary sources include the *Survey of Current Business*.

The CCI figures are available the last Tuesday of the same month to which they refer. The data are revised for the previous month.

Content

The CCI represents the combined effects of household perceptions of general business conditions; perceptions of available jobs in the respondents' local areas currently and six months ahead; and expected personal family income six months ahead. A rising index means consumers are more optimistic, and a declining one signifies greater pessimism. There are no absolute values of optimism and pessimism, but comparisons of the index levels with previous periods indicate whether consumers are more optimistic or pessimistic than in past periods.

The CCI is based currently on 1985 = 100.

The CCI is seasonally adjusted.

Methodology

Data for the CCI are obtained from a monthly household survey conducted by National Family Opinion, Inc. for The Conference Board. The survey is mailed to approximately 5,000 households in the forty-eight mainland states and the District of Columbia, and the response rate is about 80 percent. A completely new group of households is surveyed each month.

The CCI is constructed by giving equal weight to each of five questions: two on local business conditions currently and six months ahead; two on jobs in the area currently and six months ahead; and one on personal family income six months ahead. In valuing the answers, positive responses are expressed as a percentage of the sum of the total positive and negative responses. Neutral answers are not counted. Depending on the question, positive answers are "good," "better," "plenty," "more," "higher"; negatives are "bad," "worse," "hard to get," "fewer," "lower"; and neutrals are "normal," "same," "not so many."

Accuracy

The sampling error in two out of three cases is approximately plus or minus 1.5 percentage points.

Consumer Sentiment Index

The consumer sentiment index (CSI) reflects consumer attitudes toward the economy, their own financial condition, and perceptions about buying big-ticket durable goods.

Where and When Available

The CSI is provided monthly by the Survey Research Center of the University of Michigan. It is published in the monthly report, *Surveys of Consumer Attitudes.* Secondary sources include the *Survey of Current Business.*

The CSI figures are available within the first five to ten days of the month after the month to which they refer. The monthly data are not revised.

Content

The CSI combines three main categories of household attitudes toward the economy in one figure: (1) expected business conditions in the national economy for one and five years ahead, (2) personal financial well-being compared with one year earlier and expected one year later, and (3) whether the current period is a good or bad time to buy furniture and major household appliances. Upward movements of the index suggest that consumers are becoming more optimistic, and downward movements suggest a growing pessimism. While there are no absolute levels that define optimism and pessimism, comparison levels can be made between current and past periods. For example, the current period can be characterized as being more optimistic or pessimistic than past periods.

Supplementary information that can help in interpreting the reasons for changes in household attitudes is included in *Surveys of Consumer Attitudes*. The full report includes data on attitudes toward such items as employment, prices, interest rates, shortages, and government policies.

The CSI is based currently on 1966: 1Q = 100.

The CSI is not seasonally adjusted.

Methodology

Data for the CSI are obtained from a telephone survey of a sample of households conducted by the Survey Research Center. Approximately 500 households are contacted monthly in the forty-eight mainland states and the District of Columbia, with a response rate of about 80 percent. The sample is designed as a rotating panel in which one-half of the survey respondents are new each month and one-half are carryovers from the survey panel six months earlier.

Five questions are used in constructing the index. There are two questions on expected general economic conditions one year and five years ahead, two questions on personal financial well-being contrasting the current period with one year earlier and one year ahead, and one question on whether the current period is a good time to buy furniture and major household appliances. Equal weight is given to each question. In valuing the answers, only positive and negative replies are used. Depending on the question, positive answers are "up," "better," "good"; negatives are "down," "worse," "bad"; and neutrals are "same," "no change," "uncertain." The proportion of negative responses is subtracted from the proportion of the positive responses (of the sum of positives and negatives), and 100 is added to the difference to avoid negative numbers as follows:

$$\frac{\text{Positive}}{\text{Positive} + \text{Negative}} - \frac{\text{Negative}}{\text{Positive} + \text{Negative}} + 100$$

Accuracy

The sampling error for the CSI in two cases out of three is plus or minus 1.3 percentage points.

Main Differences between the Conference Board and Michigan Indexes

While the CCI and CSI indexes basically measure the same phenomena, there are clear differences in their methodologies associated with the index content, wording of questions, seasonal adjustment, household samples, data collection, and questionnaire response evaluation. The main differences are summarized below.

Index content: The CCI excludes the purchase of big-ticket items, while the CSI includes them.

Wording of questions: For general business conditions, the CCI focuses on the respondents' local economy with a short-term current and six-month outlook, while the CSI focuses on the national economy and a long-term outlook of one to five years ahead. The CCI also includes questions on both current and expected job opportunities that are not in the CSI.

For personal financial well-being, the CCI looks at family income six months ahead, while the CSI asks how well off the respondent is financially compared with one year earlier and what expectations are for one year ahead.

Seasonal adjustment: The CCI is seasonally adjusted, while the CSI is not seasonally adjusted.

Monthly household sample: The CCI sample is 5,000 households, while the CSI sample is 500 households.

Data collection: The CCI uses a mail questionnaire, while the CSI uses a telephone interview.

Survey response evaluation: The CCI and CSI apply different weights for positive and negative answers to survey questions.

Relevance

Perceptions by households of the strength of general business conditions and of their personal financial conditions are closely linked to consumers' feelings of optimism and pessimism about the economy. In theory, when consumers are optimistic, they are more willing to increase spending and incur debt to finance the higher spending. When consumers are pessimistic, they are likely to cut back on spending, pay off debts, and build nest egg savings. An individual's decision to buy a home or other "big-ticket" durable goods is typically based on advance planning and is heavily influenced by consumers' perception of changing economic conditions.

When there are large changes in the indexes, the CCI and CSI are fairly good predictors of shifts in future consumer spending and saving; however, the actual levels of the indexes are less important as harbingers of future spending and saving.

The CCI and the CSI are classified as leading indicators of economic activity by the Bureau of Economic Analysis in the U.S. Department of Commerce. (In addition, Michigan University's "index of consumer expectations," which is based only on the three questions in the CSI relating to the future [the CSI has five questions], is a component of the leading index of the *leading, coincident, and lagging indexes*). Because the monthly and even quarterly movements show erratic increases and decreases, both indexes should be viewed over longer periods to discern a change from past trends.

Recent Trends

The CCI and the CSI generally had similar movements during 1980–92, although there were some differences (Table 12.1). Both indexes were at the lowest levels in 1980–83 and 1990–

Table 12.1

Consumer Attitude Indexes

	Consumer confidence index (1985 = 100)	Consumer sentiment index (1966:1Q = 100)
1980	73.8	64.4
1981	77.4	70.7
1982	59.0	68.0
1983	85.7	87.5
1984	102.3	97.5
1985	100.0	93.2
1986	94.7	94.8
1987	102.6	90.6
1988	115.2	93.7
1989	116.8	92.8
1990	91.5	81.6
1991	68.5	77.6
1992	61.6	77.3

92, with the highest levels occurring in 1984–88. They differed in direction in 1985, 1986, 1987, and 1989. The CCI typically had larger yearly changes than the CSI.

References from Primary Data Sources

Curtain, Richard T. 1982. "Indicators of Consumer Behavior: The University of Michigan Surveys of Consumers." *Public Opinion Quarterly*. Fall.

Linden, Fabian. 1982. "The Consumer as Forecaster." *Public Opinion Quarterly*. Fall.

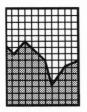

13
CONSUMER INSTALLMENT CREDIT

Consumer installment credit represents loans to households for financing consumer purchases of goods and services and for refinancing existing consumer debt. The loans are scheduled to be repaid in two or more monthly payments. Credit payable in one month or in a lump sum, such as charge accounts and single-payment loans, are excluded from the installment credit figures.

Where and When Available

Measures of consumer installment credit are provided monthly by the Federal Reserve Board. They are published in a statistical release and in the *Federal Reserve Bulletin*, the FRB's monthly journal. Secondary sources include *Economic Indicators* and the *Survey of Current Business*.

The figures are available approximately six weeks after the month to which they refer. The data are revised for the previous month and annually as part of a periodic benchmarking.

Content

The main categories of consumer credit are: auto (passenger cars and station wagons); revolving credit (credit cards used for sales transactions or for cash advances and check credit plans that allow overdrafts up to certain amounts on personal accounts); and "other" loans to consumers for items not specified in the above categories, such as home improvement, recreational vehicles, vans and pickup trucks, and student loans. Secured and unsecured loans are included, except those with secured real estate; loans secured with real estate, including home equity loans (which may be used for consumer spending), are defined as mortgage loans. Securitized consumer loans—loans made by finance companies, banks, and retailers that are sold as securities—are included.

The figures reflect consumer installment credit outstanding at the end of the month. The monthly charge in consumer credit outstanding is the net effect of credit extensions and repayments during the month. Separate data on credit extended and repaid during the month are not available.

The consumer installment credit data are seasonally adjusted.

Methodology

Monthly data on consumer installment credit are based on the following: monthly surveys of a sample of commercial banks conducted by the Federal Reserve Board; quarterly surveys of consumer finance companies, including auto finance companies, conducted by the Federal Reserve Board; monthly surveys of a sample of savings and loan associations conducted by the Office of Thrift Supervision; monthly surveys of credit unions conducted by the National Credit Union Administration (for federally insured credit unions) and by the Credit Union National Association (for other credit unions); and monthly surveys of retail sales conducted by the Bureau of the Census. Benchmark data are available annually for commercial banks, savings and loan associations, mutual savings banks, and retailers (accounts receivable), and every five years for finance companies.

Accuracy

There are no estimates of sampling or revision error for the consumer installment credit figures.

Table 13.1

Consumer Installment Credit Outstanding

	Credit outstanding (billions of dollars) December	Annual percent change Dec. to Dec.
1980	298.2	0.6%
1981	311.3	4.4
1982	325.8	4.7
1983	369.0	13.3
1984	442.6	19.9
1985	517.7	17.0
1986	572.0	10.5
1987	608.7	6.4
1988	662.6	8.9
1989	724.4	9.3
1990	738.8	2.0
1991	733.5	–0.7
1992	741.1	1.0

Relevance

Consumer installment credit supplements *personal income* as a source of consumer purchasing power. In turn, consumer purchasing power impacts *retail sales*. While consumer credit outstanding typically increases, the rate of increase is faster during expansions than during recessions. The occasional monthly declines in consumer credit occur mostly during recessions. Thus, consumer credit accentuates the cyclical movements of consumer spending, particularly for durable goods. People generally borrow more during periods of rapidly growing personal income, because prosperity leads to optimism regarding financial commitments (see *Consumer Attitude Indexes*).

Existing consumer credit is also viewed as a burden on households because they must pay the principal and interest on the loans. The proportion of personal income that consumer credit represents is a commonly used measure of this burden. As this percentage rises during expansions, the growing consumer credit can be expected to depress further consumer borrowing. The ratio of consumer installment credit outstanding to personal income is a component of the lagging index of the *leading, coincident, and lagging indexes.*

Recent Trends

Movements in consumer credit outstanding varied considerably during 1980–92 (Table 13.1). There were modest increases of 4 –5 percent in 1981–82; annual increases skyrocketed to 11–20 percent in 1983–86; the increases slowed but were still robust at 6–9 percent in 1987–89; the increases were very small at 1–2 percent in 1990 and 1992, and credit actually decreased in 1991.

Reference from Primary Data Source

Federal Reserve Board Staff. 1988. "Recent Developments in Economic Statistics at the Federal Reserve: Part 1." *Business Economics*. October.

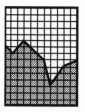

14
CONSUMER PRICE INDEX

The consumer price index (CPI) gauges the overall rate of price change for a fixed basket of goods and services bought by households. Because it prices the same items every month, this measure of inflation or deflation reflects the cost of maintaining the same purchases over time. The CPI is not a cost-of-living index because a COL index provides for pricing perfect substitutes when the substitute product is lower in price in order to measure *minimum* price changes associated with maintaining constant living conditions. A COL index also allows for the effects of changes in income tax rates on a household's after-tax income and thus the ability to buy the same goods and services over time. By contrast, the CPI focuses on pricing the same goods and service items households bought in a base period.

Where and When Available

The CPI is provided monthly by the Bureau of Labor Statistics in the U.S. Department of Labor. The data are published in a press release and in two monthly BLS journals, the *Monthly Labor Review* and *The CPI Detailed Report*. Secondary sources include *Economic Indicators*, the *Survey of Current Business*, and the *Federal Reserve Bulletin*.

The figures are published in the middle of the month immediately following the month to which they refer. They are not revised on a regular monthly basis. Major benchmark revisions are made approximately every ten years, mainly to reflect changes in the goods and services households buy. Smaller technical revisions, such as including or substituting new products or refining the methodology, are occasionally made between benchmarks.

Content

The CPI records price changes in food and beverages, housing, apparel, transportation, medical care, entertainment, education, personal care, and tobacco products. It is published in two versions, the CPI-U and the CPI-W. The CPI-U represents all urban households including urban workers in all occupations, the unemployed, and retired persons; in 1980, this accounted for 80 percent of the noninstitutional population. The CPI-W represents urban wage and clerical workers employed in blue-collar occupations; it accounted for 32 percent of the 1980 noninstitutional population. Both CPI measures exclude rural households, military personnel, and persons in institutionalized housing such as prisons, old age homes, and long-term hospital care.

CPIs are calculated for the nation as a whole, for broad geographic regions, and for large metropolitan areas. They therefore provide differential national and geographic measures of price movements. However, the CPI does not reflect the actual dollar level of living costs in the nation or in one area compared with another.

Rather, the weights of the CPI are based on the proportions of household budgets that consumers actually spend for particular goods and services. The CPI reflects actual spending patterns. It is not a "standard of living" concept that prices spending patterns aimed at achieving certain standards of nutrition, housing, health, and so on, that society considers appropriate. The indicator measures price changes associated with buying the same set of items over periods of approximately ten years (the spending patterns are updated every ten years). Currently, the CPI is based on spending patterns during the 1982–84 period. New spending patterns reflecting household expenditures in the early 1990s will be incorporated in the CPI in the late 1990s.

The CPI is based on actual transaction prices, which take into account such variations as premiums or discounts from the list price, sales and excise taxes, import duties, and trade-in allowances when the used car trade-in is part of the new car price. The CPI reflects price movements for the same or similar item exclusive of enhancement or reduction in the quality or quantity of the item (see "Methodology" below).

The CPI is currently based on 1982–84 = 100.

The CPI figures are seasonally adjusted.

Methodology

The monthly price data are obtained primarily from surveys of retail and service establishments, utilities, and households. Surveyors visit or telephone the same retail and service establishments and price the same items (or close substitutes) every month or bimonthly, depending on the city and item in the survey sample. To reduce survey costs, rental information is obtained by less frequent visits (every six months) to one of six groups of apartments and single-family homes. The monthly rental price represents the weighted change of rentals for the most recent month and the prior six-month period for the same group of housing units. For example, the same groups are surveyed at six-month intervals for January and July, February and August, and so on. For a small number of items such as used cars, air fares, and postal rates, BLS receives monthly reports on prices from trade sources and the Postal Service.

The current index weights, which represent the proportion of household budgets spent on the various components, reflect consumer purchasing patterns during 1982–84. The weights are revised approximately every ten years based on surveys of households to determine their actual purchase patterns. These surveys also obtain information on which retail establishments where purchases are made, in order that greater weight may be given to prices in stores that have the largest sales volumes. One-fifth of the retail establishments in the sample is changed every year to reflect shifts in shopping preferences such as toward discount stores.

If the quality or quantity of an item in the monthly survey has changed, an adjustment is made to reflect the improvement or decline. The goal is to price products having the same functional characteristics over time. For example, if an apartment building is renovated to include air conditioning, the increased rent attributable to the air conditioning is not represented as a price increase in the CPI. By contrast, if a loaf of bread gets smaller but the price remains the same, the price of bread per unit has in fact increased and is represented as a price increase in the CPI. Because the data needed to make the necessary adjustments are not always available, the CPI contains an unknown amount of price change caused by quality and quantity changes.

Accuracy

On average, the sampling error of the monthly percentage change in the CPI is plus or minus 0.07. For example, if the CPI increases by 0.3 percent from one month to the next, in two of three cases the increase ranges from 0.23 to 0.37 percent due to sampling error.

Relevance

The CPI is the most widely quoted figure on inflation. In the formulation of fiscal and monetary policies (see "Relevance" under *gross domestic product*), trends in the CPI are a major guide in determining whether economic growth should be stimulated or restrained.

The CPI is also contrasted with *unemployment* to analyze the tradeoff between *inflation* and unemployment. (The concept that inflation and unemployment are inversely related is referred to as the Phillips Curve.) Maintaining a better balance between inflation and unemployment was included in the goals of the Full

Table 14.1

Consumer Price Index
(annual percent change)

	CPI-U			CPI-W
	All items	All items excluding energy	All items excluding food and energy	All items
1980	13.5	11.6	12.4	13.4
1981	10.3	10.0	10.4	10.3
1982	6.2	6.7	7.4	6.0
1983	3.2	3.6	4.0	3.0
1984	4.3	4.7	5.0	3.5
1985	3.6	3.9	4.3	3.5
1986	1.9	3.9	4.0	1.6
1987	3.6	4.1	4.1	3.6
1988	4.1	4.4	4.4	4.0
1989	4.8	4.7	4.5	4.8
1990	5.4	5.2	5.0	5.2
1991	4.2	4.6	4.9	4.1
1992	3.0	3.2	3.7	2.9

Employment and Balanced Growth Act of 1978 (Humphrey-Hawkins Act). The act set a 1988 goal of zero percent inflation based on the CPI and 4 percent unemployment. The act allows a deviation from the inflation goal if it impedes achieving the unemployment goal.

The CPI is used in a variety of ways to adjust for cost escalation in commerce and government programs: inflation adjustments to wages, pensions, and income maintenance payments for cost of living allowances; inflation adjustments in business contracts; and indexing of federal individual income tax returns to limit the inflation-induced bracket creep. Many labor—management union contracts are based on CPI-W. In addition, the CPI is used to deflate various economic indicators to reflect constant prices such as the *gross domestic product*.

Recent Trends

Inflation levels and movements as gauged by the CPI-U and the CPI-W were similar during 1980–92 (Table 14.1). The CPI-U measure showed the very high 13.5 and 10.3 percent inflation rates in 1980–81 decelerating sharply in 1982–83. The annual increases then averaged 4 percent during 1984–92, with fluctuations of one to two percentage points around the 4 percent average. The basic differences in the CPI measures excluding energy and food prices are that because of the generally relatively slower price increases for food and energy products than for other items in most years, inflation excluding food and energy prices was typically slightly higher than for all goods and services over the thirteen-year period.

References from Primary Data Sources

Bureau of Labor Statistics, U.S. Department of Labor. 1992. *BLS Handbook of Methods*. Chapter 19. September.

Fixler, Dennis. 1993. "The Consumer Price Index: Underlying Concepts and Caveats." *Monthly Labor Review*. December.

Moulton, Brent R. 1993. "Basic Components of the CPI: Estimation of Price Changes." *Monthly Labor Review*. December.

Aizcorbe, Ana M., and Patrick C. Jackman. 1993. "The Commodity Substitution Effect in CPI Data, 1982–91." *Monthly Labor Review*. December.

Kokoski, Mary F. 1993. "Quality Adjustment of Price Indexes." *Monthly Labor Review*. December.

Schmidt, Mary Lynn. 1993. "Effects of Updating the CPI Market Basket." *Monthly Labor Review*. December.

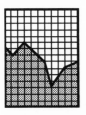

15
CORPORATE PROFITS

Corporate profits are the returns to corporate enterprise from current operations. Profits occur when operating income (receipts) exceeds operating expenses (costs), and losses (negative profits) occur when expenses exceed income. Because profits are the difference between income and expenses, both elements affect profits. From one year to the next, for example, profits decline when income rises less than expenses or when income declines more than expenses, while profits increase when income rises more than expenses or when income declines less than expenses. Profits are measured both before and after the payment of federal, state, and local government income taxes. Undistributed corporate profits are the profits retained in the business after corporate income taxes are paid and dividends are distributed to stockholders. (Profits also accrue to unincorporated sole proprietorships and partnerships; corporations differ from unincorporated businesses in the method of designating ownership in the company, liability of owners, and income taxes.)

Where and When Available

Corporate profits measures are prepared quarterly for all industries by the Bureau of Economic Analysis in the U.S. Department of Commerce as part of the *gross domestic product.* The profits estimates are available fifty-five days after the quarter to which they refer; they are revised one month later and annually every July. They are published in a press release and in BEA's monthly journal, the *Survey of Current Business*. Secondary sources include *Economic Indicators*.

Corporate profits measures are prepared quarterly for manufacturing, mining, and retail and wholesale trade corporations by the Bureau of the Census in the U.S. Department of Commerce. The data are available about two and a half months after the quarter to which they refer; they are not revised. They are published in a press release and in the Census Bureau's *Quarterly Financial Report*. Secondary sources include the *Survey of Current Business*.

Corporate profits measures are prepared annually for all industries by the Internal Revenue Service in the U.S. Department of the Treasury. Preliminary data are available about fifteen months after the fiscal year to which they refer; they are revised seven months later. They are published in the IRS report, *Statistics of Income: Corporation Income Tax Returns*.

Content

Three estimates of corporate profits are generally defined as specified by federal government laws and reported on federal income tax returns, but with some variation from the income tax laws. Variations from the income-tax-based profits occur in company financial reports to stockholders and in estimates of the *gross domestic product*. In the case of stockholder reports, which are most closely reflected in the Census Bureau's *Quarterly Financial Report,* accelerated depreciation is used less frequently than it is on income tax returns, and stockholder reports often include deductions for anticipated expenditures associated with anticipated plant closings, company reorganizations, pension liabilities, and deferred compensation when the decision to make these expenditures is made, while tax returns include these expenditures only when they are made. In the GDP estimates, profits differ from those in income tax data mainly as follows:

• In the GDP, corporations are defined to include (1) institutions required to file federal corporate income tax returns—for-profit corporations, savings and loan associations, mutual savings banks, and cooperatives—and (2) certain institutions not required to file federal corporate income tax returns—Federal Reserve Banks, federally sponsored credit unions, private noninsured pension funds, and nonprofit organizations that primarily serve business.

• In the GDP, company profits exclude profits from subsidiaries of U.S. companies abroad and include profits from subsidiaries of foreign companies in the United States.

• In the GDP, inventory profits and losses are modified in the "inventory valuation adjustment" to eliminate profits or losses on inventory holdings due to changes in inventory prices.

• In the GDP, depreciation allowances on structures and equipment are modified in the "capital consumption adjustment" to reflect the economic lifetime of capital facilities actually used in business practice in place of the service lives specified for these facilities in the income tax laws, and to reflect the current cost of replacing the existing structures and equipment in place of the original acquisition cost.

Profits including the inventory valuation and capital consumption adjustments reflect actual business practice, in contrast to profits measures excluding these adjustments, which are geared to the federal income tax laws.

• In the GDP, capital gains and losses from the sale of property are excluded from profits, except for sales of securities which are the primary activity of security dealers and brokers.

• In the GDP, depletion allowances for using up nonreplaceable mineral reserves of mining corporations are added to profits.

• In the GDP, charges for bad debts are treated as changes in asset valuation rather than as a deduction from profits.

In 1989, the difference of $47.4 billion between the GDP corporate profits estimate ($342.9 billion) and the Internal Revenue Service profits estimate ($390.3 billion) was due largely to the above factors.

The quarterly corporate profits data in the *gross domestic product* are seasonally adjusted and presented at an annual rate. The corporate profits data in the Quarterly Financial Report are seasonally adjusted at the all-manufacturing, all-durable manufacturing, and all-nondurable manufacturing levels.

Methodology

Corporate profits in the *gross domestic product* are estimated every quarter from the *Quarterly Financial Report* (QFR), company stockholder reports published in the press for certain industries not covered in the QFR, and indirect data on the economic activity for other industries such as construction. These are revised in subsequent years based on *Statistics of Income* (SOI) information, including the effects of IRS audits of corporate income tax returns. Special adjustments to the reported data for the GDP estimates of profits are made for institutional coverage, inventories, depreciation, capital gains and losses, depletion, and bad debts as noted above under "Content."

The QFR is a quarterly survey of a sample of manufacturing, mining, and retail and wholesale trade corporations that provides profits data based on company definitions used in reports to stockholders. Manufacturing accounts for 85−90 percent of the profits of all industries in the QFR. The manufacturing information collected from a sample of corporations is weighted to represent the universe of all manufacturing companies with more than $250,000 in assets. The mining and trade sample survey information is obtained from all companies in those industries above certain size thresholds, and the QFR profits measures are confined to the reports of those companies; thus, the mining and trade data are not weighted to represent the universe of all firms in those industries.

The SOI is an annual report based on a sample of corporate federal income tax returns in all industries. The sample is augmented to provide universe estimates in all industries. The IRS also publishes the results of audits of selected corporate tax returns in later years that data users may later utilize to revise the published SOI data. The SOI provides the most comprehensive coverage and detailed information of profit-and-loss statements of U.S. corporations.

Accuracy

The average revision error of corporate profits in the *gross domestic product* as a percentage of the quarterly change in profits is plus or minus 18 percent from the 55-day to the 85-day estimates, and plus or minus 46 percent from the 85-day to the final annual estimates. The sampling error of profits for the total of all manufacturing industries in the *Quarterly Financial Report* is plus or minus 0.5 percent in two of three cases for manufacturing corporations; there are no sampling errors for the mining and trade corporations because a sample is not used. The sampling error of profits for all industries in *Statistics of Income* is plus or minus 0.3 percent in two of three cases.

Relevance

Output of corporations accounts for 60 percent of *gross domestic product* and 70 percent of gross business product (gross business product excludes output of households and governments). Profits are the returns of investment and risk taking and are the prime motivating factor of the private enterprise economy. Past profits and anticipated future profits directly affect business actions on *employment, inventory*—sales ratios, and *plant and equipment expenditures*. When business conditions are buoyant, entrepreneurs and executives are optimistic about the future and likely to expand their work force, inventories, and investment in capital facilities; by contrast, when business conditions are depressed, entrepreneurs and executives are pessimistic about the future and are likely to retrench employment, inventories, and investment (see *business optimism indexes*).

Profits are one of the more volatile elements of the economy in that they tend to rise faster than the overall economy during business expansions and to decline more sharply than the rest of the economy during business recessions. While some corporations lose money, it is rare for all corporations in total to lose money. The last time total corporate profits of all companies declined was in the depth of the Great Depression in 1931 and 1932.

Undistributed profits, also referred to as retained earnings, are profits before the payment of dividends to stockholders. Undistributed profits are internally generated funds available to business for use in operations, investment, or as an addition to surplus in the balance sheet (external funds are obtained from business loans and selling new equity stock). Profits before dividends fluctuate more than dividends since companies do not change dividend payments frequently. Company actions to change dividends are an indicator of business optimism (see *business optimism indexes*), rising with dividend increases and declining with dividend decreases.

Recent Trends

Corporate profits of domestic industries generally rose during 1980–92, although within the period there were several years of decline, based on the concepts of the *gross domestic product* (Table 15.1). (Domestic industries exclude reinvested profits of U.S. affiliates abroad and reinvested profits of foreign affiliates in the United States.) Profits including the inventory valuation adjustment (IVA) and capital consumption adjustment (CCAdj) were lower than profits excluding these adjustments during 1980 –83, but profits including the IVA and CCAdj were higher during 1984–92. These shifts reflect the effects of two patterns: (1) the rate of *inflation* declined in the early 1980s, thus reducing the negative IVA substantially and the negative CCAdj by a small amount in those years, and (2) federal income tax law changes in the early 1980s resulted in faster depreciation of plant and equipment investment for calculating corporate income tax liabilities than

Table 15.1

Corporate Profits (billions of dollars)

	1 Before income taxes including IVA and CCAdj	2 Before income taxes excluding IVA and CCAdj	3 After income taxes excluding IVA and CCAdj	4 Undistributed profits excluding IVA and CCAdj
1980	142.7	205.9	121.1	78.4
1981	152.8	199.7	118.5	64.3
1982	123.7	148.5	85.4	31.5
1983	182.3	180.4	103.1	33.6
1984	233.0	209.3	115.3	44.1
1985	250.0	194.2	97.7	16.4
1986	238.7	184.9	78.4	−14.6
1987	280.3	248.4	121.3	29.7
1988	315.9	298.5	161.4	75.3
1989	303.4	283.5	142.2	34.3
1990	312.6	297.8	159.1	30.8
1991	302.6	295.5	165.6	51.6
1992	344.9	333.2	186.9	59.6

Note: Based on the gross domestic product measures.
IVA = inventory valuation adjustment. CCAdj = capital consumption adjustment.

companies actually used in practice, thus shifting the CCadj in later years substantially from a negative to a positive amount. Profits before and after taxes both rose over the twelve-year period and had the same year-to-year movements (except for 1991). Undistributed profits were lower during 1983−92 than they had been in 1980−81 (except for 1988), and they were negative in 1986. Profits showed sharp yearly changes over the entire period.

References from Primary Data Sources

Bureau of the Census, U.S. Department of Commerce. Quarterly. *Quarterly Financial Report.*

Bureau of Economic Analysis, U.S. Department of Commerce. 1985. "Corporate Profits: Profits Before Tax, Profit Tax Liability, and Dividends." *Methodology Papers.* May.

Internal Revenue Service, U.S. Department of the Treasury. Annual. *Statistics of Income: Corporation Income Tax Returns.*

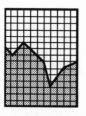

16
CRB FUTURES PRICE INDEX

The CRB Index represents futures prices of twenty-one raw and semiprocessed commodities sold up to nine months in advance of delivery. These expected prices differ from actual prices when the futures contracts expire.

Where and When Available

The CRB Futures Price Index (CRB Index) is provided daily by the Commodity Research Bureau and the New York Futures Exchange, Inc. It is disseminated electronically by the New York Futures Exchange and published in the *Wall Street Journal* and *New York Times*. The New York Futures Exchange provides an up-to-date index every fifteen seconds during trading hours.

Revisions are made when new commodities are added and existing ones deleted to reflect changing trading volumes.

Content

The twenty-one commodities and their general groupings in the index are: coffee, cocoa, and sugar (imports); live cattle, hogs, and pork bellies (meats); corn, wheat, soybeans, soy meal, and soy oil (grains); crude oil, heating oil, unleaded gasoline, copper, lumber, and cotton (industrials); gold, silver, and platinum (metals); and orange juice (miscellaneous). Separate indexes are developed for the broad components of imports, meats, grains, industrials, metals, and miscellaneous.

The CRB is currently based on 1967 = 100.

The CRB figures are not seasonally adjusted.

Methodology

Prices are based on actual sales (not bids and offers) of commodity futures on the various commodity exchanges. If the commodity is not sold during the day, the closing price of the previous day is used in calculating the current day index.

The index construction uses both arithmetic and geometric averaging. Each commodity is weighted equally in the base year of the index. The calculation is made as follows: (1) to obtain the 1967 base period, futures prices in 1967 over nine months are averaged arithmetically for each of the twenty-one commodities; (2) these twenty-one arithmetic averages are averaged geometrically into a single 1967 base period figure, say A; (3) the same procedure of arithmetic and geometric averaging is done for futures prices nine months ahead in the current month, resulting in a single current month figure, say B; (4) the CRB Index is obtained by dividing B by A and multiplying by 100.

Geometric averaging ensures that relatively large price increases or decreases for particular commodities do not influence the index more than the items having small price changes (by contrast, the *consumer price index, producer price indexes, import and export price indexes,* and *GDP price indexes* are averaged arithmetically). Technically, arithmetic averaging is the sum of n numbers divided by n, and geometric averaging is the nth root of the product of n numbers.

Accuracy

There are no estimates of sampling or revision error for the CRB Index.

Table 16.1

CRB Futures Price Index
(1967 = 100)

	December	Annual percent change (Dec. to Dec.)
1980	308.5	9.6%
1981	254.9	−17.4
1982	234.0	−8.2
1983	277.6	18.6
1984	244.2	−12.0
1985	229.4	−6.1
1986	209.1	−8.8
1987	232.5	11.2
1988	251.8	8.3
1989	229.9	−8.7
1990	222.6	−3.2
1991	208.1	−6.5
1992	202.8	−2.5

Relevance

The CRB Index is an indicator of future inflation because of its sensitivity to actual and perceived shortages and surpluses of the component commodities. The index movements are a precursor to movements in the crude materials index of the *producer price indexes* (the PPI represents current prices of a broader range of raw materials, and, as noted above under "Methodology," the PPI movements are also averaged differently). Because raw materials and commodities in the early stages of processing become a decreasing component of the production cost of semifinished and finished goods, the CRB Index is of particular interest when it shows large price movements over sustained periods. These are more likely to have a subsequent, significant impact on semifinished and finished goods prices.

In addition, businesses trade CRB Index futures on the New York Futures Exchange to hedge against price changes.

Recent Trends

The CRB Index has volatile price movements (Table 16.1). Annual price changes during 1980–92 show large price increases in one year and large price decreases in the following year, sharply accelerating and decelerating rates of inflation, and consecutive years of substantial price declines.

Reference from Primary Data Source

New York Futures Exchange, Inc. 1992. *CRB Index Futures Reference Guide.*

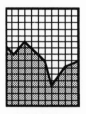

17
DISTRIBUTION OF INCOME

The distribution of income figures represent the proportion of total household money income as received by households in low-, middle-, and high-income groups. The data are typically shown in quintiles, which array the number of households from the lowest to the highest fifths based on income. For example, in 1992, after the payment of income, social security, and property taxes, the 20 percent of households with the lowest incomes received 4.5 percent of all income, while the 20 percent of households with the highest incomes received 43.6 percent of all income. Quintile income groups (or quartiles for fourths, deciles for tenths, etc.) provide a relative measure of the change in income distribution over time by comparing the position of one income group with that of others. The absolute dollar income of each income group rises over time because of *inflation* and increasing *productivity.*

Where and When Available

The Bureau of the Census in the U.S. Department of Commerce provides annual measures of the distribution of income. The data on income before the payment of taxes are published annually in *Money Income of Households, Families, and Persons in the United States.* The income data after the payment of taxes are provided on an unpublished basis.

The income measures are available in the fall after the year to which they refer. Revisions for the previous years are made in the annual publication.

Content

The income measures represent household money income (cash income) both before and after the payment of income taxes, social security taxes, federal employee retirement taxes, and property taxes. Money income is derived from wages, self-employment earnings, social security and other income maintenance benefits, interest, dividends, rent, and all other cash income that is regularly received. Noncash benefits such as food stamps, Medicare, Medicaid, and rent supplements, as well as income from nonrecurring sources such as capital gains and life insurance settlements, are excluded from money income.

Household income figures are categorized both before and after taxes in $5,000 increments (e.g., under $5,000, $5,000–9,999 . . . $95,000–99,999, $100,000 and over), as well as by the quintile percentages. Additional detail on income before taxes is shown separately for families and unrelated individuals for the different dollar income groups. (A family refers to two or more persons related by blood, marriage, or adoption and living together in a house, apartment, or rooms intended for separate living quarters. A household consists of all families and unrelated individuals living together.)

Methodology

The before-tax income data are based on the current population survey (CPS) conducted by the Census Bureau. The information is collected every March for the previous calendar year. The survey sample is approximately 60,000 households. Typically, 57,000 are interviewed and 3,000 are not available for interviews. For additional detail on the CPS, see *unemployment*.

Estimates of household income after taxes are based on tax simulations incorporating the CPS income figures with several other data sources. Federal and state income taxes are simulated based on data from the Internal Revenue Service's *Statistics of Income* and the Commerce Clearinghouse, Inc.'s *State Tax Handbook*; social security and federal employee retirement taxes are estimated using the legal percentage rates for these taxes; and property taxes are estimated from information in the U.S. Department of Housing and Urban Development's American housing survey.

Accuracy

The sampling error in two of three cases for the share of income before taxes in 1991 is 0.05 percentage point for the lowest quintile and 0.6 percentage point for the highest quintile. This differential reflects the greater proportion of income in the highest quintile.

Based on estimates derived from administrative records of the income tax, unemployment insurance, social security, and other programs, survey respondents tend to understate their income by approximately 11 percent in the aggregate for all sources of income. However, this overall underreporting is not taken into account in developing the income distribution figures because determining the variations in underreporting among income groups is difficult.

Relevance

The income distribution focuses on differences in economic well-being among groups in the population. The data show how equitably income is distributed in society and highlight how overall economic trends are affecting different income groups. A large disparity in the distribution suggests a society that is divided into "haves" and "have nots," which raises both economic and social concerns. Economic growth is hindered when purchasing power and profit-motivated incentives are not broadly based. Socially, a large disparity results in increasing discord and despair among the population. Economic growth and social harmony are regarded as essential to a democratic and stable society, even while

Table 17.1

Distribution of Income: Households' Shares
(percent)

	1992	1991	1990	1989	1988	1987	1986	1985	1980
Income Before Taxes	100.0%	100.0%	100.0%	100.0%	100.0%	100.0%	100.0%	100.0%	100.0%
Lowest fifth	3.8	3.8	3.9	3.8	3.8	3.8	3.8	3.9	4.2
Second fifth	9.4	9.6	9.6	9.5	9.6	9.6	9.7	9.8	10.2
Third fifth	15.8	15.9	15.9	15.8	16.0	16.1	16.2	16.2	16.8
Fourth fifth	24.2	24.2	24.0	24.0	24.3	24.3	24.3	24.4	24.8
Highest fifth	46.9	46.5	46.6	46.8	46.3	46.2	46.1	45.6	44.1
Income After Taxes	100.0%	100.0%	100.0%	100.0%	100.0%	100.0%	100.0%	100.0%	100.0%
Lowest fifth	4.5	4.5	4.5	4.6	4.5	4.5	4.4	4.6	4.9
Second fifth	10.6	10.8	10.8	10.8	10.9	10.9	10.9	11.0	11.6
Third fifth	16.8	16.9	16.9	16.9	17.1	17.2	17.2	17.2	17.9
Fourth fifth	24.5	24.6	24.3	24.4	24.6	24.8	24.8	24.7	25.1
Highest fifth	43.6	43.2	43.5	43.3.	42.9	42.5	42.6	42.6	40.6

Note: The quintile money income ranges before taxes in 1992 are: Lowest fifth—$12,663 and under; Second fifth—$12,664–24,299; Third fifth—$24,300–37,999; Fourth fifth—$38,000–58,199; Highest fifth—$58,200 and over.

political and economic philosophies for achieving these goals differ. Measures of *poverty* are related to the distribution of income.

Recent Trends

The quintile income distribution of households shows a declining share of the nation's money income received by each of the first four fifths of the households and an increasing share received by the top fifth during 1980–92 (Table 17.1). This pattern occurred both before and after the payment of federal and state income taxes, social security and federal employee retirement taxes, and property taxes. Each of the first four fifths of the households received a lower share of the income continuously over the twelve-year period, although the declines were sharper during 1980–85 than during 1985–92. Before taxes, the top fifth of households rose from receiving 44.1 percent of all income in 1980 to 46.5 percent in 1992 (2.4 percentage points). After taxes, the top fifth rose from 40.6 percent in 1980 to 43.6 percent in 1992 (3.0 percentage points).

Reference from Primary Data Source

Bureau of the Census, U.S. Department of Commerce. Annual. *Money Income of Households, Families, and Persons in the United States*.

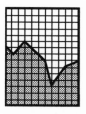

18
EMPLOYMENT

Employment represents workers engaged in gainful work. There are two official measures of employment. One is a count of jobs and is detailed here. The other, which is a count of employed persons that is provided as part of the *unemployment* figures, is detailed in that chapter. The main differences in the two measures are summarized later in this chapter.

Where and When Available

Employment data are provided monthly by the Bureau of Labor Statistics in the U.S. Department of Labor. The data are published in a press release and in two BLS monthly journals, the *Monthly Labor Review* and *Employment and Earnings*. Secondary sources include *Economic Indicators*, the *Survey of Current Business*, and the *Federal Reserve Bulletin*.

The monthly figures are available on the third Friday after the week containing the twelfth of the month, which falls on the first or second Friday of the month following the month to which they refer. On the day the data are released, the commissioner of labor statistics reports on recent employment and unemployment trends to the Joint Economic Committee of Congress. Preliminary data are provided for the immediately preceding month; these are revised in the subsequent two months. Annual revisions are made in June of the following year.

Content

Employment figures count the number of paid nonfarm civilian jobs. To be counted, a job must be on the payroll of a business, government, or nonprofit organization. Since some individuals hold two or more jobs, the number of jobs exceeds the number of working persons. Employment data exclude farm jobs, self-employment, domestic jobs in private households, unpaid family work, and the armed forces.

Persons on paid leave for illness or vacation are counted as employed because the job continues as a payroll cost. Those temporarily not working because of illness, vacation, strike, or lockout and who are not paid during this absence are not counted as employed.

The employment figures are seasonally adjusted.

Methodology

The employment data are based on employer payroll records that represent employees on payrolls during pay periods that include the twelfth day of the month. The data are obtained from a mail survey of a sample of over 370,000 employer establishments in 1992 that includes employers with only one work location as well as those with several establishments. The survey sample covered 39 percent of all nonfarm employment in 1992. The sample is weighted toward large establishments: large establishments are sure to be included in the sample while small establishments have less of a chance of inclusion. The survey sample is not a probability sample. The survey response rate rises from 56 percent in the preliminary estimate to 83 and 90 percent in the revised estimates in the subsequent two months. The employment estimates are calculated for specific industries and categories of governments, and the figures for industry and government components are summed to obtain the nonfarm economywide total.

The surveys of industry establishments and state and local

governments are conducted for BLS by state employment agencies. Data covering all federal civilian workers are provided by the U.S. Office of Personnel Management. The monthly estimates are based on changes in employment by the same establishments reporting in the preceding month.

The monthly data are revised every year based on the universe of all employers that pay unemployment insurance premiums to state employment offices. These benchmark data are obtained for March of the previous year, and the relative revisions for March are carried back through the previous eleven months and extrapolated forward to the current period.

Because of the difficulty of obtaining timely information on the startup of new firms, the payroll survey is late in capturing the employment of these firms. To compensate for this understatement of employment, the survey figures are augmented by an estimate of the additional employment generated by the new firms that have not yet been incorporated in the survey. The estimate is based on the difference between the benchmark and the sample survey data of the past three years and the relationship of the employment movement in the most recent quarter to the average employment growth over the past several years. If the current employment growth is smaller than the long-term rate, the survey figures are augmented by less-than-average additional employment for the undercoverage of new firms, and if the current employment growth is greater than the long-term rate, the survey figures are augmented by more-than-average additional employment for the undercoverage of new firms. The effect of this "bias adjustment" is to correct at an early stage for the delayed coverage of new firms and for the tendency of the sample to understate employment growth when the average size of the establishment in the industry is small.

Accuracy

The annual benchmark data typically revise employment levels within a range of plus or minus 0.5 percentage point. The average benchmark revision is 0.2 percentage point. Shorter-term revisions in the monthly data show that in two of three chances, the monthly level will be revised between plus or minus 78,000 workers between the preliminary figure and the revision two months later.

Relevance

Employment is the main source of household incomes, which, in turn, are spent on consumer goods and services. Because consumer spending accounts for approximately 65 percent of the *gross domestic product*, employment is a key factor affecting economic growth. In addition, employment is a component of the coincident index of the *leading, coincident, and lagging indexes*.

The distribution of employment between high- and low-paying jobs also affects household incomes. The types of jobs held influence economic growth as well as living conditions, because the bulk of the population depends on employment for their major source of income.

Recent Trends

Employment based on the payroll survey showed three different periods of growth in 1980–92 (Table 18.1). There was no employment growth in 1980–83, as a result of the sharp drop in 1982 reflecting the 1981–82 recession; employment rose by an average of 2.7 million workers annually in 1984–90; after declining by 1 million workers in 1991 due to the 1990–91 recession, it remained close to that level in 1992. (Comparative trends in the payroll and household surveys of employment are noted in the next section.)

Comparison of Alternative Employment Measures

This section summarizes the main differences between the employment figures obtained from surveys of employer payroll records described here and the employment data associated with *unemployment*, which are based on a household survey.

Coverage

Employment figures based on the payroll survey are limited to employees in nonagricultural industries and government civilian workers who are paid for their work or for their absence from the job. By contrast, employment figures based on the household survey cover a broader range of employment, including farm and nonfarm workers, the self-employed, government civilian workers and the U.S. resident armed forces, private household workers, unpaid workers in an family business, plus those temporarily absent from work due to illness, vacation, strike, or lockout, whether or not they are paid during their absence. The payroll figures partially compensate for their smaller coverage by including workers of all ages and multiple jobs of workers, while the household survey is limited to workers sixteen years and older and counts each worker only once regardless of how many jobs he or she may hold. (Supplementary data on multiple jobs of workers are available in the household survey beginning in 1994.) The net effect is that the household survey exceeds the payroll survey in 1992 by 9.1 million civilian workers and 10.7 million when the armed forces are included.

Recent Trends

Both the payroll and the household surveys show similar long-term movements in employment (Table 18.1). For example, over the 1980–92 period, payroll employment rose 18.1 million for an annual rate of 1.5 percent, and household employment rose by 18.3 million for an annual rate of 1.4 percent. Similarly, both surveys showed increases in employment in all years except 1982, although the decline in 1982 was noticeably sharper in the payroll survey (–2.0 percent in the payroll survey and –1.0 percent in the household survey).

   Short-term monthly movements in the two surveys occasionally show different patterns over a few months, indicating a temporary uncertainty in the job figures. However, the payroll survey

Table 18.1

Employment: Alternative Definitions
(millions)

	Payroll survey (nonfarm jobs)	Household survey (civilian workers)
1980	90.4	99.3
1981	91.2	100.4
1982	89.6	99.5
1983	90.2	100.8
1984	94.4	105.0
1985	97.4	107.2
1986	99.3	109.6
1987	102.0	112.4
1988	105.2	115.0
1989	107.9	117.3
1990	109.4	117.9
1991	108.3	116.9
1992	108.5	117.6

generally has significantly smaller month-to-month movements and, thus, a smoother short-term trend than the household survey. The smoother movement in the payroll survey results from two factors: (1) the payroll survey has a much larger sample of respondents, which makes it less affected by employment reports of a small number of respondents; and (2) employment associated with new firms that have not yet been incorporated in the payroll survey sample, but for which an estimate is added every month to the survey figures, lessens the chance of an employment decline in the payroll survey. The payroll survey aims at maintaining all existing firms in the sample and getting firms that are in the sample design, but not reporting, to become active respondents, while the household survey rotates household respondents out of the survey and replaces them with new households to reduce reporting burden. The effect of these differences on the monthly volatility of employment in the two surveys is uncertain.

Accuracy

The payroll survey has a much larger sample than the household survey—over 370,000 business establishments accounting for

39 percent of payroll employment, compared with 60,000 households accounting for under 0.1 percent of household employment. However, the household survey has a more representative sample of survey respondents; it is a probability sample while the payroll survey sample is not. This allows for reliable estimates from a much smaller sample. The payroll survey may have less response error because it uses actual employer payroll tax records rather than the subjective responses of persons in the household survey.

Because of the differences in the methodologies, error estimates based on monthly movements between the two surveys are not comparable. The payroll survey only shows errors due to revision—in two of three cases, the revision error for the monthly level is plus or minus 78,000 workers (revision estimates for the monthly movements are not available). The household survey only shows errors due to sampling—in two of three cases, the sampling error for the monthly level is plus or minus 281,000 workers, and the sampling error for the monthly movement is plus or minus 213,000 workers.

Component Detail

The household survey details the age, gender, color, and Hispanic origin of workers and consequently is useful for analyzing the demographics of employment trends. Analogously, the payroll survey details the industry composition of jobs, which is useful in analyses of the industrial structure of employment. Therefore, each measure has its particular uses because of the different detail provided.

References from Primary Data Source

Bureau of Labor Statistics, U.S. Department of Labor. 1992. *BLS Handbook of Methods*. Chapter 2. September.

Kreisler, Stephen. 1993. "BLS Establishment Estimates Revised to Incorporate March 1992 Benchmarks and Historical Corrections." *Employment and Earnings*. June.

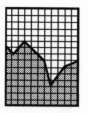

19
EMPLOYMENT COST INDEX

The employment cost index (ECI) measures changes in labor costs for money wages and salaries and noncash fringe benefits in nonfarm private industry and state and local governments for workers at all levels of responsibility. The ECI is not affected by shifts in the composition of employment between high-wage and low-wage industries or between high- and low-wage occupations within industries. Thus, the ECI represents labor costs for the same jobs over time.

Where and When Available

The employment cost index (ECI) is provided quarterly by the Bureau of Labor Statistics in the U.S. Department of Labor. The data are published in a press release and in two BLS monthly journals, the *Monthly Labor Review* and *Current Wage Developments*.

The figures are available during the last week of the month immediately following the quarter to which they refer (April for the first quarter, July for the second quarter, November for the third quarter, and February for the fourth quarter). No revisions are made in subsequent quarters.

Content

The ECI figures include money wages and salaries, fringe benefits paid leave for vacations, illness, holidays, and so on, commissions, bonuses, and noncash health, retirement, and other fringe benefits in private nonfarm industries and in state and local governments. Costs are included for all workers—production, nonsupervisory, supervisory, and executive. The wage and salary component of labor costs reflects straight-time pay only, excluding premium rates for overtime, holidays, night work, and hazardous conditions. Production bonuses, incentive earnings, commission payments, and cost-of-living adjustments are included in straight-time wage and salary rates. The fringe benefit component reflects changes in the cost of existing benefits, such as higher pay for holidays, as well as changes in the provision of benefits, such as an additional paid holiday. Wages and salaries plus fringe benefits are called compensation.

The ECI represents a fixed composition of industries and of occupations within industries. Therefore, movements over time are not affected by shifts between higher and lower paying industries and occupations. In addition to industry and occupational detail, the index distinguishes wage costs between union and nonunion workers.

The ECI is currently based on an index base of June 1989 = 100.

The ECI figures are seasonally adjusted.

Methodology

The ECI data are based on a survey of employer payrolls in the third month of the quarter (March, June, September, and December) for the pay period including the twelfth day of the month. The survey is a probability sample of approximately 4,600 private industry employers and 1,000 state and local governments, public schools, and public hospitals.

The index weights represent the wage and fringe benefit costs of each occupation within an industry. This is average wage and fringe benefits per worker multiplied by the number of workers in each occupation/industry group. The employment data are obtained from the census of population and the wage and fringe benefit data are from the ECI survey. The composition of industry and occupational employment currently reflects the distributions of the 1980 population census. These weights will be updated to the 1990 census of population in 1995. In contrast to the overall ECI, the component indexes for union and nonunion workers are based on current period distributions rather than fixed weights because of the changing union status of workers within a company.

Accuracy

In two of three cases, the twelve-month percent change in the ECI for compensation for private industry workers is statistically significant within a range of plus or minus 0.25 percentage point. For state and local government workers, in two of three cases the range is plus or minus 0.33 percentage point.

Relevance

The ECI is the most comprehensive and refined measure of underlying trends in employee compensation as a cost of production. It is used for analyzing changes in wages and fringe benefits in relation to *productivity* and *inflation*, as a guide in collective bargaining negotiations (see *collective bargaining settlements*), for cost escalators in union and other business contracts, and for adjusting pay of federal government employees including members of Congress, federal judges, and senior government executives. In distinguishing between union and nonunion workers, it also provides data for contrasting wage trends between collective bargaining and unorganized companies.

Recent Trends

The employment cost index for compensation (money wages plus fringe benefits) increased at sharply declining rates in 1980–87; the rate of increase turned upward in 1988–89, but turned down again in 1990–92 (Table 19.1). This general pattern oc-

Table 19.1

Employment Cost Index: Compensation
(annual percent change)

December	Private industry workers	Private union workers	Private nonunion workers	State & local government workers
1980	9.6%	11.1%	8.8%	NA
1981	9.9	10.7	9.5	NA
1982	6.5	7.1	6.0	7.1%
1983	5.7	5.8	5.7	6.1
1984	4.9	4.3	5.1	6.7
1985	3.9	2.6	4.6	5.6
1986	3.2	2.1	3.6	5.2
1987	3.3	2.7	3.7	4.5
1988	4.8	3.9	5.1	5.6
1989	4.8	3.7	5.1	6.2
1990	4.6	4.3	4.8	5.8
1991	4.4	4.6	4.3	3.6
1992	3.5	4.3	3.2	3.7

NA: Not available

curred in both private industry and state and local governments. It resulted in the 1992 increases being at the lowest annual rates during the 1980–92 period. The exception occurred for private union workers, which after having the sharpest declines in 1980–87, had larger increases in 1988–92 than in the immediately preceding years.

Reference from Primary Data Source

Bureau of Labor Statistics, U.S. Department of Labor. 1992. *BLS Handbook of Methods*. Chapter 8. September.

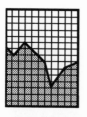

20
EXPERIMENTAL RECESSION
INDEXES

Experimental recession indexes (XRI) provide forecasts of the likelihood that the economy will be in a recession six months ahead. For example, based on data available though the month of October, the XRIs estimate the statistical probability that the economy will be in a recession the following April. The XRIs are "experimental" because they require more forecasting experience and verification before they can be considered an established economic indicator.

Where and When Available

The experimental recession indexes are prepared monthly by James Stock and Mark Watson. They are published in the "Stock and Watson Indicator Report" available from the National Bureau of Economic Research.

The XRIs are provided one month after the most recent monthly data on which the forecasts are based. Using the above example, forecasts based on October data for the following April are published about December 1. Consequently, the forecasts are published five months ahead of the forecast month. The XRIs are not revised.

Content

There are two monthly experimental recession indexes that predict the probability the economy will be in a recession six months later: one XRI includes financial variables and one XRI excludes them. The probability in each forecast ranges from zero to 100 percent.

The XRIs are derived from the relationship between a "leading index" and a "coincident index." The coincident index represents actual economic activity. The leading index indicates the expected change in the cyclical direction of the economy before it appears in the coincident index. In particular, the leading index forecasts the change in the coincident index over the next six months. Thus, the leading index forecasts the coincident index. For example, during a business expansion, the leading index turns down before the coincident index turns down into a recession, and during a recession the leading index turns up before the coincident index turns up into a recovery. The components of the experimental coincident and the two leading indexes are listed below. For further discussion of the leading index system, see *leading, coincident, and lagging indexes.*

The XRIs quantify the likelihood that the economy will be in a recession six months ahead with a statement of the following type: "The probability that the economy will be in a recession in (month, year) is X percent." For example, the XRI for January 1993 provides the probability the economy will be in a recession in July 1993. This is based on formal mathematical relationships. It differs from the *leading, coincident, and lagging indexes,* which are not rigorously linked and therefore require an assessment of the interrelationships by the analyst for forecasting future movements of the economy.

The XRIs are seasonally adjusted.

Components of the Experimental Coincident and Leading Indexes

Coincident index:

- Industrial production index *(industrial production index)*
- Personal income less transfer payments, in constant dollars *(personal income and saving)*

• Manufacturing and trade sales, in constant dollars (partly in *retail sales*)

• Employee hours in nonagricultural industries *(employment* and *average weekly hours)*

Leading index including financial variables:

• Building permits for new private housing *(housing starts)*

• Manufacturers' unfilled orders for durable goods industries, in constant dollars *(manufacturers' orders)*

• Trade-weighted index of nominal exchange rates between the United States and the United Kingdom, Germany, France, Italy, and Japan *(value of the dollar)*

• Part-time workers in nonagricultural industries due to slack work

• Ten-year Treasury bond interest rate, constant maturity *(interest rates)*

• Interest rate spread between six-month commercial paper and six-month Treasury bills *(interest rates)*

• Yield curve difference between ten-year Treasury bonds and one-year Treasury bonds

Leading index excluding financial variables:

• Building permits for new private housing *(housing starts)*

• Manufacturers' unfilled orders for durable goods industries, in constant dollars *(manufacturers' orders)*

• Trade-weighted index of nominal exchange rates between the United States and the United Kingdom, Germany, France, Italy, and Japan *(value of the dollar)*

• Help-wanted advertising *(help-wanted advertising index)*

• Average weekly hours in manufacturing industries *(average weekly hours)*

• Vendor performance (percentage of companies receiving slower deliveries)

• Capacity utilization in manufacturing industries *(capacity utilization)*

Methodology

The experimental coincident and leading indexes are composite indexes that comprise the data elements listed in "Content" above. The coincident and leading indexes underlie the preparation of the experimental recession indexes. The weights of the coincident composite index are derived from a statistical model that estimates the co-movement in time series. The weights of the leading composite index are derived from a statistical model in which the weights are chosen so that the resultant composite index is an "optimal" predictor of six-month-ahead movements in the coincident index.

The two experimental recession indexes' estimates of the probability of a future recession are based on forecasts of overall economic activity six months ahead. These six-month forecasts, which are updated every month, reflect the expected movements of each of the seven components of the two leading composite indexes (one including and the other excluding financial variables), based on statistical analysis.

The probability that the economy will be in a recession six months ahead in the XRIs is derived from a comparison of the expected future movements of the leading and coincident indexes with their behavior in previous expansions and recessions. This technique is referred to as statistical pattern recognition, in which the data set matches or is in a class of prespecified patterns.

Accuracy

There are no estimates of sampling or revision error for the experimental recession indexes. The calculation of a probability error range is not appropriate and the data are not revised.

Relevance

A major aspect of economic policy is directed at preventing a recession from occurring or moderating its length and intensity

Table 20.1

Experimental Recession Indexes
(probability of recession six months later)

	Including financial variables	Excluding financial variables
1990		
January	3%	11%
February	5	16
March	5	36
April	6	46
May	7	35
June	5	23
July	3	21
August	3	24
September	6	29
October	10	45
November	14	53
December	9	68
1991		
January	5	59
February	4	55
March	3	47
April	2	38
May	1	24
June	1	19
July	1	14
August	1	23
September	1	21
October	1	21
November	1	36
December	1	24
1992		
January	1	21
February	1	25
March	1	29
April	1	23
May	1	25
June	1	23
July	1	17
August	1	27
September	1	21
October	1	33
November	1	28
December	1	19

when it does occur. In supplementing econometric models and other forecasts of the economy, XRIs provide additional guidance on whether existing fiscal and monetary policies should be changed for counteracting prospective or actual recessions.

The XRIs were first published in 1989 and experience with them has been limited. They did not predict the 1990−91 recession, and they were late in recognizing its existence after it started, but they did predict the 1991−92 recovery. The effect of having two XRIs, one that includes and one that excludes financial variables, highlights differences in the economic outlook arising from interest rates and thus from Federal Reserve monetary policies.

Recent Trends

The experimental recession indexes did not foretell the 1990−91 recession (July 1990−March 1991) in the first half of 1990, although the XRI excluding financial variables had a much greater likelihood of a pending recession than the XRI including financial variables (Table 20.1). After the recession began, the XRI excluding financial variables had a high probability it would continue into 1991, while the XRI including financial variables had a low likelihood it would continue into 1991. After the recession ended, both XRIs in 1991 and 1992 had low probabilities of another recession in the next six months, although the pattern of the XRI including financial variables being far less recession-prone continued to prevail. Consequently, both XRIs predicted the recovery of 1991−92.

References from Primary Data Source

Stock, James H., and Mark W. Watson. 1989. "New Indexes of Coincident and Leading Economic Indicators." *NBER Macroeconomics Annual*, Vol. 4. The MIT Press.

Stock, James H., and Mark W. Watson. 1992. "A Procedure for Predicting Recessions with Leading Indicators: Econometric

Issues and Recent Experience." *Working Paper No. 4014*. National Bureau of Economic Research, Inc. March.

Watson, Mark W. 1991. "Using Econometric Models to Predict Recessions." *Economic Perspectives*. Federal Reserve Bank of Chicago. November–December.

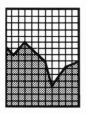

**21
FARM PARITY RATIO**

The farm parity ratio is a crude measure of changes in farmers' purchasing power. Purchasing power reflects the relationship between (1) the prices farmers pay for sales of crop and livestock products, and (2) the prices farmers pay for production and living expenses. This relationship is a limited measure of the change in purchasing power because it does not include the effects of improvements in production technology or of the changing quantities and quality of farm products sold. The 1910–14 period is used as the base for comparison because prices of farm and nonfarm items were considered to have been generally in balance in that period by the legislators who passed the Agricultural Adjustment Act of 1939, establishing the parity ratio.

Where and When Available

The farm parity ratio is provided for the months of January, April, July, and October by the National Agricultural Statistics Service of the U.S. Department of Agriculture. It is published in a press release and in the report *Agricultural Prices*. Secondary sources include *Economic Indicators* and the *Survey of Current Business*.

The figures are available at the end of the month to which they refer (the end of January, April, July, and October). Revisions are made to each of the four months in the following monthly esti-mates, and annually in January of the following year.

Content

The farm parity ratio is composed of the index of prices received for sales of crop and livestock products in the numerator, and the index of prices paid for farm production and living expenses in the denominator. The percent change in both indexes reflects the movement from 1910–14 to the current period. Currently, the ratio using 1977 = 100 is also provided to facilitate comparisons with other price indexes. Basing the ratio on 1977 does not affect percent changes from one period to another, but the number lev-els are different. Thus, when using the 1977 base, a comparison with 1910–14 is not readily observable unless back data are shown for the earlier period. When either ratio is above 100, farmers' purchasing power is higher than in the base period, and when either ratio is below 100, their purchasing power is less than in the base period.

The current weights in both the prices received and the prices paid indexes reflect the relative dollar importance of sales and expenses of the components of each index during 1971–73. In the prices received index, crops account for 44 percent of the weight and livestock products for 56 percent. Crop products in-clude food and feed grains, cotton, tobacco, oil-bearing crops (e.g., soybeans and peanuts), and fruits and vegetables. Livestock products include meat animals, dairy products, poultry, and eggs. The index represents about 90 percent of the cash receipts from all farm products: of the excluded commodities, livestock prod-ucts such as wool, horses, goats, and ducks account for 2 percent and crop products such as forest, nursery, greenhouse, and spe-cialty crops account for 8 percent.

In the prices paid index, farm production expenses are weighted 70 percent and living expenses are weighted 30 per-cent. Farm production costs include such items as feed, feeder livestock, seed, fertilizer, fuels, chemicals, equipment, cash rent, wages, interest, and real estate taxes. The living expense component is based on the *consumer price index* (CPI-U).

The farm parity ratio is currently based both on 1910−14 = 100 and 1977 = 100.

The farm parity ratio figures are not seasonally adjusted.

Methodology

Weights for the prices received and prices paid indexes are changed at intervals of several years with no set pattern. The current weights are based on the importance of the components during 1971−73. Prior to this, weights were based on the 1953−57 period.

Data for the prices received index are based on U.S. Department of Agriculture surveys of marketings and prices for various crop and livestock products. Similar data sources are used for the base period weights and the current period prices. The prices received data are not adjusted for changes in the quality of farm products.

Data for the prices paid index for the weights are based on U.S. Department of Agriculture annual surveys of farm production expenditures during 1971−73 for the production component of the index, and on a Department of Agriculture 1973 survey of farm family living expenditures. There are plans to update these factors by the mid-1990s. Current period prices are derived from surveys of firms that sell to farmers, that purchase the item directly from farmers, such as feeder pigs, the *consumer price index*, and a Department of Agriculture quarterly survey of farm labor wage rates. Since 1986, prices paid data are developed only for the first month of the quarter. The prices paid data for farm expenditures are not adjusted for changes in the quality of the goods and services bought; the living expense component of prices paid is adjusted for changes in quality in the *consumer price index*.

Table 21.1

Farm Parity Ratio
(1977 = 100)

	Farm parity ratio	Prices received index	Prices paid index
1980	97	134	138
1981	93	139	150
1982	84	133	159
1983	84	135	161
1984	87	142	164
1985	79	128	162
1986	77	123	159
1987	78	127	162
1988	81	138	170
1989	83	147	178
1990	81	149	184
1991	77	145	189
1992	73	140	191

Accuracy

There are no estimates of sampling or revision error for the farm parity ratio.

Relevance

The farm parity ratio is a broad indicator of the economic well-being of farmers. Because the ratio does not reflect improvements in farm production technology or changes in the quantity and quality of farm products sold, it is not an indicator of farm income. However, it gives a clue as to whether price movements are more or less favorable to farmers and thus provides an early indication of a change in income for farmers. Used with projections of the production of crop and livestock products, it provides a rough indication of the likely magnitude of changes in income. In addition, by focusing attention on the price component of income, the farm parity ratio may also influence the nature of farm price support laws.

Recent Trends

The farm parity ratio declined during 1980–82 (Table 21.1). Although there were scattered years of increase, the thrust was downward. From a peak of 97 in 1980, it fell to a low of 73 in 1992 (1977 = 100). The downward trend reflects the far greater increases in prices paid than in prices received.

Reference from Primary Data Source

Statistical Reporting Service, U.S. Department of Agriculture. 1983. *Scope and Methods of the Statistical Reporting Service.* September.

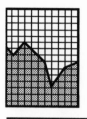

22
FLOW OF FUNDS

The flow of funds measures are a financial and economic accounting system of the sources and uses of money and credit, and of the financial assets and liabilities of households, businesses, governments, and foreigners (in their economic activities in the U.S. economy). The system relates the *gross domestic product* to the lending, borrowing, and investment funds used in financing the nation's output. It also shows the debt in the private and public sectors of the economy.

Where and When Available

The flow of funds measures are provided quarterly by the Federal Reserve Board. They are published in a statistical release and in the *Federal Reserve Bulletin*, the FRB's monthly journal. Secondary sources include *Economic Indicators*.

The figures are available two months after the quarter to which they refer. The data are revised quarterly and annually to reflect more complete information.

Content

The flow of funds represents sources and uses of money, credit, and equity funds (Table 22.1). Conceptually, the totals of all

Table 22.1

Flow of Funds (illustrative): **Net Funds Raised** (billions of dollars)

	1990	1991	1992
Domestic nonfinancial borrowing			
Borrowing sectors	418.2	164.4	283.5
Households	254.3	144.9	215.1
Corporate	86.4	3.7	53.5
Nonfarm noncorporate	26.7	−23.6	−34.2
Farm	2.5	0.9	0.9
State & local governments	48.3	38.5	48.1
Borrowing instruments	418.2	164.4	283.5
Consumer credit	17.5	−12.5	2.4
Mortgages	244.0	120.1	160.8
Corporate bonds	47.1	78.8	66.3
Tax-exempt obligations	51.2	45.8	53.3
Bank loans (unclassified)	4.4	−33.4	−16.8
Open market paper	9.7	−18.4	9.8
Other	44.2	−15.8	7.5
U.S. Government borrowing	246.9	278.2	304.0
Net foreign borrowing in U.S.	23.9	14.1	24.1
Corporate equity funds raised by nonfinancial corporations (new share issues)	−45.8	48.3	65.7

sources and uses are equal. There are two main sources of funds: (1) wage, profit, interest, and rent income generated in the production of goods and services, and (2) credit such as mortgages, bonds, bank loans, consumer credit, trade credit, and commercial paper, plus corporate stock (equity capital). Income derived from production is an "internal" source of funds, while credit and corporate stock are "external" sources that require raising funds in the marketplace and, thus, are sensitive to interest rates. The uses of funds include spending for consumer goods and services; savings in bank deposits and in life insurance and pension reserves; and investment in plant and equipment, housing, inventories, and financial assets.

Asset and liability figures are shown for bank deposits, life insurance and pension reserves, mortgages, bank loans, other credit, and corporate stock. The data on debt refer to money owed on borrowings for mortgages, bonds, bank loans, consumer credit, and commercial paper.

The flow of funds figures are seasonally adjusted.

Methodology

The flow of funds figures are based on many data sources for the financial elements, plus the *gross domestic product* for the income and product flows that are available monthly or quarterly, and on trend estimates for those elements that are available less frequently. The annual revisions incorporate the GDP revisions.

Accuracy

There are no estimates of sampling or revision error for the flow of funds measures.

Relevance

The flow of funds measures are used to assess funding requirements associated with varying rates of economic growth and inflation. The Federal Reserve Board uses the measures as a guide in evaluating the needs and availability of money and credit to influence the *money supply* and *interest rates* through monetary policy. Funding requirements are included in projections of the *gross domestic product* and *inflation* to make more realistic forecasts. The flow of funds measures help to reconcile assumed growth in spending (GDP) and supply constraints (inflation) with the availability of money, credit, and equity funds. The flow of funds is also the source of quarterly debt figures.

Contrary to other economic indicators, the flow of funds measures are not an economic barometer in their own right. That is, annual increases or decreases are not the focus of attention, and therefore there is no section below on Recent Trends. The flow of funds data are significant because they provide an integrated statistical system for measuring borrowing and lending in analyses of monetary policies and financial markets.

Reference from Primary Data Source

Board of Governors of the Federal Reserve System. 1993. *Guide to the Flow of Funds Accounts.*

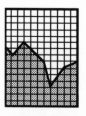

23
GDP PRICE MEASURES

There are four measures of price change associated with the *gross domestic product*: implicit price deflator, fixed-weighted price index, benchmark-years weighted price index, and chain-type annual weighted price index. The four GDP measures are the most comprehensive indicators of price change of the American economy. They include the goods and services elements of consumer, investment, government, and international economic transactions in the GDP. Because of the different methodologies used in their calculation, the four measures result in alternative trends in prices. In doing so, they provide a basis for addressing the intrinsic problem of index number construction discussed in the Introduction.

Where and When Available

The four GDP price measures are provided quarterly by the Bureau of Economic Analysis in the U.S. Department of Commerce. The data are published in a monthly press release and in BEA's monthly journal, the *Survey of Current Business*. Secondary sources include *Economic Indicators* and the *Monthly Labor Review*.

The figures are available during the fourth week of every month. Preliminary data for the immediately preceding quarter are provided in the month following the quarter (April for the first quarter, July for the second quarter, etc.). These are initially revised in the subsequent two months. More detailed revisions are made annually every July, and comprehensive benchmark revisions based largely on the quinquennial economic censuses are published about every five years.

Content

The four GDP price measures are developed for the entire GDP and for the consumer, investment, government, and international components. The four measures vary in the composition of the goods and services items covered. They utilize expenditures for goods and services items in different years as index number quantity "weights," which give each price measure a different weighting structure. This is the obverse of the alternative quantity indexes of real GDP in the *gross domestic product*, which use price weights.

The *implicit price deflator* represents the changing distribution of goods and services bought in the marketplace in every period. It includes the effect on overall price movements of the continually changing allocation of resources among the GDP components and changing preferences for goods and services consumption items within a component. For example, if there is a shift in spending within the consumer component from food to medical care, and medical care prices increase more than food prices, the implicit price deflator will rise more sharply than the other measures because of the greater spending for medical care.

The *benchmark-years weighted price index* weights change every five years according to the composition of expenditures for goods and services items in each quinquennial benchmark year. Benchmark years coincide with economic census years—1987, 1992, 1997, 2002, and so on. For historical data, two adjacent benchmark-year expenditure weights (for example, 1987 and

1992) are used in calculating price movements. For recent estimates after the last benchmark year, expenditure (that is, quantity) weights comprising the last benchmark year and the most recent subsequent year are used for the price movements. Price movements from one period to the next are based on the Fisher ideal index number formula described below under "Methodology."

The *chain-type annual weighted price index* weights change annually according to the composition of expenditures for goods and services items in each year. Two expenditure weights in adjacent years are used in calculating price movements. Price movements from one period to the next are based on the Fisher ideal index number formula described below under "Methodology."

The *fixed-weighted price index* weights change according to the composition of the goods and services items in the last GDP benchmark revision, thus holding the composition constant since the most recent benchmark for all years both before and after the benchmark. Benchmark revisions are made every five years. However, because of the time required to complete benchmarking, the current composition may be unchanged for up to 13 years after the most recent benchmarking. The most recent weights for the fixed-weighted price index reflect the GDP spending patterns in 1987.

Taken together, the four price measures are a spectrum of techniques that account for change in expenditure weights. At the extremes are the fixed-weighted price index that allows for no change in price weights and the implicit price deflator that incorporates continuous change in expenditure composition. Within these poles, the benchmark and chain price indexes include varying degrees of change in expenditures, with the benchmark index changing less frequently than the chain index.

The GDP price measures are currently based on 1987 = 100.

The GDP price measures are seasonally adjusted.

Methodology

All four GDP price measures are developed by using the price movements indicated mainly in the *consumer price index, producer price indexes*, and the *import and export price indexes*. These are supplemented with several other indexes, including those for construction and defense prices and costs.

The *implicit price deflator* is calculated by dividing current-dollar GDP by constant-dollar GDP. Since it is a byproduct of the estimation of GDP in constant dollars, it does not involve the conventional index number construction of multiplying price movements by the weights and summing the products as used in calculating the other indexes.

The *benchmark-years weighted price index* movements are calculated using the geometric mean of two price movements based on alternative goods and services expenditure weights (referred to as the Fisher ideal index number formula). For historical estimates between adjacent benchmark years such as 1987 and 1992, price changes are calculated separately using 1987 and 1992 expenditure weights, and the actual price movement is the geometric mean of the two movements. For price movements after the last benchmark year, the two expenditure weights are those in the last benchmark year and those in the most recent year based on the annual GDP revisions each July. Price changes are calculated separately using the two weighting patterns, and the actual price movement is the geometric mean of the two movements.

The *chain-type annual weighted price index* movements are calculated using the geometric mean of two price movements based on alternative goods and services expenditure weights (Fisher ideal index). The expenditure weights for the two most recent years are based on the annual GDP revisions each July. Price changes are calculated separately using the two weighting patterns, and the actual price movement is the geometric mean of the two movements.

The *fixed-weighted price index* movements are calculated

based on the single-year weights of the most recent benchmark year.

Accuracy

There are no estimates of sampling or revision error for the GDP price measures.

Relevance

The inclusion of all components of the economy in these four indexes is a unique feature of the GDP price measures. It enables comprehensive analyses of the sources of *inflation* in the consumer, investment, government, and international components integrated in a statistically consistent framework.

The alternatively weighted indexes allow flexibility in analyzing price movements. Depending on the particular analysis, one index may be more appropriate than the others. However, in the absence of a clear preference for a particular weighting scheme to assess price changes, the four measures together can be a realistic compromise to the index number dilemma. Together, the four yield a range for price movements and establish the upper and lower bounds within which the true rate of price change lies (see the section on index numbers in the Introduction).

In analyzing consumer price movements, it is also useful to compare the movements of the GDP fixed-weighted index for consumer expenditures to the *consumer price index*. Both indexes are conceptually similar in terms of the constant weighting scheme. However, there are two technical differences: the goods and services items are not identical, and the weights of the GDP index represent spending of all consumers while the CPI weights refer only to spending by urban civilian households. For example, life insurance is included in the GDP index but excluded from the CPI, and the GDP weights include rural and military households, which are excluded from the CPI. These technical differences result in different movements that provide an upper and lower bound in estimating consumer price movements; this

Table 23.1

GDP Price Measures
(annual percent change)

	Implicit price deflator	Chain-type annual weighted price index	Benchmark-years weighted price index	Fixed-weighted price index
1980	9.5	9.0	9.2	NA
1981	10.0	9.2	9.1	NA
1982	6.2	6.3	6.4	NA
1983	4.1	4.1	4.1	3.9
1984	4.4	3.6	3.6	3.4
1985	3.7	3.6	3.6	3.5
1986	2.6	2.7	2.9	2.8
1987	3.2	3.1	3.2	3.1
1988	3.9	3.9	3.9	4.0
1989	4.4	4.4	4.4	4.5
1990	4.4	4.4	4.4	4.6
1991	3.9	4.0	4.0	4.1
1992	2.9	3.1	3.2	3.3

NA: Not available

range can supplement the above-noted bounds in the consumer components of the four GDP price measures.

Recent Trends

The alternative GDP price measures showed similar inflation patterns during 1980–92 (Table 23.1). Inflation dropped sharply in the early 1980s, and then fluctuated within the 3–4.5 percent range. The annual change in the four price measures typically varied by only 0.1 percentage point. Larger differences occurred in 1980, 1981, and 1984, the main one being that the implicit price deflator had higher inflation rates than the other indexes.

Theoretically, for price movements after the most recent benchmarked base period, the implicit price deflator would be expected to show the lowest rate of inflation and the fixed-weighted price index the highest rate, with the chain and benchmark-years price indexes between the two; in contrast, before the base period benchmark, the implicit price deflator would be expected to show the highest rate of inflation and the fixed-weighted price index the lowest. This reflects the differential effects of changing the weights with every benchmark. In practice, this expected result was generally borne out during 1980–92. From 1980 to 1987, the implicit price deflator usually had the highest rate of inflation and the fixed-weighted price index had the lowest rate. These patterns reversed during 1988–92, when the implicit price deflator usually had the lowest inflation rate and the fixed-weighted price index had the highest.

Reference from Primary Data Source

Young, Allan H. 1993. "Alternative Measures of Change in Real Output and Prices, Quarterly Estimates for 1959–92." *Survey of Current Business*. March.

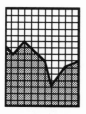

24

GOVERNMENT BUDGETS AND DEBT

Measures of government budgets represent spending and revenue for all levels of government—federal, state, and local. Spending and revenues are based, in part, on legislation appropriating funds to be spent and on tax laws specifying what items are to be taxed and the taxation rates. Actual spending and revenue are also influenced by the state of the economy. The budget is in balance when spending equals revenue, in surplus when revenue exceeds spending, and in deficit when spending exceeds revenue. There are two measures of government spending and revenue that are based on different concepts: one is based on the official budget and the other is based on statistical definitions of the national income and product accounts.

Government debt is a result of borrowing. Much of the debt represents the cumulative excess of annual budget deficits over annual budget surpluses in previous years, less the debt that has been paid off. In addition, some borrowing occurs in anticipation of spending in future years, particularly for capital construction projects of state and local governments.

Where and When Available

The U.S. Office of Management and Budget publishes annual figures on the official federal budget in the *Budget of the United*

States Government. The U.S. Department of the Treasury publishes monthly data on the federal budget in the *Monthly Treasury Statement of Receipts and Outlays of the United States Government.* The Bureau of Economic Analysis in the U.S. Department of Commerce publishes quarterly statistical measures of budgets of the federal government and of the total of all state and local governments in a press release and in BEA's monthly journal, the *Survey of Current Business.* The Bureau of the Census in the U.S. Department of Commerce publishes annual data on all governments—federal, state, and local—in a press release and in *Government Finances.* Secondary sources include *Economic Indicators* and the *Federal Reserve Bulletin.*

The official OMB federal budget figures are available every January when the president submits the budget to Congress. The Treasury figures are available fifteen working days after the month to which they refer; they are revised continuously during the year. The BEA statistical budgets are available in the month after the quarter (April for the first quarter, July for the second quarter, etc.); but these exclude data on corporate income taxes and thus the budget surplus/deficit position. They are revised in the following two months, which include corporate income taxes and the budget position, with subsequent revisions made annually every July and comprehensive benchmark revisions about every five years. The Census Bureau annual statistical budgets are available one year after the fiscal year to which they refer.

Content

Government spending represents government outlays for wages and fringe benefits of government workers; purchases of materials, equipment, structures, and services from private industry; and transfer payments to individuals, state and local governments, and business. Transfers include social security, unemployment insurance, food stamps, and other income maintenance programs; grants-in-aid to state and local governments; interest on the public debt; and subsidies to business. Government revenues encompass government receipts from income, sales, and property taxes;

customs duties; and fees, licenses, and other miscellaneous sources of income.

The main components of spending and revenue differ between the federal government and state and local governments. For example, only the federal government spends for defense, social security, and farm subsidies, and collects customs duties; only state and local governments spend for local schools and police (although financed in part with federal grants-in-aid), and collect sales and property taxes.

Official and Statistical Budgets

There are two measures of budgets. The official budget represents the legally recognized spending, revenues, and surplus or deficit that are used by governments in establishing actual figures. The statistical budget is consistent with the definitions of the national income and product accounts (NIPA), which conform to the concepts of the *gross domestic product*. (As noted below, there is another version of a statistical budget for state and local governments.) Differences in both item content and timing distinguish the official budget from the statistical budget.

The statistical budgets in the NIPA for the federal government and for the state and local governments are seasonally adjusted. The monthly figures on the official federal budget are not seasonally adjusted. The Census state and local governments statistical budgets are annual figures and therefore are not seasonally adjusted.

Differences in Item Content

For the *federal* government, examples of differences in item content between the official budget of the U.S. Office of Management and Budget and the NIPA statistical budget are: new loans and repayment of government loans are included in the official budget but excluded in the statistical budget; purchases and sales of land are included in the official budget but excluded in the statistical budget; government contributions to federal worker retirement funds are excluded in the official budget but included in the statistical budget; and spending and revenues in U.S. territories outside the United States and the Commonwealth of Puerto Rico are included in the official budget but excluded in the statistical budget.

The official federal budget distinguishes between "on-budget" and "off-budget" items. All items are on-budget except social security funds for retirement and disability insurance. Because the off-budget items impact the economy, they are presented here as a combined total with on-budget items. By contrast, the statistical budget does not distinguish between on-budget and off-budget items.

For *state and local* governments, there is no official budget total that combines all state and local budgets. However, there are two measures of statistical budgets. One is the NIPA budget and the other is the Census Bureau budget in *Government Finances*. The most significant differences in item content between these two statistical measures are: unemployment insurance payments and revenues are included in the Census budget but excluded in the NIPA budget (unemployment insurance is in the federal NIPA budget); purchases and sales of land are included in the Census budget but excluded in the NIPA budget; and government contributions to employee retirement funds are excluded in the Census budget but included in the NIPA budget.

Differences in Timing

The timing differences reflect distinctions among the cash, accrual, and delivery methods of accounting. The cash basis counts spending when governments' payment checks are issued and revenues when taxpayers' checks are received. The accrual basis counts spending when the expense is incurred; similarly, accrued tax revenues are counted when tax liabilities are incurred. The delivery basis counts spending when the purchased items are delivered to the government.

The *federal* official budget is on a cash basis, except for payment of interest on the public debt, which is on an accrual basis. The statistical budget is also on a cash basis, but with several exceptions. The primary exceptions are: for spending, payment of interest on the public debt is on an accrual basis, and payment for large defense items such as airplanes, missiles, and ships are recorded on a delivery basis; and for revenues, business income taxes are recorded on an accrual basis.

The two *state and local* statistical budgets are mainly on a cash basis. The Census Bureau figures are completely on a cash basis. The NIPA figures are on a cash basis, except for interest payments and business income taxes, which are on an accrual basis.

Debt

Government debt represents short-term and long-term interest-bearing obligations such as notes, bonds, and mortgages. It excludes noninterest-bearing obligations (with minor exceptions), rights of individuals to government employee retirement funds, financial obligations of trust funds, and advances and contingent loans from other governments. It is included in the Office of Management and Budget official budget and in the Census Bureau statistical budgets, but not in the NIPA statistical budgets.

There are two measures of federal government debt. One is gross debt and the other is debt held by the public. *Gross debt* is the total debt and includes securities owned by individuals, businesses, pension funds, and foreigners, as well as those owned by government trust funds such as social security, federal worker retirement, unemployment insurance, highway trust funds, and public enterprise "federal" funds such as the Postal Service, Overseas Private Investment Corporation, and the nuclear waste funds. *Debt held by the public* is confined to securities owned by individuals, businesses, pension funds, and foreigners, but excludes security holdings of government trust funds and federal funds. The government and federal funds invest their balances in government securities as a source of interest income.

Methodology

Official budget figures for the *federal* government are based on reports of government agencies to the Office of Management and Budget and the Treasury Department. The Bureau of Economic Analysis estimates the accrual and delivery-based elements for the NIPA budgets.

The annual NIPA figures for *state and local* governments are based on Census Bureau surveys of all state governments and a sample of local governments that provide spending and revenue information on a yearly basis. The quarterly NIPA figures are based on survey data of the Bureau of Labor Statistics and the Census Bureau for payrolls, construction, and taxes, and are supplemented by the trend of less recent actual data for the other components. The Bureau of Labor Statistics conducts a monthly survey of state and local government worker payrolls, and the Census Bureau conducts a monthly survey of state and local government-owned new construction and a quarterly survey of state and local tax revenues. The quarterly tax revenue figures are used in the historical NIPA measures but are too late for use in the current NIPA budgets. The Bureau of Economic Analysis estimates the accrual elements for the NIPA budgets.

Accuracy

There are no estimates of sampling or revision error in government budgets. There is an estimate of sampling error in the Census Bureau state and local statistical budgets. This sampling error is based entirely on the local government component because all state governments are surveyed. (Local governments accounted for 59 percent of state and local spending and 57 percent of state and local revenues in 1991, exclusive of intergovernmental state payments to local governments.) In two of three cases, the local government sampling error is less than one percent.

Estimates of revision error in the NIPA measures are available only for the "purchases" component of total spending. For the federal government, the average revision error in the quarterly change in purchases, without regard to sign, is approximately 7 percentage points. For state and local government, the average revision error in purchases is 1.5 percentage points.

Relevance

Budgets

The official and statistical government budgets have different analytic uses. The federal official budget is better for assessing trends in spending, revenues, surpluses, and deficits associated with spending appropriations and tax legislation. The federal and the state and local statistical budgets are better for analyzing the relationship between the budget on the one hand and spending in the entire economy and economic growth on the other.

A budget surplus or deficit affects spending in the entire economy both directly and indirectly. The direct effect of a surplus (or reduction in the deficit) is to remove money from the income stream and, thus, restrain spending, although not necessarily proportionately; similarly, the direct effect of a deficit (or reduction in surplus) is to add money to the income stream and, thereby, stimulate spending, although not necessarily proportionately.

The budget also affects spending indirectly through *interest rates*. These effects are in opposition to the more direct effects. Because a surplus (or reduction in the deficit) will reduce the debt (or slow down the increase in the debt), it will tend to lower interest rates and, consequently, stimulate spending; similarly, a deficit (or reduction in the surplus) will increase debt (or slow down the reduction in debt), resulting in higher interest rates, which should restrain spending. The net result of these contrasting direct and indirect effects determines the overall impact of government budgets on the economy.

In addition to the budget impacting the economy, the economy impacts the budget through feedback effects. Because economic growth (measured by the *gross domestic product*) affects tax revenues and spending for unemployment insurance, periods of high economic growth generally tend toward a budget surplus and low growth periods tend toward a deficit.

The size and components of spending and revenue also influence the economy. The amount of total spending, as well as the specific amounts spent on the defense and civilian components, impact *employment, industrial production*, and the *distribution of income*. The amount of total revenue, as well as the specific amounts from component income, and sales and property taxes affect business and employment incentives and the distribution of income.

Debt

Government debt also affects *interest rates* through sales of new securities and refinancing of existing debt in bond markets. A large debt provides substantial low-risk investment outlets as an alternative avenue for investing funds. During periods of considerable economic uncertainty, investment funds may be channeled toward government securities, resulting in higher interest rates for household and business borrowers.

Generally, debt held by the public is more relevant than gross debt for assessing the impact of debt on interest rates. The publicly held debt directly affects credit markets and bank reserves, while the government funds that are invested in gross debt are internal to the government and thus do not directly affect credit markets and bank reserves.

Recent Trends

Budgets

The federal government budget deficit rose considerably during 1980–92 (Table 24.1). This reflected the general pattern of expenditures increasing faster than receipts in most years. From $60 billion in 1980, the deficit increased to an initial peak of $201 billion in 1986, then declined to a low of $122 billion in 1989, and resumed upward, reaching $276 billion in 1992.

The above data are based on the statistical budget. Yearly differences between the official and statistical budgets fluctuate in regard to the federal deficit. The deficit in the official budget exceeded that in the statistical budget by $19 to $80 billion over 1989–92. Because these differences are difficult to predict, there is some uncertainty in relating the official budget to the statistical budget.

State and local government budgets showed a surplus during 1980–92, although the surplus diminished considerably by 1991–92 (Table 24.1). The surplus rose from $25 billion in 1980 to $58 billion in 1984, and then declined to $7 billion in 1991–92.

Social insurance (mainly Social Security in the federal budget and state government employee retirement in state and local budgets) affects the overall budget positions. Social insurance funds run a surplus in both the federal and state and local governments, as receipts from individual and employer contributions exceed expenditures in transfer payments to persons. Federal social insurance funds had a surplus of $32 billion in 1992, which reduced the deficit arising from all other operations by that amount. State and local social insurance funds had a surplus of $59 billion in 1992, which shifted the deficit of $52 billion from all other operations to an overall budget surplus of $7 billion.

Debt

Gross government debt rose much faster for the federal government than for state and local governments during 1980–92 (Table 24.1). Federal debt increased by 341 percent over the twelve-year period (based on the official budget), and state and local debt increased by 173 percent (based on statistical budgets). The state and local debt primarily results from advance borrowing for future government capital outlays, which more than offsets the annual budget surpluses. In addition, part of the state and local debt represents public debt for private purposes. Many state and local governments finance economic development by selling government bonds because of their lower interest rates, which reflect

Table 24.1

Government Budgets and Debt
(billions of dollars)

Statistical budgets

	Federal			State and local		
Calendar year	Receipts	Expenditures	Surplus, deficit (–)	Receipts	Expenditures	Surplus, deficit (–)
1980	553.0	613.1	– 60.1	361.4	336.6	24.8
1981	639.0	697.8	– 58.8	390.8	362.3	28.5
1982	635.4	770.9	–135.5	409.0	382.1	26.9
1983	660.0	840.0	–180.1	443.4	403.2	40.3
1984	725.8	892.7	–166.9	492.2	434.1	58.1
1985	788.6	969.9	–181.4	528.7	472.6	56.1
1986	827.2	1,028.2	–201.0	571.2	517.0	54.3
1987	913.8	1,065.6	–151.8	594.3	554.2	40.1
1988	972.3	1,109.0	–136.6	631.3	593.0	38.4
1989	1,059.3	1,181.6	–122.3	681.5	636.7	44.8
1990	1,111.4	1,274.9	–163.5	730.0	704.9	25.1
1991	1,127.8	1,331.2	–203.4	780.5	773.2	7.3
1992	1,183.0	1,459.3	–276.3	837.8	830.6	7.2

Comparison of federal official and statistical budget deficit
(billions of dollars)

Fiscal year	Official	Statistical	Difference
1989	–152.5	–114.3	– 38.2
1990	–221.4	–151.1	–70.3
1991	–269.5	–190.0	–79.5
1992	–290.4	–271.4	–19.0

Government debt
(billions of dollars)

End of fiscal year	Federal gross debt	Federal debt held by the public	State and local gross debt
1980	908.5	709.3	335.6
1985	1,817.0	1,499.4	571.4
1990	3,206.3	2,410.4	860.6
1991	3,599.0	2,687.9	915.5
1992	4,002.7	2,998.6	915.7

the federal tax exemption for interest income on these bonds. However, this debt is repaid by the private borrowers.

Federal debt held by the public rose less than gross debt. Publicly held debt, which excludes government funds, accounted for 75 percent of gross debt in 1992, down from 78 percent in 1980. Trust funds account for the dominant share of government funds.

References from Primary Data Sources

Office of Management and Budget, Executive Office of the President. Annual. *Budget of the United States Government*.

Bureau of the Census, U.S. Department of Commerce. Annual. *Government Finances*.

Bureau of Economic Analysis, U.S. Department of Commerce. 1988. *Government Transactions*. Methodology Paper Series MP – 5. November.

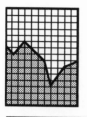

25
GROSS DOMESTIC PRODUCT

The gross domestic product (GDP) is the broadest indicator of economic output and growth. It covers the goods and services produced and consumed in the private, public, domestic, and international sectors of the economy. Two measures of the GDP are provided, one from the viewpoint of demand that shows the market for goods and services, and the other from the viewpoint of supply, showing the resource costs in producing the goods and services. The GDP is a summary measure of the national income and product accounts, which are also referred to as the "national accounts."

In addition, the GDP is presented in two ways with respect to price levels: in current dollars that represent actual prices in every period, and in constant dollars that abstract from changing prices over time. The current-dollar GDP is the market value of goods and services produced. The constant-dollar GDP, which is referred to as real GDP, represents the quantity of economic output and is the measure used to define the rate of economic growth. There are several alternative measures of real GDP growth based on different techniques for adjusting for price change. Indicators of price movements are provided for the total GDP and its major components (see *GDP price measures*).

The United States GDP will be converted to the definitions of the United Nations' system of national accounts (SNA) in the second half of the 1990s. The SNA also provides for extending the national accounts to satellite accounts that are linked statistically to the traditional accounts and encompass entire fields of economic activity such as research and development, natural resources, pensions, housing, health, transportation, and education. The United States has published satellite accounts for natural resources (referred to as "Green GDP"), is developing satellite accounts for research and development, and plans to add pensions as a third satellite.

Where and When Available

The GDP is provided quarterly by the Bureau of Economic Analysis in the U.S. Department of Commerce. The data are published in a monthly press release and in BEA's monthly journal, the *Survey of Current Business*. Secondary sources include *Economic Indicators* and the *Federal Reserve Bulletin*.

The figures are available during the fourth week of every month. Initial (referred to as "advance") data are provided in the month after the quarter to which they refer (April for the first quarter, July for the second quarter, etc.); these are revised in the subsequent two months (referred to as "preliminary" and "final," respectively), with more detailed revisions made annually every July, and still more comprehensive benchmark revisions made about every five years.

Content

The composition of the two GDP measures is shown in Table 25.1. The "product side" reflects demand or markets for goods and services, and the "income side" reflects the supply or costs of producing the goods and services. The two measures are conceptually equal, but they differ statistically because of inadequacies in the data; this difference is called the "statistical discrepancy." As noted below under "Accuracy," each measure is equally valid for calculating economic growth rates.

GDP is measured on a "value added" basis. Only the value that is added in each stage of production from raw materials to semifinished goods to final products is counted. This prevents endless

Table 25.1

Gross Domestic Product and Major Components, 1992

	Product side			Income side	
	$ billions	percent		$ billions	percent
Gross national product	6,038.5	100.0%	Gross national product	6,038.5	100.0%
Personal consumption expenditures	4,139.9	68.6	Compensation of employees	3,582.0	59.3
Durable goods	497.3	8.2	Wages and salaries	2,953.1	48.9
Nondurable goods	1,300.9	21.5	Supplements	629.0	10.4
Services	2,341.6	38.8			
Gross private domestic investment	796.5	13.2	Proprietors' income[c]	414.3	6.9
Nonresidential[a]	565.5	9.4	Farm	43.7	0.7
Residential[b]	223.6	3.7	Nonfarm	370.6	6.1
Inventory change	7.3	0.1			
Net exports	−29.6	−0.5	Rental income	−8.9	−0.1
Exports	640.5	10.6	Corporate profits	407.2	6.7
Imports	670.1	11.1			
			Net interest	442.0	7.3
Government purchases	1,131.8	18.7	Indirect business taxes[d]	502.8	8.3
Federal	448.8	7.4	Consumption of fixed capital[e]	657.9	10.9
			Business transfers, government subsidies, and government enterprises	24.9	0.4
State and local	683.0	11.3	Rest of the world[f]	−7.3	−0.1
			Statistical discrepancy	23.6	0.4

Note: Detail may not add to totals due to rounding. [a]Business plant and equipment. [b]Mainly new housing construction. [c]Profits of unincorporated business. [d]Mainly sales and property taxes. [e]Mainly depreciation allowances. [f]Factor income payments less receipts.

double counting that would occur if goods and services purchased from other business for use in production were included.

The GDP figures are seasonally adjusted.

Product Side:
Demand Components

The component markets for the nation's output represent the demand aspects of the economy and are referred to as the product side of GDP. The product-side total is the official GDP measure. It has the following main categories:

Personal consumption expenditures represent spending by households for durable goods, nondurables, and services and spending by nonprofit organizations for operating expenses.

Gross private domestic investment represents business spending for equipment and nonresidential structures by for-profit and nonprofit organizations; residential construction; and the change in business inventories, excluding profit or loss, due to cost changes between the time of purchase and sale of inventoried goods.

Government purchases of goods and services represent the federal, state, and local wages of government workers and purchases of civilian and defense goods and services, exclusive of transfer payments. (Total government spending, which also includes social security and other income maintenance payments, federal grants to state governments and state grants to local governments, interest on the public debt, and subsidy payments to business, is covered in *government budgets and debt.*)

Net exports of goods and services represent the international balance of exports minus imports in goods and services, including balance of U.S. income from investments in companies and securities abroad less that of foreigners' income from investments in the United States.

Income Side:
Supply Components

The labor, capital, and tax costs in producing the nation's output are reflected in the supply aspects of the economy and are referred to as the income side of GDP. It has the following main categories:

Compensation of employees represents the money and in-kind wages and fringe benefits of workers.

Proprietors' income and corporate profits represent business profits of unincorporated businesses and corporations, excluding the profit or loss due to cost changes between the time of acquisition and time of sales of inventories or to cost changes in replacing existing capital facilities since their acquisition.

Rental income of persons represents profits to residential and nonresidential real property owners who are not primarily engaged in real estate business, including nonmarket imputations of profits for owner-occupied housing as if such housing were rented at the market price, and royalties paid by businesses to individuals.

Consumption of fixed capital represents the depreciation allowances for the use of capital equipment and structures that are deducted as costs on business income tax returns and also are calculated for owner-occupied housing, including adjustments for the changing costs of replacing existing capital facilities from their original purchase cost.

Indirect business taxes represent sales and property taxes, customs duties, user fees, fines, and other analogous sources of government revenue.

Real GDP

GDP in constant dollars, referred to as "real GDP," represents the *quantity* of output goods and services. It eliminates the effect of price increases or decreases from one period to the next and is used for measuring the nation's economic growth. This differs from GDP in current dollars, referred to as "nominal GDP," which represents the *value* of goods and services produced, since it includes price as well as quantity change. There are three alternative quantity indexes of real GDP growth based on different procedures for adjusting for price change. They utilize different price "weights" to deal with the intrinsic problem of index number construction discussed in the Introduction. This is the obverse of the alternative price indexes in *GDP Price Indexes*, which employ quantity (expenditure) weights. The three quantity indexes of output are: fixed 1987 weights, chain-type annual weights, and benchmark-years weights. The varying price weights reflect the changing price relationships among goods and services items from period to period as some items rise in price more rapidly than others, some items remain at the same price levels, and some items decline in price.

The *fixed 1987 weighted quantity index* weights are the prices for goods and services items in 1987. These 1987 price weights are used for all years. They are also used to prepare the estimates of GDP in constant dollars. Therefore, growth rates calculated from the fixed 1987 weighted quantity index and from GDP in constant dollars are identical. *This is the most widely-accepted rate of economic growth.*

The *benchmark-years weighted quantity index* weights change every five years according to the prices of goods and services items in each quinquennial benchmark year. Benchmark years coincide with economic census years—1987, 1992, 1997, 2002, and so on. For historical data, two adjacent benchmark year price weights (for example, 1987 and 1992) are used in calculating quantity movements. For recent estimates after the last benchmark year, price weights comprising the last benchmark year and the most recent subsequent year are used for the quantity movements. Quantity movements from one period to the next are based on the Fisher ideal index number formula described below under "Methodology."

The *chain-type annual weighted quantity index* weights change annually according to the prices of goods and services items in each year. Two price weights in adjacent years are used in calculating quantity movements. Quantity movements from one period to the next are based on the Fisher ideal index number formula described below under "Methodology."

Taken together, the quantity measures are a spectrum of tech-

niques that account for changes in price structure from one period to the next. At the extremes are the fixed-weighted quantity
index, which allows for no change in price weights, and the
chain-type quantity index, which changes the price weights every
year. Within these poles, the price weights of the benchmark-
years quantity index change more frequently than the fixed-
weighted index and less frequently than the chain index.

Other Summary GDP Measures

In addition to GDP, several variants of total GDP are provided to
assist in economic analysis. These are based on adjustments related to inventories, international transactions, and statistical
problems. The most widely cited one is *final sales*, which excludes the effect of inventory increases or decreases. This results
in highlighting underlying demand as represented by purchases
of goods and services by households, business, government, or
foreigners, independent of whether the highly volatile business
inventories in stores , warehouses, and factories are accumulating
or depleting. Other summary measures are final sales to domestic
purchasers, gross domestic purchases, gross national product, and
command GDP. Typically, the largest difference in the quarterly
and annual movements between GDP and the other measures
occurs in the case of final sales.

Methodology

The GDP is calculated using secondary data that are initially
compiled for other purposes, which limits control of the quality
of the data for GDP requirements. Because of this dependence on
secondary data, the BEA directs considerable attention to un-
usual movements in the data base and raises questions with the
organizations providing primary data to determine whether errors
or special circumstances affect the figures. This close probing is
done when the GDP components are first estimated and is also
repeated a second time when the total product and income sides
are compared, particularly if there is a large difference (statistical

discrepancy) between the two GDP aggregates. This process sometimes uncovers data problems that in turn lead to changing certain components to mitigate the problems. In addition, special formulas are used to adjust inventories and depreciation to exclude profit or loss due to changing costs of inventories or capital facilities between the time of purchase and their sale or replacement. These are referred to as the "inventory valuation adjustment" and "capital accumulation adjustment," which are included in the product side under inventory change and in the income side under proprietors' income, corporate profits, and consumption of fixed capital.

The data used in constructing the GDP come from many government agencies and private organizations that provide statistics obtained from surveys, income tax returns, and regulatory reports. The items in this data base vary considerably in definition, collection technique, and timeliness, and thus are of uneven quality. Because the two measures of GPD on the product and income sides are developed independently from different data sources, the "statistical discrepancy" between the two GDP totals indicates the extent of the inconsistency in the two data bases. Formally, the "statistical discrepancy" is the product side minus the income side.

GDP in constant dollars is prepared by adjusting the current-dollar figures for the various goods and services items primarily by the price movements of the *consumer price index, producer price indexes*, and the *import and export price indexes*. These are supplemented with other indicators of price change such as those for construction and defense prices and costs.

The *fixed 1987 weighted quantity index* movements are calculated using 1987 goods and services price weights for all years. No other weighting structure is used. The movements of this index are identical to the movements of GDP in constant dollars.

The *chain-type annual weighted quantity index* movements are calculated using the geometric mean of two quantity movements based on two goods and services price weights (Fisher ideal index). The price weights for the two most recent years are based on the annual GDP revisions each July. Quantity changes are calculated separately using the two weighting patterns, and the actual quantity movement is the geometric mean of the two movements.

The *benchmark-years weighted quantity index* movements are calculated using the geometric mean of two quantity movements based on alternative goods and services price weights (referred to as the Fisher ideal index number formula). For historical estimates between adjacent benchmark years such as 1987 and 1992, the actual quantity changes are calculated separately using 1987 and 1992 price weights, and the actual quantity movement is the geometric mean of the two movements. For quantity movements after the last benchmark year, the two price weights are those in the last benchmark year and those in the most recent year based on the annual GDP revisions each July. Quantity changes are calculated separately using the two weighting patterns, and the actual quantity movement is the geometric mean of the two movements.

Accuracy

There are no estimates of sampling error for the GDP figures. The statistical discrepancy indicates the extent to which unknown errors in the data bases, in which some are above and others below the "correct" values, do not cancel each other. However, because some of these errors are offsetting, the statistical discrepancy is a net figure of the consistency of the data bases rather than a gross measure of all errors regardless of whether the high and low figures are offsetting. As noted earlier, the product side GDP is regarded as the official measure, although the availability of the product and income sides allows the calculation of alternative growth rates that provide a lower and upper range for use in analysis (by comparing movements of the product side against the product side minus the statistical discrepancy). Thus, one way of viewing the accuracy of the GDP figures is to treat it as being within the growth rate range indicated by the product and income sides movements.

Another perspective of GDP accuracy is provided by considering the size of the revisions to provisional GDP figures. These are shown in terms of the confidence that the percentage growth rates in GDP and prices are likely to be revised upward or downward within a specified range based on past experience. For example, the growth rate of the estimate of the constant-dollar GDP that is published in the third month after the quarter to which it refers is revised in the succeeding annual revisions each July as follows: in two of three cases in a range of –1.9 to +1.9 percentage points and in nine of ten cases in a range of –2.8 to +3.0 percentage points.

Relevance

The GDP provides the overall framework for analyzing and forecasting economic trends. It has the unique attribute of integrating the markets for goods and services (demand or spending) with the production of the goods and services (supply or costs) in one format. Because the costs of production also generate wage and profit incomes, the GDP measures are the basis for analyzing the feedback effects between spending and incomes from one period to the next. The analyses are used to assist the president and Congress in formulating fiscal and income policies and the Federal Reserve Board in formulating monetary policies that are aimed at maximizing employment growth and minimizing inflation. Fiscal policies are enacted through federal spending and taxes (*government budgets and debt*), fiscal and income policies and the Federal Reserve Board in formulating monetary policies through the *money supply* and *interest rates*, and income policies through price and wage voluntary guidelines and mandatory controls. Analyses of the cyclical expansion and recession movements and of the longer- term periods that span several cycles can suggest the likely future implications of adopting particular policies for moderating cyclical fluctuations and stimulating noninflationary long-term economic growth. The GDP is the main framework of such analyses, although it is supplemented by and integrated with data from other indicators.

Recent Trends

Gross domestic product in constant dollars showed three different periods of growth during 1980–92 (Table 25.2). The years

Table 25.2

Gross Domestic Product

	Current dollars (billions)	1987 dollars (billions)	1987 dollars (percent change)
1980	2,708.0	3,776.3	−0.5%
1981	3,030.6	3,843.1	1.8
1982	3,149.6	3,760.3	−2.2
1983	3,405.0	3,906.6	3.9
1984	3,777.2	4,148.5	6.2
1985	4,038.7	4,279.8	3.2
1986	4,268.6	4,404.5	2.9
1987	4,539.9	4,539.9	3.1
1988	4,900.4	4,718.6	3.9
1989	5,250.8	4,838.0	2.5
1990	5,546.1	4,897.3	1.2
1991	5,722.9	4,861.4	−0.7
1992	6,038.5	4,986.3	2.6

	Alternative quantity indexes (percent change)		
	Fixed-weighted index	Chain-type weighted index	Benchmark-years weighted index
1980	−0.5	−0.2	0.0
1981	1.8	2.5	2.7
1982	−2.2	−2.2	−1.9
1983	3.9	3.8	3.9
1984	6.2	7.0	6.7
1985	3.2	3.2	3.3
1986	2.9	2.9	2.9
1987	3.1	3.1	3.2
1988	3.9	3.9	3.8
1989	2.5	2.6	2.5
1990	1.2	1.2	1.2
1991	−0.7	−0.8	−0.8
1992	2.6	2.3	2.4

1980 – 82 had a negative growth rate, with real GDP declining in two of the three years; growth was 3 percent or more over 1983 – 88; and growth slowed considerably in 1989–92, including one year of one percent growth and another of declining growth. The alternative quantity indexes of GDP growth typically varied by only 0.1 percentage point. Larger differences

4

occurred in 1980, 1981, and 1984, the main one being that the fixed-weighted index had lower growth rates than the other indexes.

References from Primary Data Source

Bureau of Economic Analysis, U.S. Department of Commerce. 1992. *National Income and Product Accounts of the United States*. Volume 2, 1959–88. September.

Bureau of Economic Analysis, U.S. Department of Commerce. 1993. *National Income and Product Accounts of the United States*. Volume 1, 1929–58. February.

Carson, Carol S. 1987. "GNP: An Overview of Source Data and Estimating Methods." *Survey of Current Business*. July.

Carson, Carol S., and Bruce T. Grimm. 1991. "Satellite Accounts in a Modernized and Extended System of Economic Accounts." *Business Economics*. January.

Carson, Carol S., and Jeanette Honsa. 1990. "The United Nations System of National Accounts: An Introduction." *Survey of Current Business*. June.

Carson, Carol S., and J. Steven Landefeld. 1994. "Integrated Economic and Environmental Satellite Accounts," and "Accounting for Mineral Resources: Issues and BEA's Initial Estimates." *Survey of Current Business*. April.

Young, Allan H. 1987. "Evaluation of the GNP Estimates." *Survey of Current Business*. August.

Young, Allan H. 1993. "Alternative Measures of Change in Real Output and Prices, Quarterly Estimates for 1959–92." *Survey of Current Business*. March.

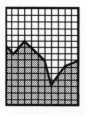

26
GROWTH CYCLES

Growth cycles represent pronounced deviations in the short-term movements of aggregate economic activity from the long-term rate of economic growth. The peak of a growth cycle occurs when economic output is furthest above its long-term trend and the trough occurs when economic activity is furthest below the long-term trend. Growth cycles differ from business cycles, which simply reflect the direction in which economic activity is moving during cyclical expansions and recessions—that is, expansions represent periods of increasing economic activity, and recessions represent periods of declining economic activity. Data on growth cycles are prepared for eleven countries encompassing North America, Europe, and the Pacific region.

Where and When Available

Growth cycle measures are prepared monthly by the Center for International Business Cycle Research, Graduate School of Business, Columbia University. They are published in the center's monthly report, *International Economic Indicators Outlook*.

The composite indexes for all eleven countries are available two months after the month to which they refer. The components of the indexes for the individual countries are available five to seven weeks after the reference month. The data are revised on an ongoing basis as new information becomes available.

Content

Growth cycles reflect fluctuations in economic growth that occur during business cycle expansions and recessions. When the growth rate of overall economic activity during a cyclical expansion remains below the average long-term growth rate for a sustained period, which is defined as six months or more, the period is referred to as a "growth recession." Thus, growth recessions occur during business cycle expansions. A growth recession may signal an oncoming cyclical recession, or it may reflect a less serious slowdown in economic growth.

Analogously, when growth in economic output during a cyclical expansion exceeds the long-term growth rate for a period of six months or more, the period is referred to as a "growth expansion." Because some growth recessions do not turn into cyclical recessions, and because business cycle recessions, by definition, constitute growth recessions, there are more growth cycles than business cycles.

Growth cycle measures are prepared for eleven countries: the United States, Canada, United Kingdom, West Germany, France, Italy, Japan, South Korea, Taiwan, Australia, and New Zealand. (Data for the former East Germany are not available to calculate growth cycles for the united Germany.) The country measures are also combined to provide growth cycles collectively for North America (two countries), Europe (four countries), Pacific region (five countries), all eleven countries, ten countries excluding the United States, and the G-7 countries (the United States, Japan, Germany, France, the United Kingdom, Italy, and Canada).

The measure of economic growth is the level of economic activity based on a composite coincident index. The coincident index contains similar but not identical elements for the eleven countries. These typically are *industrial production,* gross national product (see *gross domestic product*), *retail sales, employment,* and *unemployment.* The peaks and troughs in the deviations from the long-term trend in the coincident index, and its components, are the reference criteria for dating the peaks and troughs of growth cycles. The peak is reached when the index is furthest above the long-term trend, and the trough is reached when the index is furthest below the long-term trend.

Leading and long-leading indexes are also prepared for growth cycles. The leading indexes change direction before a significant change occurs in the sustained growth rate of the coincident index. The leading index for the eleven countries typically leads the coincident index by four months, and the long-leading index typically leads the coincident index by six to twelve months. The growth cycle leading indexes have the same properties of business expectations and profits as the *leading, coincident, and lagging indexes.*

The components of the composite leading index are similar but not identical for all eleven countries. The elements of the U.S. leading index are: unemployment insurance initial claims, net business formation (business incorporations and *business failures*), consumer goods and materials new orders (*manufacturers' orders*), plant and equipment contracts and orders (*plant and equipment expenditures*), housing building permits (*housing starts*), business inventories change, industrial materials price change, stock market prices (*stock market price indexes*), corporate profits after taxes (*corporate profits*), price/labor cost ratio in the nonfarm business economy (*GDP price measures* and *unit labor costs*), and consumer installment credit change (*consumer installment credit*). The elements of the U.S. long-leading index are: bond prices, price to unit labor cost ratio in manufacturing, money supply (M2) in constant dollars, housing building permits, output per hour in manufacturing, and consumer price index for services (inverted)

Most of the components of the leading and coincident composite indexes are seasonally adjusted. The composite indexes are not seasonally adjusted at the overall level.

Methodology

The elements of the coincident and leading indexes for each country are combined into the composite indexes by a method that gives the same influence to all data series regardless of whether they typically show small or large month-to-month changes. This prevents data series with typically large monthly movements from dominating the index. Other adjustments are made to have the coincident and leading indexes for each country consistent with each other in terms of the cyclical amplitude (the amount of the rise during a cyclical expansion and the amount of the decline during a cyclical recession) and the long-term trend. Generally, this is done by superimposing the monthly movement of the industrial production index (for the amplitude) and the long-term growth of the gross national product (for the trend) on the coincident and leading indexes. In addition, the monthly movements of the composite indexes are calculated as a six-month smoothed percentage change at an annual rate.

The dating of the monthly peak and trough of each growth cycle is based on the monthly deviation of the coincident index from its long-term trend. The general rule is that the peak month occurs when the index is furthest above the long-term trend, and the trough is the month when the index is furthest below the long-term trend. This is modified by a visual inspection of the data to avoid the situation when strict adherence to the rule would result in cycles with relatively small amplitudes or when atypical events such as hurricanes or strikes/lockouts create the appearance of a cycle.

Growth cycles for the eleven countries are combined into the North American, European, Pacific, and other groupings by weighting each country by its gross national product in 1980 in U.S. dollars.

Accuracy

There are no estimates of sampling or revision error for the international growth cycles.

Relevance

Growth cycles aid in the analysis of traditional business cycle recessions in two principal ways. First, growth cycles reflect

Figure 26.1 **Growth Cycles: 1981–93**

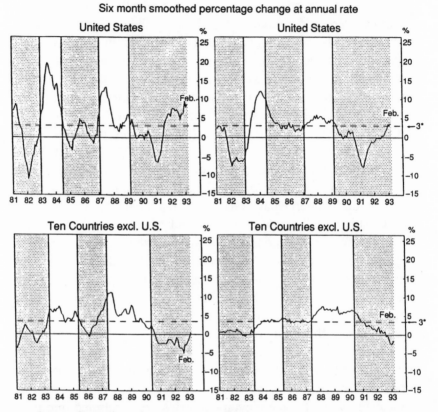

Source: Center for International Business Cycle Research, Columbia University.
Note: Vertical bars are growth cycle recession periods. The ten countries excluding the United States are: Canada, United Kingdom, West Germany, France, Italy, Japan, Australia, Taiwan, South Korea, and New Zealand.
*Dash lines are the long-term average annual rate of change in the index and in the real gross national product.

slowdowns in economic activity that are sometimes followed by cyclical recessions; this is an "early warning" function. Second, growth cycles identify slowdowns that are sometimes followed by sustained periods of low economic growth; this is the "growth recession" phenomenon. Thus, growth cycles provide additional perspectives for analyzing business cycle movements.

Recent Trends

Growth recessions were longer than growth expansions during 1981–92 for the eleven countries covered in the growth cycle measures (Figure 26.1). Comparisons of growth cycles between the United States and the ten countries excluding the United States show that the United States had a shorter growth recession in the early 1980s and longer growth recessions in the mid-1980s and in the late 1980s into the early 1990s. The amplitudes of the U.S. growth cycle expansion and recession periods were greater than those for the ten countries excluding the United States. The lead times of the leading index at growth cycle peaks and troughs show no consistent patterns in which the United States or the ten countries excluding the United States had substantially different lead times (see Figure 26.1).

Reference from Primary Data Source

Center for International Business Cycle Research, Graduate School of Business, Columbia University. 1992. "International Economic Indicators: Appendix A." December.

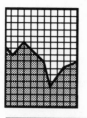

27
HELP-WANTED ADVERTISING INDEX

The help-wanted advertising index tracks employers' advertisements for job openings in the classified section of newspapers in fifty-one labor market areas. The index represents job vacancies resulting from turnover in exiting positions such as workers changing jobs or retiring and from the creation of new jobs. It excludes nonadvertised job vacancies and jobs advertised in non-classified sections of newspapers such as display ads in business or news sections.

Where and When Available

Measures of the help-wanted advertising index are provided monthly by The Conference Board. The figures are published in a press release and in the Conference Board's monthly *Economic Times*. Secondary sources include the *Survey of Current Business*.

The figures are available about thirty-five days after the month to which they refer. The data are revised in the following month.

Content

The help-wanted advertising figures cover jobs in many fields—professional, technical, crafts, office, sales, farm, custodial, and so on. They include a higher proportion of all junior and middle-level vacancies than of managerial, executive, or unskilled levels. In addition to the national help-wanted index, local indexes for fifty-one labor markers are provided.

The index is currently based on 1967 = 100.

The help-wanted figures are seasonally adjusted.

Methodology

The help-wanted advertising figures are obtained from classified advertisements in one daily (including Sunday) newspaper in each of the fifty-one labor markets (fifty-one cities including their suburbs). Newspapers are selected according to how well their ads represent jobs in the local labor market area. The labor markets accounted for approximately one-half of nonagricultural employment in 1992.

The index reflects the number of job advertisements. Each advertisement is weighted equally regardless of whether it is an ad for one job or for multiple positions or whether for full-time or part-time work. Advertisements of both employers and employment agencies and advertisements for the same job on successive days are included in the count.

Index weights for the fifty-one labor markets are based on the proportion of nonagricultural *employment* accounted for by each of the labor markets. These weights are updated every two years. Within each market area, help-wanted advertisements in the Sunday newspaper are weighted according to the ratio of the average Sunday advertising volume to average daily advertising volume.

Accuracy

There are no estimates of sampling or revision error for the help-wanted advertising figures.

Relevance

The help-wanted advertising index indicates the direction of employers' hiring plans. In theory, it provides an advance signal of future changes in *employment* and cyclical turning points. In

Table 27.1

Help-Wanted Advertising Index
(1967 = 100)

1980	128
1981	118
1982	86
1983	95
1984	130
1985	138
1986	138
1987	153
1988	157
1989	150
1990	129
1991	94
1992	92

practice, the help-wanted index leads the downturn from the expansion peak to a recession, but it lags the turning point in moving from recession to expansion, based on analyses conducted as part of the *leading, coincident, and lagging indexes*. The lag in timing as the economy is recovering from a recession results from the tendency of employers to increase *average weekly hours* of existing workers when business improves or to call back workers on layoff before advertising for new workers.

The help-wanted index is inversely related to *unemployment*. When help-wanted advertisements increase, unemployment declines, while a decline in help-wanted advertisements is accompanied by a rise in unemployment. The help-wanted movements sometimes are sharper than unemployment movements because of changing advertising practices. For example, during periods of low unemployment, employers may rely more heavily on help-wanted advertisements than on alternative means of finding workers. During high unemployment, employers may find workers more easily through alternative means such as through workers initiating the contact on their own or on the advice of a friend.

Some advertised jobs may not be filled because employers are not satisfied with the applicants, there is an overall shortage of applicants, or employers decide not to fill the jobs.

Recent Trends

The help-wanted advertising index showed three periods of different movements during 1980–92 (Table 27.1). After declining in the early 1980s to a low of 86 in 1982, it rose in subsequent years to a peak of 157 in 1988 (1967 = 100). It then declined to 92 in 1992.

Reference from Primary Data Source

Preston, Noreen L. 1977. *The Help-Wanted Index: Technical Description and Behavioral Trends.* The Conference Board.

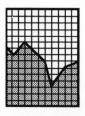

28
HOME SALES

Sales of new and existing privately owned single-family homes represent the number of housing units sold. Each house is counted as one unit regardless of the sales price. New homes are newly constructed houses that are sold by the developer to the first owner. Existing homes are houses that have been occupied that are sold to a new owner. The number of new and existing homes available for sale indicates the inventory of unsold houses that are on the market.

Where and When Available

Measures of new home sales and of new homes available for sale are prepared monthly by the Bureau of the Census in the U.S. Department of Commerce and the U.S. Department of Housing and Urban Development. The data are available twenty-one work days after the month to which they refer. They are revised in the three succeeding months. They are published in a press release and in the Census/HUD report, *New One-Family Houses Sold*. Secondary sources include *Economic Indicators*.

Existing home sales and existing homes available for sale are prepared monthly by the National Association of Realtors. The data are usually available twenty-five days after the month to which they refer. They are revised one month later and annually every March. They are published in the NAR report, *Home Sales*.

Content

Single-family homes are unattached houses and townhouses, including individually owned and operated housing units as well as townhouse condominiums. Multifamily condominium and cooperative apartment buildings and mobile homes are not included in the measures of single-family homes.

A *new home sale* is recorded when a sales contract is signed or a buyer's deposit is accepted by the developer or the developer's real estate broker, whichever occurs first. Although some contracts or deposits are conditional and subsequently canceled, the data are not revised to show this change.

New homes available for sale are the inventory of unsold new homes. They are recorded when a building permit to construct the house is issued or, in non-permit-issuing places, when work begins on the foundation if there is no sales contract or sales deposit at that time. Although a building permit may not be followed by actual construction (that is, a *housing start*), the data are not revised to show this change.

Sales of existing homes include transactions conducted through a real estate broker and those made directly by the owner. A sale of an existing home is recorded when a sales contract is signed, which is typically sixty days before the closing. The data are not revised if the contract is subsequently canceled.

Existing homes available for sale are the inventory of unsold existing homes. They are recorded when a house is put on the market through a contract with a real estate broker. The data are not revised if the house is later removed from the market.

The new and existing home sales data are seasonally adjusted.

Methodology

New home sales and new homes available for sale data are obtained from a monthly survey of a sample of developers conducted by the Bureau of the Census. The response rate is virtually 100 percent for the final estimate; imputations are made for 40 percent of the preliminary estimate and decreasing percentages for successive revisions as late reported sales are processed. There are no imputations for new homes available for sale; instead, the inventory of homes available for sale is reduced by the expected late reported sales.

Existing home sales and existing homes for sale data are obtained from monthly surveys of a sample of over 600 boards/associations of realtors and multiple-listing systems conducted by the National Association of Realtors. The samples of realtor boards and multiple-listing systems account for approximately 75 percent of all existing home sales. The data are primarily for metropolitan areas, but they are considered to be representative of nonmetropolitan counties surrounding the metropolitan areas, based on biennial information in the *American Housing Survey* of the U.S. Department of Housing and Urban Development. The local area data are summed to the four broad Census Bureau regions of the U.S. encompassing the states classified in the Northeast, South, Midwest, and West. The regional data are in turn augmented by a "blow-up" factor to account for total sales of each region, including those not captured in the sample of realtor and multiple-listing reporting systems and including sales made directly by the owner. The blow-up factor is based on sales data in the American Housing Survey and the decennial Census of Housing. The blow-up factor is revised approximately every five years.

The monthly survey data on new homes available for sale and existing homes available for sale are checked for reasonableness with an alternative measure of the inventory of unsold homes estimated by accounting for changes in the inventory from one period to the next. This indirect estimate of unsold homes is illustrated below using the December 31 inventory as the example.

New homes available for sale:
    Inventory on November 30
        plus: building permits issued during December for which there is no sales contract or sales deposit

minus: new home sales during December
equals: inventory on December 31.

   Existing homes available for sale:
     Inventory on November 30
      plus: existing homes put on the market during December
      minus: existing home sales during December
      equals: inventory on December 31.

Accuracy

The sampling error in two of three cases for new home sales data is plus or minus 6 percent and for new homes available for sale is plus or minus 3 percent. There are no estimates of sampling or revision error for the existing home sales data.

Relevance

About 60 percent of all households own single-family homes. The purchase of a home is typically the largest single item bought by householders (outlays of comparable magnitude are associated with financing college educations and major medical bills). Economic output is increased far more by the purchase of a new house than of an existing house because of the materials and construction work required in building a new house, although renovation work is sometimes done when an existing house is purchased. While existing home sales have a much smaller direct impact on the economy than new home sales, existing and new home sales are in fact closely linked because existing home owners often can afford to buy a new home only by selling their current home. Thus, the market for existing homes strongly influences sales of new homes. In addition, both new and existing home sales generate purchases of furniture, appliances, and other house furnishings, which is a secondary stimulus to the economy.

Home sales are sensitive to changes in economic conditions

Table 28.1

Home Sales
(thousands of housing units)

	New home sales	Existing home sales	New homes available for sale*	Existing homes available for sale*
1980	545	2,973	342	NA
1981	436	2,419	278	NA
1982	412	1,990	255	1,910
1983	623	2,719	304	1,980
1984	639	2,868	358	2,260
1985	688	3,214	350	2,200
1986	750	3,565	361	1,970
1987	671	3,526	370	2,160
1988	676	3,594	371	2,160
1989	650	3,440	366	1,870
1990	534	3,296	321	2,100
1991	509	3,221	284	2,130
1992	610	3,520	265	1,760

*As of December 31
NA: Not Available.

related to *employment, personal income and saving, interest rates,* and housing prices. Although housing is a necessity of living, home sales are highly cyclical because households are most likely to purchase a home during prosperous times when they can best afford it, but they tend to defer a home purchase during depressed times when they can least afford it.

Recent Trends

Sales of new single-family homes fluctuated during 1980–92 (Table 28.1). After declining from approximately 550,000 in 1980 during the next two years, home sales rose to a peak of 750,000 in 1986. They declined during 1987–91, and then rose to 600,000 in 1992. Sales of existing homes generally rose during the twelve-year period, although they declined in several years. They peaked at 3.6 million in 1986 and 1988, declined more slowly than new home sales during 1989–91, and totaled 3.5 million in 1992.

New homes available for sale fluctuated within 250,000–370,000 during 1980–92. They followed the general pattern of new home sales over the period, although not in all years. Existing homes available for sale peaked at 2.3 million in 1984, and fluctuated within 1.8–2.2 million during 1985–92.

References from Primary Data Sources

Bureau of the Census, U.S. Department of Commerce, and U.S. Department of Housing and Urban Development. Monthly. *New One-Family Houses Sold.*

National Association of Realtors. Monthly. *Home Sales.*

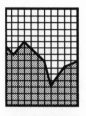

29
HOUSING STARTS

The housing starts indicator tracks the beginning of construction of new privately owned single-family homes, townhouses, and multifamily apartment buildings. Each single-family house and each separate apartment within apartment buildings (including cooperative and condominium buildings) is counted as one housing start. The measure excludes publicly owned housing, placements of mobile homes, additions and alterations to existing housing, and conversions from nonresidential structures to residential use.

Where and When Available

Housing starts figures are provided by the Bureau of the Census in the U.S. Department of Commerce. The data are published in the report *Housing Starts*. Secondary sources include *Economic Indicators*, the *Survey of Current Business*, and the *Federal Reserve Bulletin*.

The data are available in a press release during the third week of the month after the month to which they refer. Each monthly report contains revised figures for the two previous months. The seasonally adjusted figures are revised every year for the preceding three years based on revised seasonal adjustment factors.

Content

Data on housing starts are confined to privately owned housing. Data collection of publicly-owned housing was discontinued in 1988. A housing start is counted as occurring in the month that excavation work begins for the foundation. While each single-family house and apartment unit is counted as one housing start, the effect of differences in size and amenities of each start with respect to the volume of construction work is only captured in figures on the dollar value of housing construction. (Other monthly information is available on the number of housing units for which construction is completed every month, and annual information on the size and amenities of new housing units is in *Characteristics of New Housing*.)

The housing starts figures are seasonally adjusted.

Methodology

Housing starts figures are estimated separately for housing in local areas that require building permits for construction and for housing in non-permit-issuing localities. For the permit-issuing areas, two monthly sample surveys are used: (1) a mail survey of 8,300 of 17,000 permit-issuing localities to determine the total number of permits issued, and (2) a survey of 840 areas by on-site interviewers to determine in which month construction started on housing units that were authorized in previous months and the current month. The information obtained on-site about the rates of construction started for permits issued for each month to date is applied to the current permit figures to develop the total number of housing starts every month. The figures are adjusted upward to reflect starts begun in permit areas without a permit based on factors developed from surveys conducted in the late 1960s. The figures are also adjusted upwards to reflect units started before permit authorization and those for which late reports are received. These upward adjustments are based on factors derived from annual reviews of the extent to which these events occur.

Private housing starts in nonpermit areas are estimated from monthly on-site surveys of ongoing construction work in a sample of 120 localities.

Accuracy

The sampling error for the level of housing starts in two cases out of three is plus or minus three percent. The sampling error for the monthly movement of housing starts in nine of ten cases is six percentage points.

Relevance

New housing construction is important to the overall economy. Construction results in the hiring of workers, the production of construction materials and equipment, and the sale of large household appliances such as ranges and refrigerators. In addition, when owners or tenants occupy the housing, they often buy new furniture, carpeting, and other furnishings.

The rate of new housing construction is heavily influenced by the growth of the number of households in the long run and by the growth of real family income and the level of mortgage interest rates over shorter periods. Because housing lasts for many years and there is little need to replace it frequently, the purchase of new housing usually is deferred until incomes and interest rates make it affordable. Typically, housing starts increase when interest rates are low or incomes in general are rising, and they fall when interest rates are high or incomes are growing slowly or declining.

Housing starts fluctuate considerably during business cycles. They are also classified as a leading indicator of business activity by the Bureau of Economic Analysis in the U.S. Department of Commerce. Housing permits are a component of the leading index of *leading, coincident, and lagging indexes*. The permit to construct a house is typically issued shortly before the beginning of construction, as reflected by the housing start—usually within three months in advance of the start of construction for single family homes, and within six months in advance for apartment buildings.

Table 29.1

Housing Starts (thousands)

		Privately owned		
	Total	Total privately owned	Single family	Multi-family	Publicly owned
1980	1,313	1,292	852	440	20
1981	1,100	1,084	705	379	16
1982	1,072	1,062	663	400	10
1983	1,713	1,703	1,068	635	9
1984	1,756	1,750	1,084	665	6
1985	1,745	1,742	1,072	669	3
1986	1,807	1,805	1,179	626	2
1987	1,623	1,621	1,146	474	2
1988	NA	1,488	1,081	407	NA
1989	NA	1,376	1,003	373	NA
1990	NA	1,193	895	298	NA
1991	NA	1,014	840	174	NA
1992	NA	1,200	1,030	170	NA

Note: Detail may not add to totals due to rounding.
NA: Not available.

Recent Trends

Housing starts fluctuated within 1.0 to 1.8 million during 1980–92 (Table 29.1). After declining to 1.1 million in 1981–82, starts rose to a peak of 1.8 million in 1986. They subsequently declined to an average of 1.1 million in 1991–92. As a proportion of all starts, single-family units drifted downward from 66 percent in 1980 to 62 percent in 1982–85. The single-family share rose continuously in subsequent years, peaking at 86 percent in 1992. Publicly owned housing declined from 20,000 units in 1980 to 2,000 units in 1986–87, after which no estimates are provided.

Reference from Primary Data Source

Bureau of the Census, U.S. Department of Commerce. Monthly. *Housing Starts.*

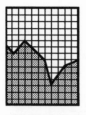

30
IMPORT AND EXPORT
PRICE INDEXES

The import and export price indexes measure price changes in agricultural, mineral, and manufactured products for goods bought from and sold to foreigners. They represent increases and decreases in prices of internationally traded goods due to changes in the value of the dollar and changes in the markets for the items.

Where and When Available

Import and export price indexes are provided monthly by the Bureau of Labor Statistics in the U.S. Department of Labor. The data are published in a press release and in the BLS monthly journal, the *Monthly Labor Review*.

The figures are published at the end of the month immediately following the month to which they refer. They are revised in the following three months. Major benchmark revisions, which include updating the weighting structure, are made approximately every five years. Smaller technical revisions such as introducing new products are made between benchmarks.

Content

The import and export price indexes cover most foreign traded goods. The broad product categories of the indexes are food;

beverages and tobacco; crude materials; fuels; intermediate manufactured products; machinery and transportation equipment; and miscellaneous manufactured products. The monthly figures cover approximately 10,000 products. Additional product detail is provided quarterly. Military equipment, works of art, commercial aircraft, and ships are excluded. Commodity detail is provided in three classifications systems: Standard International Trade Classification, Harmonized System, and End-Use.

(Supplementary price indexes are provided for a limited number of transportation services. These are not included in the above indexes for goods.)

Prices represent the actual transaction value including premiums and discounts from list prices and changes in credit terms and packaging. The preferred price definition for imports is the value at the U.S. border including overseas transportation and insurance costs (c.i.f., cost-insurance-freight), but if c.i.f. values are not readily available, then value at the foreign port of export port (f.o.b., free-on-board) is used. For example, imports of food, beverages, and intermediate manufactured products are priced on an f.o.b. basis. Import duties are excluded in both cases. The preferred price definition for exports is the value at the U.S. port of export before loading (f.a.s., free alongside ship), but if f.a.s. values are not readily available, the value f.o.b. at the U.S. factory or mine is used. In some cases, supplementary information on transport costs between the production facility and the export port is used to adjust the reported f.o.b. data to a f.a.s. basis. Regardless of these variations between products, the same definition of prices is maintained for individual products to ensure consistency in the monthly price movements.

Prices usually are based on the time the item is delivered, not the time the order is placed. The indexes reflect movements for the same or similar items exclusive of enhancement or reduction in the quality or quantity of the item.

The import and export pricer indexes are not seasonally adjusted.

Methodology

The price data are obtained by a Bureau of Labor Statistics mail survey from a sample of over 4,800 importers and exporters, including a limited number of foreign trade brokers. The overall response rate to the BLS survey is 90 percent. In addition, prices of crude petroleum imports are based on U.S. Department of Energy data, and those for grain exports (excluding rice) are based on U.S. Department of Agriculture data. Price quotations are sought for the first transaction of the month, which typically occurs within the first week of the month.

The weights of the indexes for 1993 and subsequent years are based on the 1990 dollar value of imports or exports for each item as reported by the Census Bureau. The weights were based on the 1985 value of foreign trade for 1985–92, and on the 1980 foreign trade value before 1985.

If the reported import or export price includes a change in the quality or quantity of the item, an adjustment is made to compensate for the improvement or decline in order to measure price movements for items having the same functional characteristics over time. Because data to make the necessary adjustments are not always available, the import and export price indexes contain an unknown amount of price change caused by quality and quantity changes. (See the *consumer price index* and *producer price indexes* for examples.)

Accuracy

There are no estimates of sampling or revision error for the import and export indexes.

Relevance

The import and export price indexes help to gauge changes in the competitive position of U.S. imports and exports and to analyze the effect of this changing competitive position on the volume of

Table 30.1

Import and Export Price Indexes
(annual percent change)

December to December	All imports	Imports excluding fuels	All exports
	Dollar price	Dollar price	Dollar price
1985	1.0%	NA	−0.9%
1986	−0.1	8.0%	−0.7
1987	10.1	8.7	6.0
1988	4.4	6.7	6.4
1989	2.5	−0.2	0.7
1990	7.4	3.0	2.2
1991	−4.2	0.2	−0.4
1992	0.2	0.8	0.5

NA: Not available.

import and export trade. The price indexes are useful in evaluating the effect of changes in the *value of the dollar* on import and export prices. This information also makes it possible to perform a limited analysis of the effect of changes in the dollar on U.S. domestic price *inflation*.

Recent Trends

Import prices for all goods varied considerably during 1985−92 (Table 30.1). International oil price movements affected overall import prices substantially in 1986, 1990, and 1991. Export prices were more stable than import prices. Export prices changed within a range of minus 1 to plus 2 percent in six of the eight years.

Reference from Primary Data Source

Bureau of Labor Statistics, U.S. Department of Labor. 1992. *BLS Handbook of Methods*. Chapter 17. September.

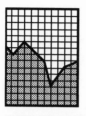

31
INDUSTRIAL PRODUCTION INDEX

The industrial production index (IPI) measures the change in output in U.S. manufacturing, mining, and electric and gas utilities industries. Output refers to the physical quantity of items produced, as distinct from sales value, which combines quantity and price. The index covers the production of goods and power for domestic sales in the United States and exports. It excludes production in the agriculture, construction, transportation, communication, trade, finance, and service industries; government output; and imports. While the excluded industries and imports are not directly in the IPI, they are indirectly incorporated to the extent that the manufacturing, mining, and utilities industries use them as intermediate items, in which case they are a component of the product or power produced.

Where and When Available

The IPI is prepared monthly by the Federal Reserve Board. It is published in a press release and in the *Federal Reserve Bulletin*, the FRB's monthly journal. Secondary sources include *Economic Indicators* and the *Survey of Current Business*.

The figures are available in the middle of the month after the month to which they refer. Preliminary data are provided for the preceding month; these are revised in the subsequent three months. Annual revisions are made in the fall.

Content

The IPI is provided from two perspectives: (1) output originating in the producing industries (supply) and (2) selected consumer and business markets of the items produced (demand). The component groups of the supply perspective are the producing industries: manufacturing, mining, and electric and gas utilities. For the market perspective, these components are categorized as products according to their typical usage. These are: consumer goods, business equipment, defense and space equipment, intermediate products including construction and business supplies, and materials including parts, containers, and raw materials.

The official monthly index is based on the total in the market grouping because of the greater interest in the cyclical aspects of the economy associated with changes in demand. The two alternative totals typically differ by no more than 0.1 percentage point from month to month.

The IPI is currently based on 1987 = 100.

The IPI figures are seasonally adjusted.

Methodology

The IPI is developed by weighting each component according to its relative importance in the base period. (See the section on index numbers in the Introduction.) The information for weights is obtained from the value-added measures of production in the quinquennial economic censuses of manufacturers and minerals industries and from value-added information for the utility industries in Internal Revenue Service statistics of income data. The value added weights for utilities in future years may be based on the new economic census for utilities which was first done for 1992. Value added generally refers to the wages, profits, and depreciation of capital facilities in the producing industry, that is, the value an industry adds to goods and services it buys from other industries, although there are technical differences in the definition of value added as it is used in the economic censuses and the *gross domestic product*. The weights are updated at five-

Table 31.1

Industrial Production Index (1987 = 100)

		Market categories			
	Total	Consumer goods	Equipment	Intermediate products	Materials
1980	84.1	85.3	74.6	77.0	91.3
1981	85.7	85.8	78.2	77.0	92.8
1982	81.9	84.5	77.0	75.1	85.1
1983	84.9	88.8	76.8	80.3	88.3
1984	92.8	92.8	89.2	86.2	96.6
1985	94.4	93.7	94.8	88.3	96.6
1986	95.3	96.8	94.5	91.9	95.9
1987	100.0	100.0	100.0	100.0	100.0
1988	104.4	102.9	107.6	101.8	105.0
1989	106.0	104.0	110.9	102.0	106.7
1990	106.0	103.4	112.1	101.2	106.8
1991	104.1	102.8	108.9	96.5	105.5
1992	106.5	105.2	112.7	97.6	107.9

		Industry categories			
	Total	Percent change	Manufacturing	Mining	Utilities
1980	84.1	− 1.9%	78.8	110.0	95.9
1981	85.7	1.9	80.3	114.3	94.3
1982	81.9	− 4.4	76.6	109.3	91.8
1983	84.9	3.7	80.9	104.8	93.6
1984	92.8	9.3	89.3	111.9	97.0
1985	94.4	1.7	91.6	109.0	99.5
1986	95.3	0.9	94.3	101.0	96.3
1987	100.0	4.9	100.0	100.0	100.0
1988	104.4	4.4	104.7	101.3	105.0
1989	106.0	1.5	106.4	100.0	108.7
1990	106.0	0.0	106.1	102.0	109.9
1991	104.1	−1.8	103.7	100.4	112.2
1992	106.5	2.3	106.9	97.6	112.0

year intervals that coincide with the economic censuses. The monthly movements of the index are based on the following information: production of actual items (39 percent); production worker hours in producing industries (34 percent); and electric kilowatt hour consumption by producing industries (27 percent).

In the annual revisions, monthly movements of the IPI components that were estimated from indirect sources (kilowatt hours and worker hours) are corrected to reflect more extensive direct data on production, which is obtained mainly from the Census Bureau's annual survey of manufactures.

Accuracy

The typical revision to the monthly IPI level between the preliminary estimate and the third monthly revision is 0.35 percent. The typical revision to the monthly movement is 0.25 percentage point.

Relevance

The coverage of the IPI makes it a sensitive gauge of the most cyclical aspects of the economy. Although the industries covered amounted to only 23 percent of the GDP in 1990, they account for the bulk of the more volatile movements in expansions and recessions. Consequently, the IPI tends to rise more in expansions and fall more in recessions than the overall economy. The IPI is a component of the coincident index of the *leading, coincident, and lagging indexes.*

For short-run cyclical analysis, the market categories are of particular interest. They are helpful in assessing the effect of changes in demand on industrial output. For longer-run analysis, the IPI industrial categories are more significant. These industries are important customers of the noncovered industries such as agriculture, transportation, communication, and services, and thus have a significant secondary effect on the growth of the rest of the economy. Generally, the overall economy does not grow rapidly unless the IPI expands even more robustly.

Recent Trends

The industrial production index showed different movements in three time segments during 1980–92 (Table 31.1). Industrial production was level over 1980–83; production grew at an average rate of 4 percent annually over 1984–88; and it was level over 1989–92. There were substantial yearly variations in the 1980–83 and 1984–88 periods.

Marked differences in growth among the market and industry components occurred during 1980–92. Equipment and intermediate products had the highest overall growth, although output of intermediate products declined in 1990–92. Consumer goods and materials had the slowest growth. Manufacturing increased more than utilities output, while mining production declined.

References from Primary Data Source

Board of Governors of the Federal Reserve System. 1986. *Industrial Production*—1986 Edition: *With a Description of the Methodology.*

Raddock, Richard D. 1993. "Industrial Production, Capacity, and Capacity Utilization Since 1987." *Federal Reserve Bulletin.* June.

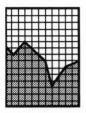

32
INFLATION

Inflation is a rise in the general level of prices. A decline in overall prices, which occurs less frequently, is known as deflation. Five measures of inflation are covered in this book: the *consumer price index, GDP price measures, producer price indexes, import and export price indexes,* and the *CRB futures price index.*

Because the prices of particular goods and services, such as food, housing, transportation, clothing, medical care, energy, equipment, containers, lumber, chemicals, and metals, rise and fall at different rates, price measures that include different items and combine the items in different ways show different overall rates of price change. And because the five price measures cover different items and are constructed using different methodologies, they show different rates of price change.

In addition, prices of food and energy are highly volatile due to the effect of unpredictable weather conditions on crop harvests and the uncertainty of the Organization of Petroleum Exporting Countries as an effective cartel in managing oil production and prices. Movements in the prices of food and energy sometimes diverge noticeably from those of other items. Because food and energy prices are linked to vagaries like the weather and OPEC, economists have developed a concept called "core inflation" or the "underlying rate of inflation," which refers to price movements of goods and services except for food and energy. These measures are regularly published for the consumer price index and the producer price indexes. They provide a gauge of price pressures in the economy that are attributable to macroeconomic forces, rather than to the special factors cited earlier.

Various terms are used to distinguish differing rates of price change. Overall, price increases are referred to as inflation and price decreases are called deflation. More specifically, price increases below 2 percent annually are known as "creeping inflation" or "price stability"; price increases that become progressively larger each year are "accelerating inflation"; price increases either approaching or above 10 percent annually are "hyperinflation"; a reduction in the rate of inflation is "disinflation"; and no change in the annual price level is "zero inflation."

Inflation affects the purchasing power of people's income and wealth (*personal income and saving*); the ability to manage the economy through fiscal and monetary policies (*government budgets and debt, money supply, interest rates*). the tendency to channel funds into different types of investment (*plant and equipment expenditures, housing starts, stock market prices and dividend yields*); and our ability to compete in world markets (*balance of trade, balance of payments, value of the dollar*). A low rate of inflation is a basic goal of economic policy because it protects purchasing power; helps in designing fiscal and monetary policies to promote economic growth; encourages investment in the production of goods and services as distinct from speculation in stocks, real estate, art work, and gambling; and makes U.S. goods more competitive at home and abroad. Inflation sometimes moves inversely to *unemployment*, where an increase in inflation is accompanied by a decrease in unemployment. When this occurs, the goal of lower inflation may be relaxed in favor of lower unemployment, as provided for in the Full Employment and Balanced Growth Act of 1978 (Humphrey-Hawkins Act).

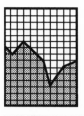

33
INTEREST RATES

Interest represents the cost of borrowing money. Thus, interest rates are the price of money. An interest rate, also referred to as a yield, is the annualized percentage that interest is of the principal of the loan. The level of interest rates for different loans reflects the length and risk of the loan. Generally, short-term loans have lower interest rates than long-term loans, and loans subject to little risk of not being repaid have lower interest rates than those with higher risk. The main exception occurs during periods of high *inflation* when the Federal Reserve Board tightens bank credit to lower the inflation rate, which may temporarily raise short-term interest rates above the long-term rates.

Where and When Available

Measures of interest rates for different types of loans are provided variously on a daily, weekly, or monthly basis by the Federal Reserve Board, Federal Reserve Bank of New York, Federal Housing Finance Board, Moody's Investors Service, Standard & Poor's Corporation, and American Banker-Bond Buyer. They are published in press releases, the *Federal Reserve Bulletin, Moody's Bond Survey,* Standard & Poor's *Current Statistics* and the American Banker-Bond Buyer *Bond Buyer Index.* Secondary sources include *Economic Indicators* and the *Survey of Current Business.*

The figures are available within a day to a week after the period to which they refer. Some of the measures are revised for the previous month.

Content

The ten interest rate measures covered here show the different costs of borrowing for short-term, medium-term, and long-term loans of high quality. Loans of high quality have the least risk of nonpayment. While all of these ten types are high-quality loans, some are more secure than others — for example, U.S. Treasury securities are default-free and, thus, are the highest quality. Loan periods may be broadly defined as up to one year (short-term), one to three years (medium-term), and more than three years (long-term). Some interest rates are for new loans, while others are for outstanding loans that are traded in securities markets. The loans are made to federal, state, and local governments; households; nonbank industries; and commercial banks.

Depending on the type of loan instrument, interest rates are measured according to one of three methods: (1) paying a certain amount at regularly specified intervals with a bond coupon or through negotiated terms of the loan, (2) the extent to which the par value (redemption price when the security expires) of a non-coupon security is above the discounted market price of the security or, (3) a hybrid of regular interest and a premium or discounted market price from the par value of the security.

Interest rates are not seasonally adjusted.

The ten interest rates are summarized below. Sources of the interest rate figures are in parentheses.

U.S. Treasury Three-Month Bills (U.S. Treasury): Short-term default-free borrowing of new issues sold at a discount from the par value.

U.S. Treasury Notes and Bonds with Average Constant Maturities of Three and Ten Years (Federal Reserve Board): Medium-term and long-term default-free outstanding issues sold with a coupon interest rate and at a premium or discount from the par value. These are averages of securities that encompass a range of maturities from under three years to over ten years and thus do not focus on a particular issue.

High-Grade Municipal Bonds (Standard & Poor's): Long-term outstanding issues of state and local governments sold with a coupon interest rate and at a premium rate or discount from the par value. They are exempt from federal taxes.

Bond Buyer Index for Municipal Bonds (American Banker-Bond Buyer): Theoretical yields for long-term new issues of state and local governments representing a hypothetical new issue sold at par value. They are not actual yields, but representative of what yields would be if issues were offered on the market. They are rated as AA twenty-year maturities. The bonds would be exempt from federal taxes.

Corporate AAA Bonds (Moody's Investors Service): Long-term industrial and public utility outstanding issues sold with a coupon interest rate and at a premium or discount from the par value.

Prime Commercial Paper (Federal Reserve Bank of New York): Short-term borrowing by large companies sold at a discount from the par value.

Federal Funds (Federal Reserve Bank of New York): Loans between commercial banks to enable the borrowing bank to meet its reserve requirements with the Federal Reserve. They are primarily overnight loans but also include term loans ranging from a few days to over one year. The daily effective rare is a composite of the varying interest rates on the different loan maturities.

Federal Reserve Discount Rate (Federal Reserve Bank of New York): Short-term borrowing by commercial banks from regional Federal Reserve banks to maintain certain reserve levels over a two-week period, to meet huge outflows at the end of a day, or to keep bank reserves from falling close to or below legal minimum requirements. This includes extended credit to banks with special problems for up to thirty days, after which a higher market-type rate may be charged.

Prime Rate Charged by Commercial Banks (Federal Reserve

Board): Threshold interest rate for short-term business loans, with loans to small companies above the prime rate and loans to large companies below the prime rate.

New Home Mortgage Yields (Federal Housing Finance Board): The "effective rate" at closings of conventional first mortgage loans for fixed and variable rate mortgages for newly built, single-family, nonfarm homes amortized over ten years. This rate includes the contract interest rate and all fees, commissions, discounts, and points paid by the borrower and/or seller to the lender in order to obtain the loan. The ten-year amortization period is a rough approximation of the average life of a conventional mortgage.

(The Federal Home Loan Mortgage Corporation provides a weekly home mortgage rate based on mortgage commitments [prospective interest rates] for new and existing single-family homes. This differs from the above FHFB rate, which represents closings (actual interest rates) for new homes on a monthly basis. The FHLMC rate is noted here to acquaint the reader with an indicator of future mortgage interest rates.)

Methodology

The bonds, loans, and commercial paper for particular companies and governments that are used in calculating the interest rate measures are changed from time to time. They are replaced with others, as needed, in order to maintain the measure's criteria for the length of maturity and quality of the loans and to prevent extraordinary price movements in a single security from distorting the total measure.

U.S. Treasury Three-Month Bills: The discounted price of the auction conducted every Tuesday is the weekly yield. These weekly yields are averaged to obtain the monthly figure.

U.S. Treasury Notes and Bonds with Average Constant Maturities of Three and Ten Years: Yield curves are constructed by plotting interest rates on the vertical axis of a graph and years to maturity on the horizontal axis. A line is drawn through the middle of the plotted points and the interest rate is read from the line that corresponds to three and ten years. The daily closing yields are averaged to obtain the weekly figure, and the weekly figures are averaged for the monthly yield.

High-Grade Municipal Bonds: The yields of general obligation issues for fifteen states and localities with a maturity of approximately twenty years are averaged arithmetically using equal weights for each issue. The Wednesday closing bid quotation is used as the weekly yield, and the weekly figures are averaged for the monthly yield.

Bond Buyer Index for Municipal Bonds: Municipal bond dealers and banks are surveyed each week for their opinions on what a hypothetical new coupon bond for eleven states and localities would yield if the issue sold at par value. The eleven yields are averaged arithmetically using equal weights.

Corporate AAA Bonds: Yields for samples of less than ten industrial issues and of ten public utility issues with maturities of more than fifteen years are averaged arithmetically using equal weights in two steps: (1) separate averages are calculated for the industrial and public utility groups, and (2) the two group figures are averaged into a single figure. Daily closing prices (or the average of the closing bid and asked price) are averaged to obtain the weekly and monthly figures.

Prime Commercial Paper: Based on surveys of New York City dealers, daily quotation prices of issues with six-month maturities (four to six months before 1980) are averaged arithmetically with equal weights for the weekly and monthly figures.

Federal Funds: Daily rates for federal funds of varying maturities are obtained from federal funds brokers in New York City. The daily effective rate is the average of these rates weighted by the volume of loans transacted through brokers for each rate.

Federal Reserve Discount Rate: These administered rates of the twelve regional Federal Reserve Banks must be approved by the Federal Reserve Board. The rates of all twelve regional banks are the same, except for periods of a day or two when changes are not made simultaneously. Officially, the rate for the Federal Reserve Bank of New York is used, but in practice the New York rate is the same as those of the other regional banks.

Prime Rate Charged By Banks: The daily rates charged by the majority of the twenty-five largest domestically chartered commercial banks based on assets. These rates are identical in at least thirteen of the banks, and are referred to as the "predominant rate."

New Home Mortgage Yields: A sample of savings and loan associations, commercial banks, mutual savings banks, and mortgage bankers are surveyed for yields on mortgage loans for newly built, single-family homes. The survey covers mortgage closings during the last five working days of the month. Interest rates of the various lenders are weighted by the share of the mortgages originated by each type of lender. The weights are updated quarterly.

Accuracy

There are no estimates of sampling or revision error for the interest rate figures.

Relevance

Interest rates have a significant impact on borrowing and spending. Generally, household, business, and government borrowings are stimulated when interest rates are perceived as high. The "low" and "high" designations are based on borrowers' assessments of past levels and prospective movements. If interest rates are expected to rise, there is an incentive to borrow immediately, but if interest rates are expected to fall, there is an incentive to delay borrowing. Interest rates react to and influence movements of the *gross domestic product, money supply, inflation,* and *value of the dollar.* The Federal Reserve focuses on interest rates as the ultimate tool in conducting monetary policy to foster economic growth and moderate inflation. In 1993, the Federal Reserve announced it is emphasizing real interest rates (market interest rates

Table 33.1

Interest Rates (percent)

	Federal funds	U.S. Treasury 3-month bills	Discount rate: Federal Reserve Bank of New York*	Prime commercial paper	Prime rate charged by banks	Bond buyer index (11 bonds)
1980	13.36%	11.51%	11.77%	12.29%	15.27%	8.15%
1981	16.38	14.03	13.42	14.76	18.87	10.98
1982	12.26	10.69	11.02	11.89	14.86	11.26
1983	9.09	8.63	8.50	8.89	10.79	9.26
1984	10.23	9.58	8.80	10.16	12.04	9.98
1985	8.10	7.48	7.69	8.01	9.93	9.01
1986	6.81	5.98	6.33	6.39	8.33	7.21
1987	6.66	5.82	5.66	6.85	8.21	7.53
1988	7.57	6.69	6.20	7.68	9.32	7.57
1989	9.21	8.12	6.93	8.80	10.87	7.12
1990	8.10	7.51	6.98	7.95	10.01	7.13
1991	5.69	5.42	5.45	5.85	8.46	6.77
1992	3.52	3.45	3.25	3.80	6.25	6.33

	High-grade municipal bonds	U.S. Treasury 3-year constant maturities	U.S. Treasury 10-year constant maturities	Corporate AAA bonds	New home mortgage yields
1980	8.51%	11.55%	11.46%	11.94%	12.66%
1981	11.23	14.44	13.91	14.17	14.70
1982	11.57	12.92	13.00	13.79	15.14
1983	9.47	10.45	11.10	12.04	12.57
1984	10.15	11.89	12.44	12.71	12.38
1985	9.18	9.64	10.62	11.37	11.55
1986	7.38	7.06	7.68	9.02	10.17
1987	7.73	7.68	8.39	9.38	9.31
1988	7.76	8.26	8.85	9.71	9.19
1989	7.24	8.55	8.49	9.26	10.13
1990	7.25	8.26	8.55	9.32	10.05
1991	6.89	6.82	7.86	8.77	9.32
1992	6.41	5.30	7.01	8.14	8.24

*Average effective rate for year.

minus inflation) and lessening its use of the money supply in conducting monetary policy. This reflects the weakening relationship between the gross domestic product and the money supply.

Recent Trends

All categories of interest rates generally declined during 1980–92 (Table 33.1). Exceptions to this overall downward trend typically occurred in 1981, 1984, 1988, and 1989. Among the loan categories, short-term loans (federal funds, Treasury three-month bills, Federal Reserve discount rate, and commercial paper) usually had lower rates than medium- and long-term loans (Treasury three- and ten-year constant maturities, prime rate, state and local bonds, corporate bonds, and home mortgages). The main exceptions to this pattern occurred for some loan categories in the high inflation years of 1980 and 1981.

References from Primary Data Sources

American Banker-Bond Buyer. 1993. *The Bond Buyer*.

Board of Governors of the Federal Reserve System. Annual. *Annual Statistical Digest*.

Federal Home Loan Bank Board. 1986. "Interest Rates and Other Characteristics of Conventional First Mortgage Loans Originating on Single Family Homes: Data Users Guide." Unpublished. May.

Federal Housing Finance Board. Annual. *RATES & TERMS on Conventional Home Mortgages*.

Federal Reserve Bank of Richmond. 1993. *Instruments of the Money Market*. Seventh edition.

Moody's Investors Service. Updated continuously. "Moody's Bond Yield Averages—Description of Averages and Methods of Computation." Unpublished.

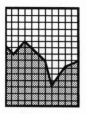

34
INTERNATIONAL INVESTMENT
POSITION OF THE UNITED STATES

The U.S. international position represents the difference between the value of foreign assets held by U.S. parties abroad and of U.S. assets held by foreign parties in the United States. It is commonly referred to as the overall creditor or debtor status of the nation, although technically it only partially represents debt because it also includes equity ownership of foreign companies. Nevertheless, in this discussion, the creditor and debtor designations will be used because they reflect the general perception of the meaning of the figures. If American assets abroad exceed foreign assets in the United States, the United States is a creditor nation, and if foreign assets in the United States exceed American assets abroad, the United States is a debtor nation. International assets include production facilities, bonds, stocks, loans, official U.S. reserves of gold, the U.S. reserve position and special drawing rights in the International Monetary Fund, and U.S. holdings of foreign currencies.

Where and When Available

The Bureau of Economic Analysis in the U.S. Department of Commerce provides annual measures of the U.S. international investment position. They are published in a press release and in BEA's monthly journal, the *Survey of Current Business*. Secondary sources include the *Economic Report of the President*.

The figures are available every June for the preceding year; they are revised in the succeeding years as part of the annual *balance of payments* revisions. The annual revisions also change the figures for several of the preceding years.

Content

The net investment position of the United States is defined as foreign assets held by U.S. parties abroad minus U.S. assets held by foreigners in the United States. The items included in assessing this investment position are the official, government, and private asset and liability components of the *balance of payments*. (U.S. assets abroad are "assets" and foreign assets in the United States are "liabilities.") The net investment position reflects the total U.S. and foreign assets outstanding at the end of each year, while the figures in the balance of payments reflect the annual increase or decrease in assets. The investment position figures include both the actual capital flows of these items in the balance of payments plus valuation changes. Geographic detail is provided for the countries of Canada and Japan, and the regions of Western Europe, Latin America, and other western hemisphere areas, other countries, plus international organizations.

The annual change in the investment position is attributable to four separately identified factors: (1) capital flows of the official, government, and private assets; (2) changes in the prices of bond and stock securities; (3) the effect of foreign exchange rate changes on the value of securities and on the U.S. official reserve; and (4) other changes associated with methodology, such as one-time changes in the item and respondent coverage in statistical surveys or one-time changes in the valuation of assets. Methodological changes result in a break in the comparability of the data series.

Methodology

The main data sources used in developing the investment position indicator are: Treasury Department surveys conducted by the

Federal Reserve Bank of New York on international assets and liabilities; BEA surveys of foreign direct investment abroad and in the United States; bilateral financial data provided by other countries; and the *value of the dollar* based on Federal Reserve Board and Treasury Department measures. Breakdowns of the factors contributing to the changes in position from year to year are also derived from these data.

Direct investment and portfolio investment are two major components of international investment. Direct investment is associated with a long-term interest in and sometimes control of corporate and noncorporate business enterprises. It is defined as when a foreign investor owns 10 percent or more of the voting securities or equivalent equity of an enterprise. Portfolio investment is associated with short-term activity in financial markets that emphasizes the ability to move funds between countries and investments. It is defined as when a foreign investor owns less than 10 percent of the voting securities or equivalent equity of a business enterprise plus the total amount of an investor's holdings of foreign private and government bonds and other debt instruments. An exception to this distinction between direct and portfolio investment is that intracompany holdings of bonds and other debt instruments between the parent company and a foreign affiliate of the parent company are defined as direct rather than portfolio investment.

The valuation of the investment position is made in current-cost and market-value prices. Current cost is the dollar outlays necessary to replace the tangible plant, equipment, and land assets of direct investments. Market value is the dollar worth of the direct investment tangible assets as measured by stock market prices, which also implicitly includes the value of intangible assets such as patents, trademarks, management, and name recognition. (Separate measures of historical cost of direct investment represent the original purchase price of tangible assets; however, historical-cost estimates are not included in the investment position measures.) Portfolio investments are measured only in market-value prices. Thus, the alternative current-cost and market-valuer price measures of the investment position only reflect these distinctions for direct investment.

Accuracy

There are no estimates of sampling or revision error in the investment position figures. Increases and decreases in the position from year to year attributable to methodological changes in the data sources ("other changes") indicate the net effect of inconsistencies in the various data sources. This is an overall minimum assessment of the inconsistencies because offsetting errors among the data elements reduce the net effect. In addition, the "statistical discrepancy" in the *balance of payments* shifts between a net inflow of unrecorded funds into the United States and a net outflow of unrecorded funds from the United States. If the unrecorded flows are capital funds, foreign assets in the United States would be understated (inflows) or overstated (outflows). For all of these reasons, the international investment position is an order of magnitude rather than a precise figure.

Relevance

The international investment position reflects the international industrial and financial base of the United States. A creditor status signifies that Americans own more capital abroad than foreigners own in the United States, while a debtor status indicates that Americans own less capital abroad than foreigners own in the United States. Because a creditor nation is less dependent on outside sources of financing than a debtor nation, its capital funding requirements are less vulnerable to changes in international financial markets. Therefore, a creditor nation is more independent than a debtor nation in conducting monetary policies to manage its economy with respect to the economic effects of *interest rates* at home and abroad and the *value of the dollar*.

A creditor nation has a net inflow and a debtor nation has a net outflow of interest and dividend incomes paid on international

Table 34.1

International Investment Position of the United States
(billions of dollars)

Year end	Net investment position (market value)	Net investment position (current cost)	U.S. assets abroad	Foreign assets in the U.S.
1980	NA	392.5	936.3	543.7
1981	NA	374.3	1,004.2	629.8
1982	265.0	379.2	1,119.4	740.2
1983	268.1	338.0	1,169.7	831.8
1984	177.3	234.2	1,178.9	944.7
1985	142.3	139.1	1,252.6	1,113.6
1986	109.7	19.2	1,410.7	1,391.5
1987	46.8	−34.0	1,557.3	1,591.4
1988	5.4	−140.3	1,698.0	1,838.3
1989	−128.9	−288.5	1,857.0	2,145.5
1990	−269.7	−291.9	1,924.8	2,216.7
1991	−396.4	−364.9	1,998.4	2,363.2
1992	−611.5	−521.3	2,003.4	2,524.7

loans and investments. If a nation is creditor, the income flows increase exports, which results in a surplus (or reduction in the deficit) in its *balance of payments*; if the nation is a debtor, the income flows increase imports, which results in a deficit (or reduction in the surplus) in its *balance of payments*. The income flows also tend to raise the wealth and standard of living in creditor nations relative to debtor nations. However, creditor nations risk adverse actions by debtor nations — default on foreign debt and expropriation of foreign-owned properties.

Recent Trends

The U.S. international investment position changed dramatically during 1980–92 (Table 34.1). Foreign assets held by U.S. parties abroad rose slower than United States assets held by foreign parties in the United States, changing the United States from an international creditor to a debtor nation. The United States had been a creditor nation since 1915. From a net creditor of approximately $400 billion in 1980, the position shifted continuously toward a declining creditor status and then to an increasing debtor status. Based on the market value measure, the United States became an international debtor nation in 1989, and the debt totaled $612 billion in 1992. Based on the current cost measure, the United States became a debtor nation in 1987, and the debt was $521 billion in 1992.

Reference from Primary Data Source

Bureau of Economic Analysis, U.S. Department of Commerce. 1990. *The Balance of Payments of the United States: Concepts, Data Sources, and Estimating Procedures.* May.

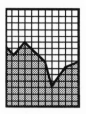

35
INVENTORY-SALES RATIOS

The inventory—sales ratio, in which inventories are in the numerator and sales in the denominator, represents the monthly turnover of inventories at current sales rates. For example, a ratio of 1.6 means that existing inventories will be used up in 1.6 months if sales continue at the current rate (assuming that inventories are not replenished during the period).

Two basic measures of inventory—sales ratios are published. They differ in the definition of sales and in industry coverage. One is provided by the Bureau of the Census and the other is provided by the Bureau of Economic Analysis.

Where and When Available

Bureau of the Census

The Census Bureau in the U.S. Department of Commerce publishes monthly inventory—sales ratios in a press release. Secondary sources include *Economic Indicators* and the *Survey of Current Business*.

The figures are available forty-five days after the month to which they refer; they are revised in the next month. Annual revisions are made in the spring of the following year, and comprehensive benchmark revisions are made about every five years.

Bureau of Economic Analysis

The BEA in the U.S. Department of Commerce provides quarterly inventory–sales ratios as part of the *gross domestic product*. The measures are published in the *Survey of Current Business*.

The figures are available during the fourth week of the month after the quarter to which they refer (April for the first quarter, July for the second quarter, etc.); they are revised in the subsequent two months. More detailed revisions are made annually every July, and comprehensive benchmark revisions are made about every five years.

Content

Bureau of the Census

The Census Bureau's inventory – sales ratios reflect inventories and sales of manufacturers, merchant wholesalers, and retailers. They include sales of raw materials, supplies, and semifinished goods to other businesses that reprocess them for later sale; sales of finished goods by manufacturers to wholesalers and retailers who resell them in the same state; and sales of finished goods to ultimate users. The inventory – sales ratios are provided in current dollars.

The inventory–sales ratios are seasonally adjusted.

Bureau of Economic Analysis

The BEA's inventory – final sales ratios are confined to final sales of domestic business. Final sales exclude sales of raw materials, supplies, and semifinished goods that are used up as intermediate products in the production process. They also exclude sales of finished goods from manufacturers to wholesalers and retailers who resell them in the same state. The inventory–final sales ratios are provided in current and constant dollars. (Inventory–sales ratios, as distinct form inventory–final sales ratios, are provided separately for manufacturing and trade industries in constant dollars.)

Domestic business includes agriculture, mining, construction, transportation, utilities, and services, as well as manufacturing and wholesale and retail trade industries. Domestic business excludes gross products of households and institutions, governments, and the rest of the world.

The inventory–final sales ratios are seasonally adjusted.

Methodology

Bureau of the Census

The inventory and sales data are obtained from Census Bureau monthly surveys of manufacturers, merchant wholesalers, and retailers. The inventory figures are defined at current cost valuation, which is the book value acquisition cost before the companies convert inventories to an LIFO (last-in, first-out) valuation.

Bureau of Economic Analysis

The inventory data for manufacturing and trade are based on the above-noted Census Bureau surveys. The BEA adjusts these inventory data to put them on a replacement-cost basis. That is, the inventories' current book value is based on prices when the inventories were acquired; BEA revalues them to reflect prices in the current period. BEA also adjusts the inventory data for other industries to reflect replacement cost. The inventory figures for these other industries are obtained from the U.S. Department of Agriculture, the U.S. Department of Energy, and the Internal Revenue Service. The IRS annual figures are the main source for the inventory levels of these other industries. These data are in turn extrapolated to the current quarter based on current data, such as is available for petroleum bulk stations and electric utilities, or by recent annual trends.

Final sales are based on the final sales figures in the *gross domestic product*, excluding gross product of households and institutions, governments, and the rest of the world. The constant dollar figures are based mainly on price changes in the *producer price indexes*.

Accuracy

Bureau of the Census

There are no estimates of sampling or revision error for the inventory–sales ratios for the combined total of manufacturing and trade industries. Estimates of sampling error are available for the wholesale and retail trade components separately.

Bureau of Economic Analysis

There are no estimates of sampling or revision error for the inventory–final sales figures.

Relevance

Inventory–sales ratios have significant implications for future production levels. Inventories are a business cost. Businesses finance inventories by borrowing funds or tying up their own money. Thus, high inventory–sales ratios suggest that businesses will tend to cut back on orders to suppliers because it is expensive to hold goods that are not selling rapidly. The resulting lower *manufacturers' orders* lead to lower production and employment levels. Analogously, low inventory–sales ratios suggest increased orders to replenish inventories, because the ability to furnish items readily off the shelf and maintaining a wider selection of goods for customers will promote sales. In this case, the growth in orders results in higher production and employment.

These general tendencies hold true, more or less, depending on the extent to which inventory movements result from deliberate action by businesses to build up or deplete inventories through sales incentives, cost cutting, changes in production and orders

Table 35.1

Inventory–Sales Ratios (months)

	Ratio for total sales: manufacturing and trade (current dollars) Annual average	Ratio for final sales: nonfarm industries (current dollars) 4th quarter	Ratio for final sales: nonfarm industries (constant dollars) 4th quarter
1980	1.55	3.38	2.65
1981	1.53	3.38	2.75
1982	1.67	3.12	2.65
1983	1.56	2.90	2.56
1984	1.53	2.94	2.66
1985	1.55	2.76	2.62
1986	1.55	2.56	2.56
1987	1.50	2.60	2.61
1988	1.49	2.59	2.56
1989	1.53	2.62	2.62
1990	1.53	2.55	2.60
1991	1.54	2.43	2.58
1992	1.50	2.30	2.48

(planned inventory change), or from unanticipated inventory accumulations or depletions due to unexpected shifts in customer demand (unplanned inventory change). Unplanned inventory changes may affect future production more because of the surprise effect they have on business expectations. Unanticipated changes are not quantifiable because the inventory data do not distinguish the planned and unplanned components. The inventory – sales ratio in constant dollars is a component of the lagging index of the *leading, coincident, and lagging indexes.*

Recent Trends

Because total sales are larger than final sales, inventory–sales ratios are smaller for total sales than for final sales.

Bureau of the Census

The inventory–sales ratios for manufacturing and trade industries fluctuated within 1.50 to 1.56 during 1980–92 except for 1982 (Table 35.1). There was a slight downward trend over the twelve-year period.

Bureau of Economic Analysis

The inventory–final sales ratio for nonfarm industries in both current and constant dollars drifted downward during 1980–92 (Table 35.1). The current-dollar measure declined from 3.4 in 1980–81 to 2.3 in 1992. The constant-dollar measure declined from an average of 2.7 in 1980–81 to 2.5 in 1992.

References from Primary Data Sources

Bureau of the Census, U.S. Department of Commerce. Annual. *Manufacturers' Shipments, Inventories, and Orders.*

Bureau of the Census, U.S. Department of Commerce. Monthly. *Manufacturing and Trade Inventories and Sales.*

Bureau of the Census, U.S. Department of Commerce. Annual. *Retail Trade.*

Bureau of the Census, U.S. Department of Commerce. Annual. *Wholesale Trade.*

Carson, Carol S. 1987. "GNP: An Overview of Source Data and Estimating Methods." *Survey of Current Business.* July.

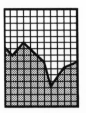

36
LEADING, COINCIDENT,
AND LAGGING INDEXES

The leading, coincident, and lagging (LCLg) indexes are an analytic system for assessing current and future economic trends, particularly cyclical expansions and recessions. The system is based on grouping some key indicators according to their tendency to change direction before, during, or after the general economy turns from a recession to an expansion or from an expansion to a recession. Indicators in the leading index change direction before a cyclical turning point in the general economy; those in the coincident index change direction at the same time; and those in the lagging index change direction after the general economy. In substance, the leading index reflects business commitments and expectations, the coincident index reflects the current pace of the economy, and the lagging index reflects business costs. The three indexes are called composite indexes because they group several component indicators. Other indicators that focus on business cycle movements are the *experimental recession indexes, growth cycles,* and the *purchasing managers' index.*

Where and When Available

The Bureau of Economic Analysis in the U.S. Department of Commerce provides monthly measures of the LCLg indexes. They are published in a press release and in BEA's monthly journal, the *Survey of Current Business.*

The figures are available one month after the month to which they refer; they are revised in the subsequent five months as new source data become available. Annual revisions in the fall incorporate revised source data for earlier years. Comprehensive revisions affecting the content and methodology are made every ten to fifteen years.

Content

The LCLg system is based on the concept that profits are the prime mover of a private enterprise economy and that the recurring business cycles of expansion and recession are caused by changes in the outlook for profits. When the outlook for profits is positive, business expands production and investment, but when the outlook is negative, business retrenches. The outlook for profits is reflected in the LCLg system in the leading index and in the ratio of the coincident index to the lagging index, which is an alternative leading index.

The leading index represents business commitments and expectations regarding labor, product, and financial markets, and thus points to future business actions. The coincident index represents the current level of actual production and sales, while the lagging index represents business costs. The ratio of the coincident to lagging index therefore suggests whether profits will rise or fall in the future due to the differential between sales and costs. If the coincident index increases faster than the lagging index, profits are likely to rise, and if the coincident index increases slower or declines in relation to the lagging index, profits are likely to fall. In this way, the coincident/lagging ratio is also a leading measure of trends in the economy.

Table 36.1 lists the component indicators included in the three indexes. The *leading index* components reflect: the degree of tightness in the labor markets due to employer hiring and firing; the buildup of orders and contracts that affect future production; materials prices that reflect shortages or gluts of raw materials for which some time will be required to expand or reduce exist-

ing inventories; financial conditions associated with the availability of funds in credit markets and the optimism and pessimism generated by price movements in the stock market; and
consumer psychology that affects household spending plans. The
coincident index components reflect: employment; real incomes
generated from production; output in cyclically sensitive manufacturing and mining industries; and real manufacturing and trade
sales depicting the flow of goods from manufacturers to other
consuming businesses, as well as to distributors and households.
The *lagging index* components reflect: the effect of the duration
of unemployment on business costs of recruitment and training;
the cost of maintaining inventories; labor cost per unit of output;
the burden of paying back business and consumer loans; interest
payments as a cost of production; and prices of consumer services as an indicator of production cost pressures in labor-inten-
sive industries.

The LCLg indexes are currently based on 1987 = 100.

Most of the component indicators of the LCLg indexes are
seasonally adjusted. The three composite indexes are not seasonally adjusted at the overall level.

Methodology

The component indicators of the LCLg indexes are selected
based on tests conducted for the following criteria: theoretical
rationale for the leading, coincident, and lagging properties; differences in the timing of their change in direction in relation to the
cyclical turning points of the overall economy; consistency with the
general upward and downward direction of the business cycle; clear
upward or downward trends as distinct from erratic monthly movements from which it is difficult to discern a trend; the quality of the
survey used in collecting the data; promptness of the availability of
monthly data; and the extent of revisions to preliminary data.

Data for the components of the LCLg indexes are based on
many of the indicators discussed elsewhere in this book. These
indicators are referenced in Table 36.1, although they are not

Table 36.1

Leading, Coincident, and Lagging Indexes

Leading Index

1. Average weekly hours of manufacturing production workers
   (Average Weekly Hours)
2. Average weekly initial claims for unemployment insurance, state programs
3. Manufacturers new orders for consumer goods and materials industries in
   constant dollars *(Manufacturers' Orders)*
4. Vendor performance (percentage of companies receiving slower deliveries)
5. Contracts and orders for plant and equipment, in constant dollars
6. New private-housing building permits, index *(Housing Starts)*
7. Manufacturers unfilled orders for durable goods industries, in constant
   dollars, monthly change (Manufacturers' Orders)
8. Prices of crude and intermediate materials, monthly percent change
   (Producer Price Indexes)
9. Prices of 500 common stocks, index *(Stock Market Price Indexes and
   Dividend Yields)*
10. Money supply (M2), in constant dollars *(Money Supply)*
11. Consumer expectations, index *(Consumer Attitude Indexes)*

Coincident Index

1. Employees on nonagricultural payrolls *(Employment)*
2. Personal income less transfer payments, in constant dollars (*Personal
   Income and Saving*)
3. Industrial production index *(Industrial Production Index)*
4. Manufacturing and trade sales, in constant dollars

Lagging Index

1. Average duration of unemployment, weeks *(Unemployment)*
2. Inventory to sales ratio for manufacturing and trade, in constant dollars
   (Inventory–Sales Ratios)
3. Labor cost per unit of output in manufacturing, monthly percent change
   (Unit Labor Costs)
4. Commercial and industrial loans outstanding, in constant dollars
   (Bank Loans: Commercial and Industrial)
5. Consumer installment credit outstanding to personal income ratio
   (Consumer Installment Credit and Personal Income and Saving)
6. Average prime rate charged by banks, percent *(Interest Rates)*
7. Consumer price index for services, monthly percent change
   (Consumer Price Index)

always definitionally identical to the LCLg components.

The components are combined in the three indexes and weighted equally. Several statistical procedures are used in calculating the indexes. They include: (1) preventing the components that have sharp monthly movements from dominating the indexes; (2) smoothing short-term erratic movements of the components in order to better represent their cyclical patterns; and (3) setting the long-term growth trend of the indexes equal to the trend of real *gross domestic product*.

Accuracy

There are no estimates of sampling or revision error for the LCLg indexes.

Relevance

The LCLg indexes help assess the current momentum and future direction of the economy. Because the coincident index reflects actual economic activity, it indicates whether the economy is currently expanding or in a recession. Movements in the leading index and the coincident/lagging ratio suggest whether the existing trend measured by the coincident index will continue. A change in direction in the leading index and the coincident/lagging ratio tends to foreshadow movement in the coincident index.

Figure 36.1 shows that the lead time between the change in direction of the leading measures and the coincident index is noticeably longer at the cyclical downturn than at the upturn. On average, over the nine business cycles since World War II, the leading index declines for eight months and the coincident/lagging ratio declines for twelve months before the onset of a recession; by contrast, the lead time before the beginning of an expansion is four months for the leading index and two months for the coincident/lagging ratio. Changes in the lagging index follow the coincident index and are thus used to confirm that a directional change has occurred. Because each cycle has unique characteristics, the advance signals of a pending recession in the

Figure 36.1 **Leading, Coincident, and Lagging Indexes**

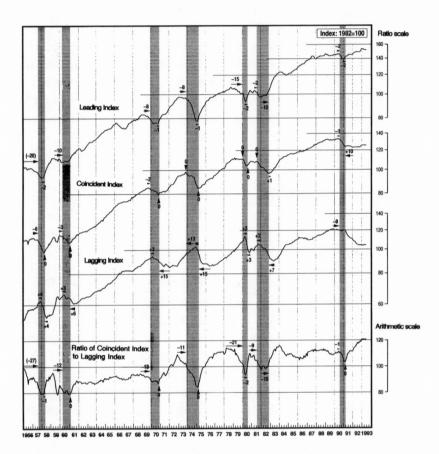

Note: Based on Bureau of Economic Analysis data. Lined bars are recession periods. Numbers are monthly leads (−) and lags (+) from cyclical turning points.

leading index and the coincident/lagging ratio vary noticeably from expansion to expansion. Therefore, the average lead times noted above are only a rough guide for when a particular expansion will slide into a recession according to the LCLg system.

The LCLg indexes are a useful tool for gauging strengths and weaknesses in the economy. However, they are limited for forecasting future economic trends. First, the preliminary contempo-

raneous data that are available during the months before a downturn into a recession or an upturn into a recovery do not always
provide advance signs of a cyclical turning point. The leading
index systematically "leads" at cyclical turning points only in the
revised data that become available several years later. Second,
the LCLg indexes do not forecast quantitative economic growth
rates or the time of future cyclical turning points. Third, the
indexes occasionally give false signals of a pending change in the
direction of the economy, such as prospective recessions in 1951,
1966, and 1984 that did not materialize.

Recent Trends

The leading index and the coincident/lagging ratio showed similar directional movements in all years over the 1980−92 period,
except in 1984, 1985, and 1988; the leading index rose in those
years, while the coincident/lagging ration declined in 1984 and
1985 and was level in 1988 (Figure 36.1). (In prior decades the
two leading indexes diverged most noticeably in the 1960s.)
Generally, when the directional movements of both of these leading measures were similar, they were accompanied by similar
movements in the coincident index in the same or following year.
The exceptions were 1991 and 1992, when both leading indexes
rose but the coincident index was level.

References from Primary Data Source

Bureau of Economic Analysis, U.S. Department of Commerce. 1984. *Handbook of Cyclical Indicators: A supplement to
the Business Conditions Digest.*
Green, George R., and Barry A. Beckman. 1992. "The Composite Index of Coincident Indicators and Alternative Coincident
Indexes." *Survey of Current Business.* June.
Hertzberg, Marie P., and Barry A. Beckman. 1989. "Business
Cycle Indicators: Revised Composite Indexes." *Survey of Current Business.* January.

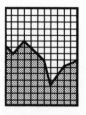

37
MANUFACTURERS' ORDERS

Manufacturers' orders measure commitments by customers to pay for subsequent delivery of goods produced by manufacturers. Orders are generally defined to be legally binding documents such as signed contracts, letters of award, or letters of intent, although there are exceptions. Orders figures are provided for new orders and for the backlog of unfilled orders.

Where and When Available

Measures of new orders and the backlog of unfilled orders for manufacturers' products are provided monthly by the Bureau of the Census in the U.S. Department of Commerce. They are published for durable and nondurable goods industries in the monthly report, *Manufacturers' Shipments, Inventories, and Orders*, and for durable goods industries only in *Advance Report on Durable Goods Manufacturers' Shipments and Orders*. Secondary sources include *Economic Indicators* and the *Survey of Current Business*.

The full report is available one month after the month to which the data refer. The advance report is available approximately five working days earlier. The figures for the previous month are initially revised in every monthly report. These are subsequently revised based on annual benchmark information in March of the following year, and comprehensive benchmark revisions are made about every five years.

Content

New orders represent the dollar value of additional orders received each month for delivery during that month or later. They include contract changes that raise or lower the value of unfilled orders received in previous months. Unfilled orders represent, in dollar terms, the backlog of orders that have accumulated from previous months for goods that have not yet been delivered. They are a running total from one month to the next of the backlog at the beginning of the month, plus the new orders received during the month, and minus shipments of goods to customers and cancellations of existing orders during the month. The data on orders are broken down for durable and nondurable industries and for market categories of various consumer goods, capital goods, defense products, and materials.

The manufacturers' orders figures are seasonally adjusted.

Methodology

Manufacturers' orders figures are based on monthly surveys of manufacturers. These surveys also obtain information on shipments and inventories. While respondents are asked about both new and unfilled orders, the survey on new orders is incomplete. Due to a lack of readily accessible records, some survey respondents do not report new orders and others do not report new orders for goods that were shipped from existing inventories in the same month. Consequently, new orders are estimated indirectly from unfilled orders, shipments, and cancellations as follows:

	Unfilled orders (end of current month)*
plus:	Shipments (during month)
minus:	Unfilled orders (end of previous month)*
equals:	New orders (during month)

---

*Unfilled orders are net of cancellation during the month.

The survey sample of manufacturing companies originally included all companies with 1,000 or more employees and a probability sample of companies with 100–999 employees. Smaller companies are not included because of poor response rates in previous attempts to include them. The survey still has response problems, which prevents it from being a probability sample: only about 55 percent of the companies with 1,000 or more employees respond. Overall, the survey sample accounts for about 50 percent of manufacturing shipments.

The monthly data are revised every year to reflect more complete information in the Annual Survey of Manufactures. They are revised every five years to benchmark information in the Census of Manufactures.

Accuracy

There are no estimates of sampling error for the manufacturers' orders figures. Revisions, based on annual figures for new orders, were 0.1 percent in 1991 and 0.2 percent in 1992. Revisions for end-of-year unfilled orders were 1.1 percent in both 1991 and 1992.

Relevance

Manufacturers' orders are significant because they indicate levels of demand and future levels of production and employment for manufacturing industries. There is a direct relationship between orders and production. Although determining when orders become production is not an exact science, rising orders are associated with higher current demand in the economy and subsequent increased production and employment, while falling orders indicate lower current demand followed by decreased production and employment. This relationship is true for both new and unfilled orders. However, new orders, which typically result in shipments of goods from existing inventories, are a good indicator of current levels of demand; unfilled orders are more closely linked to future production. Orders for market categories of certain

Table 37.1

Manufacturers' Orders
(billions of dollars)

	New orders (monthly average)	Unfilled orders (end of year)
1980	156	327
1981	168	327
1982	162	312
1983	175	347
1984	193	374
1985	196	387
1986	195	393
1987	209	430
1988	227	472
1989	236	510
1990	241	525
1991	234	511
1992	242	475

consumer goods and materials in constant dollars are a component of the leading index of the *leading, coincident, and lagging indexes.*

The market category of capital goods is particularly significant because of its relation to *plant and equipment expenditures.* While capital goods orders are analogous in many ways to plant and equipment spending, several differences sometimes cause varying trends in the two figures. For example, capital goods orders cover only certain types of equipment that are made domestically, while plant and equipment spending includes structures and all equipment items whether produced domestically or imported. The two also differ in the dollar valuation and timing of the investment.

Recent Trends

Manufacturers' new orders generally increased, although with some interruptions, during 1980—92 (Table 37.1). Orders declined in 1982 and 1991, and were level in 1985 and 1986. Unfilled orders had similar but not identical patterns during the same period. These backlogs rose in most years; the exceptions were no change in 1981 and declines in 1982, 1991, and 1992.

Reference from Primary Data Source

Bureau of the Census, U.S. Department of Commerce. Annual. *Manufacturers' Shipments, Inventories, and Orders.*

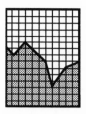

**38
MONEY SUPPLY**

The money supply measures represent the value of certain financial assets held by households, businesses, nonprofit organizations, and state and local governments. The types of assets included—which vary with each of the four money supply measures—are cash, bank deposits, money market instruments, federal securities, and trade credit notes. Financial assets such as stocks, commercial bonds, and life insurance, as well as all nonfinancial assets broadly defined as real estate and tangible goods, are excluded. The money supply therefore reflects assets that are very liquid and, consequently, are readily available for future spending.

Where and When Available

Money supply measures are provided weekly and monthly by the Federal Reserve Board. They are published in a statistical release and in the *Federal Reserve Bulletin*, the FRB's monthly journal. Secondary sources include *Economic Indicators* and the *Survey of Current Business*.

The weekly figures are available every Thursday for the week ending Monday of the previous week. The monthly figures are available in the middle of the month after the month to which they refer. The measures are revised on a continuing basis with the receipt of more accurate underlying data.

Content

There are four alternative measures of the money supply—M1, M2, M3, and L (liquid assets). In order, each measure represents an increasing number of financial assets. The measures progress from assets that are most liquid and most subject to Federal Reserve influence (M1) to assets that are least liquid and least subject to Federal Reserve influence (L). Liquidity refers to how readily assets can be converted to cash with minimal loss in value. The Federal Reserve influences the growth rate of the money supply through buying and selling of federal securities in open market operations.

Table 38.1 shows the composition of assets covered by the four measures. Each measure following M1 builds on the items in the previous one. For example, M1 is composed of currency, demand deposits, NOW accounts, and travelers checks. M2 includes all of M1 plus small savings accounts, money market holdings, overnight repurchase agreements, and Eurodollars. Similarly, M3 is M2 plus additional assets, and L is M3 plus still more assets.

The money supply figures are seasonally adjusted.

Methodology

The money supply measures are based on data from several sources. The main sources are: demand, savings, and time deposits (from weekly reports of large commercial banks and quarterly reports of small and large commercial banks and savings and loan associations); money market mutual funds (from a survey by the Investment Company Institute); Treasury securities (from data supplied by the U.S. Department of the Treasury); commercial paper (based on data from brokers who deal in commercial paper and from firms that issue commercial paper directly); bankers' acceptance and term Eurodollars (from surveys by the Federal Reserve Bank of New York); and repurchase agreements and overnight Eurodollars (from Federal Reserve Board surveys of

Table 38.1

Money Supply: Alternative Definitions (billions of dollars)

	December 1992
M1	$1,026.6
Currency (excludes bank-owned cash in bank vaults)	292.3
Demand (checking) deposits	340.9
NOW accounts (used for checking and saving)	385.2
Travelers checks, nonbank (e.g., American Express)	8.1
M2	3,496.9
M1	1,026.6
Small time deposits (less than $100,000) including open accounts and certificates of deposit	870.1
Savings deposits and money market deposit accounts	1,186.0
Money market mutual funds (households, business, broker-dealers	342.3
Overnight repurchase agreements (used in open market operations)	52.5
Overnight Eurodollars held by U.S. residents at overseas branches of U.S. banks	21.3
M3	4,166.4
M2	3,496.9
Large time deposits ($100,000 and more)	357.5
Term Eurodollars (maturities longer than one day)	45.6
Money market mutual funds (institutions only)	202.3
Term repurchase agreements (longer than one day)	80.7
L	5,043.6
M3	4,166.4
Short-term Treasury securities (maturities less than one year, excluding savings bonds)	331.6
Commercial paper (unsecured promissory notes of well-known businesses)	368.4
Savings bonds (Treasury securities)	156.8
Bankers' acceptances (bankers agreements to pay bills of customers)	20.4

Note: The totals are seasonally adjusted but some components are not seasonally adjusted. The sums of the components do not equal the totals because certain adjustments are made at the total level to avoid double counting.

large banks). The weekly figures are derived from reports of large banks with trend estimates for small banks and other data sources. The monthly figures include a broader base of monthly reported data plus interpolated figures for data reported quarterly.

The data are adjusted to avoid double counting. For example, deposits of one bank held by another bank are excluded, as are assets held by money market mutual funds in other components of M2, M3, and L. In addition, estimates of float (checks credited to bank reserve accounts but not yet collected) are used to ensure that all demand deposits are accounted for.

The money supply definitions were substantially revised in 1980 to reflect the growing impact for new financial instruments associated with monetary deregulation. Minor changes have been made since then.

Accuracy

There are no estimates of sampling or revision error for the money supply figures.

Relevance

Money supply trends are significant because of their effect on *interest rates,* real *gross domestic product,* and *inflation.* Generally, a rapid growth in the money supply tends to lower interest rates as lenders more actively seek borrowers as an outlet for their funds, and slow money supply growth raises interest rates as lenders have a smaller amount of funds available for loans. However, this relationship is sometimes reversed during periods of high inflation when rapid growth in the money supply is accompanied by higher interest rates because the money growth is perceived as fueling inflation through making more bank reserves available for loans.

The Federal Reserve uses the money supply figures through their effect on *interest rates* as a major guide in formulating monetary policies to stimulate economic growth and moderate inflation. Under the Full Employment and Balanced Growth Act of 1978 (Humphrey-Hawkins Act), the Federal Reserve reports to Congress twice a year, in February and July, on its money

Table 38.2

Money Supply (annual percent change)

December to December	M1	M2	M3	L
1980	6.8%	8.9%	10.2%	9.8%
1981	6.8	10.0	12.4	11.7
1982	8.7	8.9	9.3	9.8
1983	9.9	12.0	10.3	10.7
1984	6.0	8.7	11.0	11.9
1985	12.3	8.3	7.2	8.5
1986	16.8	9.5	9.0	7.9
1987	3.5	3.6	5.2	4.9
1988	4.9	5.5	6.6	7.8
1989	1.0	5.0	3.6	4.6
1990	4.1	3.5	1.5	1.6
1991	8.7	3.0	1.2	0.3
1992	14.2	1.5	0.0	1.2

supply targets for the current year. These reports indicate the targeted percentage increases in the money supply measures. The targets presented as a range—for example, 2–6 percent—with the Federal Reserve exercising judgment in pursuing the upper or lower end of the range depending on the state of the economy. Targets typically are supplied only for M2 and M3 because the relationship between the M1 and economic growth became more tenuous during the 1980s. In 1993, the Federal Reserve announced it was emphasizing real interest rates (market interest rates minus inflation) and lessening its use of the money supply in conducting monetary policy. This reflects the weakening relationship between the gross domestic product and the money supply.

M2 in constant dollars is a component of the leading index of *leading, coincident, and lagging indexes.*

Recent Trends

The money supply M1 measure moved at noticeably different rates than M2, M3, and L measures during 1980 – 92 (Table 38.2). The latter three measures tended to have similar yearly movements.

Compared with the M2, M3, and L measures, M1 rose at slower rates in the early 1980s, and at faster rates in 1985, 1991, and 1992.

References from Primary Data Source

Board of Governors of the Federal Reserve System. 1994. *The Federal Reserve System: Purposes and Functions*.

Federal Reserve Board Staff. 1989. "Recent Developments in Economic Statistics at the Federal Reserve: Part 2." *Business Economics*. July.

Simpson, Thomas D. 1980. "The Refined Monetary Aggregates." *Federal Reserve Bulletin*. February.

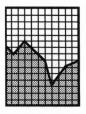

39
PERSONAL INCOME AND SAVING

Personal income (PI) mainly measures the income received by households from employment, self-employment, investments, and transfer payments. It also includes small amounts for expenses of nonprofit organizations and income of certain fudiciary activities. Disposable personal income (DPI) refers to personal income after the payment of income, estate, and certain other taxes and payments to governments. Personal saving is the residual of DPI minus consumer outlays, and the saving rate is saving as a percentage of DPI. The personal income and savings measures are definitionally consistent with those for the *gross domestic product.*

Where and When Available

Measures of personal income and saving are provided monthly by the Bureau of Economic Analysis in the U.S. Department of Commerce. The data are published in a monthly press release and in BEA's monthly journal, the *Survey of Current Business.* Secondary sources include *Economic Indicators* and the *Federal Reserve Bulletin.*

The figures for PI, DPI, and personal saving are available during the fourth week of the month after the month to which they refer. These are revised initially in the subsequent two months. More detailed revisions are made annually every July, and comprehensive benchmark revisions are made about every five years. Figures on the saving rate are available one month after the above noted dollar measures.

Content

PI mainly measures income of households. Household income is derived from wages, fringe benefits, self-employment, cash rent from rental housing, noncash rent imputed from owner-occupied homes, interest, dividends, social security and unemployment benefits, food stamps, and other income maintenance programs. PI also includes operating expenses (excluding depreciation) of not-for-profit organizations and investment income of life insurance companies, noninsured pension funds, nonprofit organizations, and trust funds. PI reflects these income flows before the payment of income, estate, gift, and personal property taxes plus fees, fines, and penalties paid to federal, state, and local governments. Social security taxes paid by employees and employers are excluded from PI.

DIP is income excluding the tax and nontax payments to governments included in PI. DPI is provided in current and constant dollars.

Personal saving is the income remaining from DPI after deductions for consumer spending for goods and services (see *gross domestic product*), interest payments on consumer loans (excluding home mortgage interest), and money sent as gifts abroad (net transfer payments to foreigners). The saving rate is saving represented as a percentage of DPI. In addition to savings deposits, money market deposit accounts, and certificates of deposits, saving figures include increases of household equity in housing and real estate investments and financial investments such as stocks and bonds, as well as reductions in consumer loans as the principal is paid off if the loans are financed from current income. Saving is reduced when consumers finance spending from existing savings or by selling real estate and financial assets to business, governments, or foreigners. Saving is not affected by gifts between households (such as when parents give a house to their children) and by sales of homes, cars, and other assets between households (except for payments to intermediaries such as brokers' commissions and used car dealer markups).

The personal income and saving figures are seasonally adjusted.

Methodology

Data for the components of PI are obtained from several government and nongovernment sources with varying degrees of currency. Fore example, wages are based on the monthly *employment* payroll survey, and social security and unemployment benefit figures are based on monthly reports from the Social Security Administration and Department of Labor. Stock dividend income is derived from the Census Bureau's Quarterly Financial Report and from corporate quarterly reports to stockholders (these quarterly data are interpolated through the three months of the quarter in estimating the monthly figures). Data for other PI components, such as income from fringe benefits, self-employment, rent, interest, and life insurance benefits, typically are available only annually, and the monthly historical and current figures are mainly estimated indirectly.

DPI is calculated by subtracting income, estate, gift, and personal property taxes plus miscellaneous fines, fees, and penalties from PI. Data for these deductions are obtained from two sources. The Department of the Treasury provides monthly data for the federal component, and the Census Bureau provides a quarterly survey of state and local governments. However, the state and local survey are used only in the historical quarterly figures because they are available too late for the current figures every quarter; indirect estimates are made for the current figures. DPI in constant dollars is calculated by dividing DPI in current dollars by the implicit price deflator for personal consumption expenditures (see *GDP price measures*).

Personal saving represents the difference between DPI and the sum of consumer spending for goods and services and interest payments on consumer loans (referred to as personal outlays). The saving rate for each month is calculated as a three-month moving average of saving as a percentage of DPI in order to dampen erratic month-to-month movements. For this reason, the saving rate is published one month after the income and saving dollar figures.

Accuracy

There are no estimates of sampling or revision error for the personal income figures.

Relevance

PI represents the main component of consumer purchasing power, and thus has a prime influence on consumer spending. Because consumer spending accounts for approximately 65 percent of the GDP, PI has a major effect on overall economic activity. DPI in constant dollars provides a better analytic measure of consumer purchasing power and its effect on real GNP than current-dollar personal income. Because personal saving indicates consumers' willingness to spend, the saving rate is an important element in predicting future spending trends.

Recent Trends

Personal income and disposable personal income increased in all years during 1980–92 (Table 39.1). DPI rose slightly faster than PI in eight of the twelve years. This pattern occurred through the entire period, despite the various changes in the income tax laws in the 1980s and in 1990. On average, DPI in constant dollars increased one-fourth as much as PI and DPI, although this average differential varied considerably in some years.

The personal saving rate drifted downward from over 8 percent in the early 1980s to a low of 4 percent in 1989. It then turned upward, reaching 5.3 percent in 1992.

Table 39.1

Personal Income and Saving
(billions of dollars)

	Personal income	Disposable personal income	Disposable personal income (1987 dollars)	Personal saving	Saving rate (percent)
1980	2,265.4	1,952.9	2,733.6	153.8	7.9%
1981	2,534.7	2,174.5	2,795.8	191.8	8.8
1982	2,690.9	2,319.6	2,820.4	199.5	8.6
1983	2,862.5	2,493.7	2,893.6	168.7	6.8
1984	3,154.6	2,759.5	3,080.1	222.0	8.0
1985	3,379.8	2,943.0	3,162.1	189.3	6.4
1986	3,590.4	3,131.5	3,261.9	187.5	6.0
1987	3,802.0	3,289.5	3,289.5	142.0	4.3
1988	4,075.9	3,548.2	3,404.3	155.7	4.4
1989	4,380.3	3,787.0	3,464.9	152.1	4.0
1990	4,673.8	4,050.5	3,524.5	170.0	4.2
1991	4,850.9	4,230.5	3,529.0	201.5	4.8
1992	5,144.9	4,500.2	3,632.5	238.7	5.3

Reference from Primary Data Source

Bureau of Economic Analysis. U.S. Department of Commerce. 1989. *State Personal Income 1929—87*: Estimates and a Statement of Sources and Methods. July.

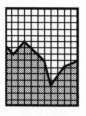

40
PLANT AND EQUIPMENT EXPENDITURES

Plant and equipment (P&E) expenditures measure capital invest-ment spending by private nonfarm business for new plant (build-ings, roads, bridges, and other structures) and new equipment (machinery, vehicles, furniture, and other items that last more than one year). They include capital spending to expand existing productive capacity and replace inefficient or outmoded capacity, and cover spending for domestically produced as well as im-ported capital goods. They exclude capital spending by farm in-dustries and governments. The spending figures are provided in current and constant dollars.

Where and When Available

P & E expenditure for both historical and projected future outlays are provided quarterly by the Bureau of the Census in the U.S. Department of Commerce. These data are published in a press release. Secondary sources include *Economic Indicators*, the *Sur-vey of Current Business,* and the *Federal Reserve Bulletin.*

The P & E spending figures are available in April, June, Sep-tember, and December, usually during the second week of the month. The figures published in December project spending for the full calendar year ahead, and those for April, June, and Sep-tember project spending for the balance of the year. Preliminary historical and projected future data are revised in succeeding quarters.

Content

The quarterly P & E figures cover companies in the mining, construction, manufacturing, transportation, communication, public utilities, trade, finance, insurance and personal and business services industries. The sum of these quarterly figures is the typically cited total for "all industries." The annual total also includes data from the forestry, agricultural services, fishery, real estate, professional services, membership organizations, and social services industries, so that the annual total is cited as "total nonfarm business." The industry detail refers to the industry of the company that owns the P & E facilities, even though facilities may be leased and used by a company in another industry.

Expenditures are counted as occurring when payments to contractors and suppliers are made. Separate figures distinguishing plant from equipment are available annually.

The P & E figures are seasonally adjusted.

Methodology

The P & E expenditure figures are based on data from quarterly and annual surveys of private nonfarm business. The quarterly survey is based on a sample of approximately 8,000 profit-making businesses, while the annual survey canvasses an additional 8,000 business and nonprofit organizations. Both the quarterly and annual surveys are based on nonprobability samples of these companies because of the difficulty of maintaining a representative sample of companies in various size categories for each industry.

The survey data will be benchmarked annually to the Census Bureau's new "Annual Capital Expenditures Survey." Previous benchmarking was done using the five-year economic censuses (the last such benchmarking was done for the year 1982).

The spending projections include adjustments to the survey information for biases that have been observed in previous spending plan data. The bias adjustments raise or lower the projected survey data for each industry by the difference between actual and planned spending for the particular quarter based on experience of the past eight years. The constant-dollar historical P & E spending data are calculated by dividing the current-dollar survey data by the nonresidential fixed investment implicit price deflator in the *gross domestic product*. The projected constant-dollar P & E figures are obtained by assuming that the rate of change of the deflator in the previous four quarters will continue for the coming year.

Accuracy

There are no estimates of sampling or revision error in the P & E figures. The average error in the projections over the 1955–83 period, without regard to whether the projection was above or below the actual spending, ranged from 1.8 percent for projections one quarter ahead to 3 percent for projections one year ahead.

Relevance

P & E expenditures affect the economy over both the short and long term. Over the short term, investment spending generally has extreme cyclical movements, rising more during expansions and falling more during recessions than the overall economy, because investment is closely related to past and anticipated business profits (see *corporate profits*). As the residual of sales minus costs, actual profits are intrinsically volatile, and anticipated profits are subject to business' changing optimistic and pessimistic perceptions of the future economic climate. This innate volatility is accentuated by the durability of existing P & E, which allows additional spending to be deferred until businesses believe

Table 40.1

Plant and Equipment Expenditures*
(billions of dollars)

	Current dollars	1987 dollars
1980	286.4	354.6
1981	324.7	360.8
1982	326.2	342.2
1983	321.2	337.7
1984	373.8	390.9
1985	410.1	424.5
1986	399.4	405.9
1987	410.5	410.6
1988	455.5	443.2
1989	507.4	482.3
1990	532.6	496.3
1991	528.4	488.6
1992	546.1	512.9

*Nonfarm industries surveyed quarterly. The broader measure of P & E spending for "total nonfarm business" that includes industries only surveyed annually as well as those surveyed quarterly was $607 billion in 1992, compared with $546 billion for industries surveyed quarterly.

it is a good time to obtain new facilities. Over the long term, P & E contributes to *productivity* because the use of more and better equipment tends to increase the nation's output.

Recent Trends

Plant and equipment expenditures generally increased during 1980–92, although there were several years of slow growth or actual decline (Table 40.1). There were three years of decline in the current-dollar measure and four years of decline in the constant-dollar measure. Spending in constant dollars also had a slower rate of growth than in current dollars.

Reference from Primary Data Source

Seskin, Eugene P., and David F. Sullivan. 1985. "Revised Estimates of New Plant and Equipment Expenditures in the United States, 1947–83." *Survey of Current Business.* February.

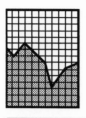

41
POVERTY

Measures of poverty count the number of persons or families with incomes below a specified minimum level. This income threshold defines subsistence living conditions according to current societal standards. Incomes below the threshold are regarded as subjecting the recipients to living conditions below currently accepted standards of decency. At any given point in time, the poverty level is defined as a specific income figure. However, what is regarded as the poverty level also has a relative dimension over longer periods of time. From the 1930s to the 1960s, the absolute value of the income threshold was raised as the nation changed its perceptions about what constitutes subsistence living. Standards typically are raised over time to reflect better living conditions afforded by advancements in technology. When the standard is raised, the number of persons defined as living in poverty increases.

There is one official measure of poverty. It counts cash income only. Fourteen supplementary measures are based on various treatments of government cash and noncash transfer payments, taxes, and capital gains.

Where and When Available

The Bureau of the Census in the U.S. Department of Commerce provides annual measures of poverty. The figures are published annually in *Poverty in the United States* and *Measuring the Effect of Benefits and Taxes on Income and Poverty*. Secondary sources include the *Economic Report of the President*.

The measures are available in the fall after the year to which they refer. Revisions for previous years are made in the annual publications.

Content

The poverty measures indicate the number of persons and families with money incomes below the poverty income threshold. Money income is cash income derived from employment, self-employment, dividends, interest, rent, royalties, social security and other income maintenance benefits, and life insurance. It excludes capital gains and losses and in-kind income. The official income threshold is based on the poverty standard developed by the Social Security Administration in 1964. This threshold measures income before the payment of income, social security, and all other taxes. Income requirements are differentiated for households depending on such characteristics as family size, age of the family members, and age of the family householder (householder is the person in whose name the home is owned or rented; when the home is jointly owned or rented by married couples either spouse's name may be used). The standard in the mid-1990s reflects the same minimum living conditions specified when it was developed in 1964. It is routinely updated for inflation only, in order to maintain the 1964 living conditions. For example, the annual threshold income before taxes for a four-person family rose from $3,200 in 1964 to $14,300 in 1992. (There was no official poverty standard before 1964; as noted below under "Relevance," there was an implied standard in the 1930s.)

Fourteen alternative nonofficial poverty measures that use different definitions of household income are also provided. The definitions vary in terms of the treatment of government cash and noncash transfer payments, federal and state income taxes, social security payroll taxes, capital gains, and an imputed return on the equity of home ownership. In 1992, under the official measure, 14.5

percent of the population is defined as being in poverty, with the alternative measures ranging from 10.4 to 23.2 percent of the population. The major factor accounting for these differences is the inclusion and exclusion of government cash transfer payments.

Methodology

The poverty standard is based on estimates made by the U.S. Department of Agriculture in 1961 about how much money a three-or-more-person family must have to meet minimal acceptable nutritional requirements under its economy food plan. This figure was multiplied by three to determine total income necessary to meet all living expenses, including housing, health, transportation, and all other nonfood items. This blowup factor is based on a 1955 study indicating that food accounts for one-third of the average household budget for families made up of three or more persons. Thus, the nonfood components are estimated indirectly as a statistical aggregate rather than by estimating each component separately with specific minimum standards for each.

The money income figures are based on the current population survey (CPS) conducted by the Census Bureau. This information is collected every March for the previous year. The survey sample is approximately 60,000 households, of whom typically 57,000 are interviewed and 3,000 are not available for interviews. For additional detail on the CPS, see *unemployment*.

Accuracy

The sampling error is that in two of three cases, the count of persons in poverty varies by approximately 550,000.

Based on estimates derived from administrative records of income tax, unemployment insurance, social security, and other programs, survey respondents are considered to understate their income by approximately 10 percent in the aggregate for all sources of income. This overall underreporting is not taken into account when developing the poverty count because determining the amount of underreporting among income groups is difficult.

Relevance

The poverty measure reflects societal concerns about how well the nation is providing for the minimal subsistence needs of the people at the bottom of the income ladder, It focuses attention on the most needy in the population and the progress made in alleviating their condition. As an absolute figure, it quantifies the magnitude of the poverty problem for purposes of political debate regarding appropriate ways to deal with it. Measures of the *distribution of income* are related to poverty.

Poverty is a relative concept that changes over time to reflect the economic aspirations of society. The poverty standard adopted in the early 1960s by President Lyndon Johnson is approximately 90 percent higher than the one used in the mid-1930s when President Franklin Roosevelt said one-third of the nation was ill-housed, ill-fed, and ill-clothed. Thus, perceptions of what constitutes a minimally acceptable standard of living changed significantly over the twenty-five-year period. These perceptions have also changed between the 1960s and the 1990s, although the standard has not been changed since the 1960s. If it raised on the basis of a political consensus of higher minimal subsistence needs in the 1990s, the number of persons defined to be in poverty would increase. The federal budget deficit (*government budgets and debt*) operates as a major constraint to reviewing the standard. It is feared that even with noncash benefits included, a new standard would raise the poverty count, and thus increase federal spending for income maintenance programs.

Nevertheless, a step has been taken toward revising the poverty standard. The U.S. Bureau of the Census, Department of Health and Human Services, and the Bureau of Labor Statistics have contracted with the National Academy of Sciences to conduct a methodological study of the concepts, information needs, and measurement methods for updating the poverty standard. The report will be completed in 1994. It will provide a framework on the basis of which the government may develop and adopt a new poverty standard later in the 1990s.

Table 41.1

Poverty Measures

	Persons in poverty		Families in poverty	
	Number (millions)	Percent of population	Number (millions)	Percent of population
1980	29.3	13.0%	6.2	10.3%
1981	31.8	14.0	6.9	11.2
1982	34.4	15.0	7.5	12.2
1983	35.3	15.2	7.6	12.3
1984	33.7	14.4	7.3	11.6
1985	33.1	14.0	7.2	11.4
1986	32.4	13.6	7.0	10.9
1987	32.2	13.4	7.0	10.7
1988	31.7	13.0	6.9	10.4
1989	31.5	12.8	6.8	10.3
1990	33.6	13.5	7.1	10.7
1991	35.7	14.2	7.7	11.5
1992	36.9	14.5	8.0	11.7

Persons below the poverty income ievel: Alternative measures
(percent of population)

	Money income*	Money income less government cash transfers
1980	13.0%	20.8%
1985	14.0	21.3
1990	13.5	20.5
1991	14.2	21.8
1992	14.5	22.6

*Official measure in above panel.

Recent Trends

The number of persons and families living in poverty and their share of the population generally rose during 1980–92, although declines occurred in six of the twelve years (Table 41.1). Poverty increased in 1981–83, decreased in 1984–89, and increased in

1990–92. Persons in poverty rose by 7.6 million from 1980 to 1992, and from 13.0 to 14.5 percent of the population over the same period. The percentage of the population in poverty was highest in 1983, when it reached 15.2. The number and proportion of families in poverty had similar yearly movements. The Government cash transfer payments for social security, unemployment insurance, and other cash income maintenance payments reduced the poverty population considerably. For example, excluding such income maintenance payments, persons living in poverty in 1992 would have accounted for 22.6 percent of the population, compared with the actual proportion of 14.5 percent. There were 37 million persons and 8 million families in poverty in 1992.

References from Primary Data Sources

Bureau of the Census, U.S. Department of Commerce. Annual. *Poverty in the United States*.

Bureau of the Census, U.S. Department of Commerce. Annual. *Measuring the Effect of Benefits and Taxes on Income and Poverty*.

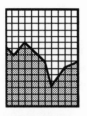

42
PRODUCER PRICE INDEXES

The producer price indexes (PPIs) track the rate of price change of domestically produced goods in the manufacturing, mining, agriculture, fishing, forestry, and electric utility industries. The PPIs exclude prices of construction, services, and imports. The PPIs most often used for economic analysis are stage-of-processing indexes. One group is based on commodities and another on industries. They distinguish between finished goods and those that need further fabrication in the commodities indexes, and between goods produced and goods purchased in the industry indexes. The separate commodities indexes are also consolidated into the "all commodities" index.

Where and When Available

The PPIs are provided monthly by the Bureau of Labor Statistics in the U.S. Department of Labor. The data are published in a press release; in the BLS monthly magazine, the *Monthly Labor Review*; and in the report, *Producer Price Indexes*. Secondary sources include *Economic Indicators,* the *Survey of Current Business*, and the *Federal Reserve Bulletin*.

The figures are published approximately in the middle of the month immediately following the month to which they refer. The monthly figures are revised for the preceding fourth month — for example, revisions to January data are supplied in June with the release of May data. Plans call for a periodic update of the weighting structure usually every five years.

Content

There are three stage-of-processing commodities PPIs. *Finished goods* covers items used by a household, business, government, or foreign buyer in the form in which they were sold without further fabrication. These include household goods ranging from fresh foods to cars and capital goods such as tractors, trucks, and machine tools. *Intermediate materials, supplies, and components* covers items that have been fabricated but are not ready for independent use and, thus, become part of other products, require further fabrication, or are otherwise used as inputs, such as cotton yarns, chemicals, containers, office supplies, electric power, and internal combustion engines. *Crude materials for further processing* covers items that are not sold directly to households and are either sold for the first time in their initial state of production, such as livestock or crude petroleum, or are being reused, such as scrap metal.

The three indexes reflect a theoretical typology of goods based on production, moving sequentially from a product's initial state to its end result. Classifying products by end user (household, business, government, or foreigner) and by degree of fabrication is referred to as stage-of-processing classification. Although the stage-of-processing concept theoretically represents a step-by-step flow from crude to intermediate to finished products, in practice this flow does not always occur. For example, there are reverse flows of intermediate containers to crude materials and of finished equipment to both intermediate and crude material groups; there are also products that skip the intermediate stage, such as when crude live poultry becomes finished processed poultry.

The industry-based stage-of-processing indexes are output and input price indexes assocoated with industry production. Output prices represent the prices of goods produced in each industry, while input prices represent the prices of goods purchased by each industry for its production plus prices of goods bought by consumers and business as part of the *gross domestic product*. This differs from the commodities-based indexes, which are associated with the stage of fabrication of the product. The industry indexes also differ from the commodities indexes in product classification. The industry indexes combine products made in companies grouped in the same four-digit Standard Industrial Classification industry; this results in heterogeneous product combinations since companies in the same industry produce similar but not identical products. By contrast, the commodities indexes represent the same products regardless of the industry in which they are produced because the products are combined homogeneously.

There are four industry output price indexes: crude products processors, primary products processors, semifinished goods processors, and finished goods processors. There are also four, but slightly different, industry input price indexes: primary products processors, semifinished products processors, finished products processors, and the personal consumption and producers durable equipment components of the gross domestic product. The industry indexes, while conceptually based on a production process flowing forward from crude and primary products producers to finished goods producers and to households and business purchases of capital goods, are not fully statistically consistent in this regard. Similar to the commodities indexes, the industry indexes include cases of industry outputs and inputs that sometimes flow backward in the industry stage of processing and also sometimes skip processing stages.

Prices reflect the first sale of the goods resulting in net revenue to the producer, and thus exclude price changes associated with resales and markups for the same item through wholesalers, retailers, or other producers as well as excise taxes. They represent the actual producer transaction price of goods meant for immediate delivery, including premiums and discounts from list prices and changes in the terms of sale such as distinctions for household and business customers and the size of the order. Prices of items with long production lead times are based on the time the item is delivered, not when the order is placed. The price quote is from the site of the producer (f.o.b., free-on-board), unless the price quote includes transportation charges when the producer provides such services directly and not through an outside transportation company or contractor. Exceptions to this include the use of list prices when transaction prices are not available (for example, some fabricated steel products), and prices quoted at central markets, particularly for farm products. The indexes reflect price movements for the same or similar item exclusive of enhancement or reduction in the quality or quantity of the item. Prices on futures markets are excluded.

The PPIs are currently based on 1982 = 100.

The PPI figures are seasonally adjusted.

Methodology

Monthly price data are obtained from a mail survey conducted by the Bureau of Labor Statistics. The survey samples prices for over 3,200 commodities. These data are supplemented by price information provided by the U.S. Department of Agriculture for farm products. Nearly all price quotes are reported by the sellers rather than the buyers.

The weights for the stage-of-processing PPIs are based on the value of sales of the component commodities and industries. These reflect data in the five-year economic censuses, unless the industry is not covered in the censuses. For example, sales weights for electric power are based on Department of Energy data. Since 1992, the weights represent 1987 sales volumes; during 1987−91 they were based on 1982 sales. The structuring of commodities and industries in a stage-of-processing chain in the commodity and industry indexes is based on the commodity and industry ordering in the input−output tables prepared by the Bureau of Economic Analysis in the U.S. Department of Commerce.

If the reported monthly price includes a change in the quality of the item, an adjustment is made to reflect the improvement or decline. Thus, the PPIs aim at measuring price movements of items having the same functional characteristics over time. For example, if better brakes are included on a car, the price increase attributable to the improved brakes does not appear as a price increase in the PPI, but if an auto bumper is weakened because of relaxed standards and there is no change in market price, the weaker auto bumper is considered a price increase in the PPI. Because product cost data required to make the necessary adjustments are not always available, the PPI contains an unknown amount of price change caused by quality and quantity changes.

One approach for adjusting quality change in price indexes when product cost data are not available is through hedonic price indexes. Hedonic indexes are based on statistical regressions that reflect historical relationships between quality change and price change. Hedonic indexes are used for computers in the PPIs.

Accuracy

There are no estimates of sampling or revision error for the PPIs.

Relevance

The PPIs help assess rates of price change for goods at the production level. This is useful because production cost trends may differ from delivery and distribution costs. The PPIs provide a basis for analyzing whether *inflation* is caused by higher demand or by supply bottlenecks in the production of goods, independent of costs and markups associated with getting the goods to the buyer.

The stage-of-processing grouping in the PPIs also theoretically helps predict potential price changes in the sequential development of crude materials to intermediate materials to finished goods. However, the stage-of-processing concept does not establish a complete unidirectional flow of materials in the production process from crude to intermediate to finished goods. While theoretically, crude prices should predict intermediate prices, and intermediate prices should predict finished prices in the commodities indexes, these lead-lag relationships are not exact because of

Table 42.1

Producer Price Indexes (annual percent change)

	Finished goods	Intermediate materials, supplies, and components	Crude materials for further processing
1980	13.4%	15.2%	10.9%
1981	9.2	9.2	8.1
1982	4.1	1.4	−2.9
1983	1.6	0.6	1.3
1984	2.1	2.5	2.2
1985	1.0	−0.4	−7.4
1986	−1.4	−3.5	−8.5
1987	2.1	2.4	6.8
1988	2.5	5.5	2.5
1989	5.2	4.6	7.4
1990	4.9	2.2	5.6
1991	2.1	−0.1	−7.1
1992	1.2	0.3	−0.8

the failure to maintain a unidirectional flow in the stage-of-processing groups. The same is true for the industry stage-of-processing indexes. More research on the properties of these classifications is needed to realize their analytic potential in the transmission of price change.

The PPIs are also used to determine cost escalation in business contracts and to deflate the gross *domestic product* to constant dollars.

Recent Trends

Producer prices showed varying rates of price change during 1980–92 (Table 42.1). The finished goods index had a sharp drop in *inflation* in the early 1980s, small price increases (including a year of price decline) in 1983–88, large price increases in 1989–90, and a return to low price increases in 1991–92. Intermediate price indexes had the same general pattern, although with some differences: compared with finished goods, intermediate products had lower price increases in most years, more years of decline or virtual no change, and price changes of intermediate products in 1988–90 foreshadowed those of finished goods in 1989–91.

Prices of crude materials were far more volatile than those of finished and intermediate goods. Some of these differences result from fluctuations in oil prices, which have their initial and heaviest impact on crude materials. The effect of price changes of crude oil is successively dampened as an increasing number of nonpetroleum products are incorporated in the finished and intermediate product indexes.

References from Primary Data Source

Bureau of Labor Statistics, U.S. Department of Labor. 1992. *BLS Handbook of Methods*. Chapter 16. September.

Gaddie, Robert, and Maureen Zoller. 1988. "New stage of process price system developed for the Producer Price Index." *Monthly Labor Review*. April.

Sinclair, James, and Brian Catron. 1990. "An experimental price index for the computer industry." *Monthly Labor Review*. October.

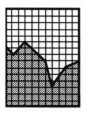

43
PRODUCTIVITY

Productivity represents the nation's efficiency in producing goods and services. It is estimated as output per unit of input. There are two measures of productivity. Labor hour productivity, which is the traditional measure, encompasses the labor and capital equipment used in production as well as factors affecting their efficiency, such as worker and management skills, worker effort, technology, and energy and materials usage. Multifactor productivity focuses solely on the factors affecting the efficiency of labor and capital facilities—worker and management skills, technology, and the like.

Where and When Available

Labor Hour Productivity

This measure of productivity for broad economy-wide sectors and the total of all manufacturing industries is provided on a quarterly basis by the Bureau of Labor Statistics in the U.S. Department of Labor. The data are published in a press release and in two BLS monthly journals, the *Monthly Labor Review* and *Employment and Earnings*. Secondary sources include *Economic Indicators* and the *Survey of Current Business*. Another set of labor hour productivity measures, covering specific industries and based on different definitions from the economy-wide measures, is published annually in *Productivity Measures for Selected Industries and Government Services*.

Preliminary data for the immediately preceding quarter are provided in the second month following the quarter (May for the first quarter, August for the second quarter, November for the third quarter, and February for the fourth quarter). The data are available at the same time as the *unit labor cost* figures and follow soon after publication of the *gross domestic product* measures. The data are initially revised in the subsequent two months. Annual revisions are made every September , and still more comprehensive benchmark revisions are made about every six years.

Multifactor Productivity

This measure of productivity for broad economywide sectors and the total of all manufacturing industries is provided annually by the Bureau of Labor Statistics in the U.S. Department of Labor. The data are published in a press release. The figures are available in October for the preceding year. There are no revisions for earlier years. Another set of multifactor productivity measures, covering specific industries and based on different definitions from the economy-wide measures, is published every one to two years.

Content

Labor Hour Productivity

This measure is defined as output per hour of labor expended. Output per hour encompasses the combined influences of all factors affecting the use of labor, such as *plant and equipment expenditures*, the substitution of plant and equipment for labor, worker skills and effort, technology, managerial skills, level of output, *capacity utilization*, energy and materials usage, and the interactions among them. By excluding labor hours, labor hour productivity also excludes the effect on output of labor hours. The productivity measure does not separate the specific contributions to productivity of labor, capital, or any other element. Labor hour productivity is typically expressed as an index, although absolute figures in constant dollars are also available.

Separate elements are developed for the business sector, the nonfarm business sector, and the total of all manufacturing industries. They are based on real *gross domestic product* data adjusted to eliminate those components of the GDP that would cause an inappropriate measure of productivity because (1) the output indicator used is also an input measure or (2) the output and input data are inconsistent. The business sector figures cover private for-profit enterprise and government enterprise. They exclude not-for-profit organizations; general government (general government is financed mainly by taxes while government enterprises are financed mainly by user fees); household employment; owner-occupied housing; and profit flows of American companies abroad into the United States. The nonfarm business sector figures also exclude farming.

The output definitions of the three economy-wide measures are based on the value-added concept of the GDP. This method counts output ad the sum of labor, profits, interest depreciation allowances, and indirect business taxes, but excludes purchased materials and services. By contrast, output measures for the specific industries include both value added and purchased materials and services.

The labor hour productivity indexes are currently based on 1982 = 100.

The labor hour productivity figures are seasonally adjusted.

Multifactor Productivity

This measure estimates efficiency as output per unit of labor and capital combined. It is the component of labor hour productivity that focuses on the underlying efficiency and external conditions of production operations. These include labor skills and worker effort, technology, managerial skills, level of output, *capacity utilization*, energy and materials usage, and the interactions among them. Labor hour productivity includes these items plus plant and equipment usage and the substitution of plant and equipment for labor. By excluding from labor productivity both labor hours and plant and equipment facilities, multifactor productivity also excludes the effect on output of the substitution of plant and equipment for labor. The figures are provided as an index.

As in the case of labor hour productivity, separate multifactor figures are developed for the business sector, the nonfarm business sector, and the total of all manufacturing industries, which are based on the *gross domestic product* value-added definitions of output. Also following labor productivity, output definitions for the multifactor figures for specific industries include both value added and purchased materials and services.

The multifactor productivity indexes are currently based on 1982 = 100.

Methodology

Labor Hour Productivity

Productivity is defined as the ratio of output (the numerator) to input (the denominator). Output is represented by either the *gross domestic product* business sectors or the total of all manufacturing industries, and input is represented by the corresponding labor hours. This leaves the sum total of all capital and multifactor elements as the items affecting the efficiency of labor. Labor hours are the product of *employment* multiplied by *average weekly hours* converted to average annual hours. The employment data are based on the sum of paid jobs counted in the payroll survey and the number of self-employed and unpaid family workers counted in the household survey (see *employment*).

$$\text{Labor hour productivity} = \frac{\text{Output}}{\text{Input}} = \frac{\text{Real GDP* (or manufacturing)}}{\text{Labor hours**}} = \text{Real GDP per labor hour}$$

* Gross domestic product in the business sector or nonfarm business sector.
** Paid employees, the self-employed, and unpaid family workers.

Multifactor Productivity

This measure is also a ratio of output to input. The output figure in the numerator is the same as was used above for labor hour productivity. The input figure in the denominator is the weighted average of the dollar value of labor hours and of capital services from plant and equipment, land, and inventories. This leaves the sum total of all multifactor elements — worker and management skills, technology, and so on — as the items affecting the efficiency of labor and capital resources.

$$\text{Multifactor productivity} = \frac{\text{Output}}{\text{Input}} = \frac{\text{Real GDP (or manufacturing)}}{\text{Labor hours and capital services}} = \text{GDP per unit of labor and capital services}$$

Definition of Labor Hours

Labor hours are based on "hours at work," which is limited to time at the job site, including paid time to travel between job sites, coffee breaks, and machine downtime. It excludes time associated with paid vacation and sick leave, which is called "hours paid."

Accuracy

Labor Hour Productivity

In nineteen of twenty cases, the second quarterly revision (two months after the preliminary figure) differs from the preliminary index by plus or minus two index points.

Multifactor Productivity

There are no estimates of sampling or revision error.

Relevance

Labor Hour Productivity

Productivity is important because greater efficiency increases the quantity of goods and services available for civilian and defense needs. The relationship of productivity to *inflation, average weekly earnings,* and *employment* is also important. When productivity increases rapidly, more goods and services are available at lower prices because of lower production costs. High productivity growth permits higher wages without increasing production costs and inflation.

High productivity can cause employment dislocation, however, because the introduction of new technology changes or eliminates some jobs. Displaced workers with outmoded skills may not be able to find new jobs or may only find work at lower rates of pay. While some individuals may therefore be adversely affected by higher productivity, higher productivity does not lead to *unemployment* or lower wages at the economy-wide level. The greater incomes and lower prices attributable to productivity growth cause overall spending and employment to increase.

Because quarterly movements of productivity are heavily influenced by cyclical changes in output, short-term changes in productivity mainly reflect cyclical changes in economic activity rather than basic changes in efficiency. Such basic changes are discerned by examining trends over at least several quarters that have relatively steady rates of economic growth. Over the longer run, the basic changes are seen more directly in the annual movements in multifactor productivity noted below.

Multifactor Productivity

This measure of underlying productivity suggests the extent to which labor, capital, materials, and other aspects of production are improving, in terms of both technology and efficient usage. Changes in multifactor productivity indicate fundamental changes

Table 43.1

Productivity (annual percent change)

	Business sector		Manufacturing	
	Labor hour	Multifactor	Labor hour	Multifactor
1980	−0.7%	−2.0%	−2.2%	−3.0%
1981	1.3	0.4	3.6	0.1
1982	0.1	−2.4	4.0	−0.6
1983	2.3	2.3	2.2	5.2
1984	2.4	3.3	1.3	5.9
1985	1.4	1.6	3.2	3.5
1986	2.1	1.4	2.6	3.7
1987	1.0	1.2	6.5	5.2
1988	1.0	2.4	2.3	5.1
1989	−0.7	−0.4	0.5	0.6
1990	0.7	−0.8	1.2	1.5
1991	1.0	*	1.7	*
1992	3.4	*	4.6	*

*Not available when book went to press.

are occurring that impact productivity. However, because multi-factor productivity encompasses all of the causal factors, further analysis is necessary to identify which elements are changing significantly.

Recent Trends

Productivity in the business sector and manufacturing industries differed during 1980 – 92 (Table 43.1). Based on the labor hour measure, business sector productivity typically increased 1 to 2 percent annually, while manufacturing productivity had some years of noticeably higher increases. The multifactor measure of annual productivity change typically diverged from the labor hour measure by no more than one percentage point in the business sector, while the differential between multifactor and labor hour productivity was several percentage points in some years in manufacturing industries.

References from Primary Data Source

Bureau of Labor Statistics, U.S. Department of Labor. 1992. *BLS Handbook of Methods.* Chapters 10 and 11. September.

Bureau of Labor Statistics, U.S. Department of Labor. 1993. *Labor Composition and U.S. Productivity Growth, 1948−90.* Bulletin 2426. October.

Mark, Jerome A., William H. Waldorf, et al. 1983. *Trends in Multifactor Productivity, 1948−81.* Bulletin 2178. Bureau of Labor Statistics, U.S. Department of Labor. September.

Sveikauskas, Leo. 1989. *The Impact of Research and Development on Productivity Growth.* Bulletin 2331. Bureau of Labor Statistics, U.S. Department of Labor. September.

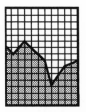

44
PURCHASING MANAGERS' INDEX

The purchasing managers' index reflects several aspects of economic activity in manufacturing industries that suggest future movements of manufacturing production and overall economic growth. It is constructed as a "diffusion index," which has intrinsic forecasting properties. A diffusion index provides an inference of the direction of change of one period to the next. This contrasts with traditional indexes of economic activity that provide the actual direction and magnitude of the change.

Where and When Available

The purchasing managers' index is prepared by the National Association of Purchasing Management. It is published on the first business day of every month in the "Report on Business." The seasonal factors of the index are updated by the U.S. Department of Commerce; they are revised for the previous one to three years every January. No other revisions are made to the index.

Content
The purchasing managers' index (PMI) is a composite of five indexes of manufacturing activity: new orders (*manufacturers' orders*), production (*industrial production index*), employment

(*employment*), the promptness of manufacturers' deliveries (the deviation from when an order for a purchased item is scheduled to arrive and when it actually arrives), and total purchased inventories. The index numbers for the composite and for each component are the proportion of the surveyed companies that report a positive change in activity from the previous month; this includes one-half of the companies reporting "no change." For example, if 56 percent report a positive change, 10 percent report no change, and 34 percent report a negative change, the index is 61.

This type of index, which provides an inference of the direction of change, and which weights all firms equally regardless of size, is a diffusion index. A diffusion index indicates the pervasiveness of increases and decreases among a surveyed population. Use of a diffusion index assumes that the cyclical movements of small and large firms are similar in terms of their percentage rates of growth and decline, although the timing of the cyclical movements varies among the firms. This implies a direct relationship between the number of firms reporting activity in a particular direction and changes in the magnitude of the rate of growth or decline. Thus, as increasing numbers of firms report a rise or decline in economic activity, similar patterns of change would be expected in the percentage rates of growth or decline for the total of all firms. A diffusion index of 50 occurs when equal numbers of firms have increases and decreases, and therefore the rate of growth from the previous period is approximately zero. When the index is above 50 the rate of growth tends to be positive, and when the index is below 50 the rate of growth tends to be negative. In addition, the further the index rises above 50 the greater is the magnitude of growth, while the further the index falls below 50 the greater is the magnitude of decline.

The PMI has forecasting properties. When it is above 50 and rising, it tends to peak when the percentage rate of increase in output as measured by the *industrial production index* is greatest, and the subsequent decline in the PMI is associated with a slowdown in the rate of increase in the industrial production index. As

Table 44.1

Purchasing Managers Index

	Weight
New Orders	0.30
Industrial production	0.25
Employment	0.20
Delivery schedules	0.15
Inventories	0.10
	1.00

the index approaches 50 from above 50, growth in the industrial production index nears zero. When the PMI declines below 50, the industrial production index is likely to decrease absolutely. Analogously, when the index is below 50 and declining, it tends to bottom out when the percentage rate of decrease in the industrial production index is greatest, and the following upturn in the index is related to a slowdown in the rate of decrease in the industrial production index. As the index rises toward 50, the decline in the industrial production falls toward zero. When the index rises above 50, the industrial production index is likely to increase absolutely.

The PMI is seasonally adjusted based on separate seasonal adjustments for each component.

Methodology

The PMI is a composite formed from the five component indexes in Table 44.1. The components reflect various aspects of operations of manufacturing companies. The component weights are assigned judgmentally based on qualitative assessments of their importance.

The survey data for each component are obtained monthly from a sample of over 300 manufacturing companies that are members of the National Association of Purchasing Management. The number of companies included in the sample for each manufacturing industry is based on the proportion of total manufacturing output accounted for by each industry. These industry shares are derived from data in the *gross domestic product* and the *industrial production index* for broad two-digit Standard Industrial Classification codes such as food, chemicals, and machinery, and for finer industry classifications within each broad group such as dairy, meat, and grains within the food group. Each company is weighted equally regardless of the size of the firm.

The survey obtains data on directional movements of each item in comparison to its level in the previous month. Depending on the item surveyed, positive responses are designated "higher," "better," or "faster" than last month; negative responses are designated "lower," "worse," or "slower" than last month; and no-change responses are designated "the same" as last month. Because the responses are supplied by the third week of the month, the survey is based on only partial information for which the entire month is estimated.

Accuracy

There are no estimates of sampling or revision error for the PMI.

Relevance

The PMI number 50 is an analytic threshold for forecasting cyclical turning points in the manufacturing component of the *industrial production index*. During manufacturing expansions, when the index drops below 50, the average lead time before a downturn in the manufacturing component of the industrial production index is three months. In the case of manufacturing recessions, when the index rises above 50, there is an average lag of two months after the onset of a recovery. These average figures mask considerable variation among the nine business cycles since World War II.

In relation to the cyclical turning points of the overall economy as designated by the National Bureau of Economic Research (see introduction), the PMI has an average lead time of about

Figure 44.1 **Purchasing Managers' Index: 1945–93**

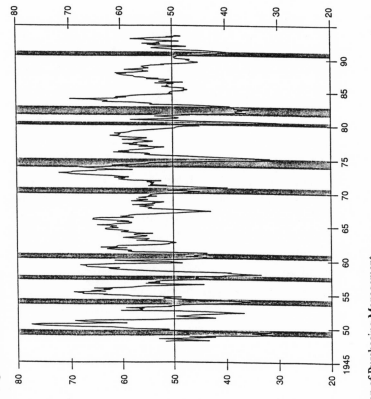

Source: National Association of Purchasing Management.
Note: Vertical bars are recession periods.

twelve months before the expansion turns down into a recession (the index reaches a peak twelve months before the onset of the recession); and the index has an average lead time of about four months before the recession turns up into a recovery (the index bottoms out four months before the onset of the recovery). However, these lead times vary widely over the nine post–World War II business cycles, ranging from six to twenty-one months during expansions and one to nine months during recessions. Such variations highlight the fact that each business cycle has unique characteristics, requiring special analysis, and that long-term averages are of limited use in assessing current economic conditions.

Recent Trends

As indicated in Figure 44.1, the PMI has signaled future recessions in reaching peaks before the cyclical downturn (it does not always give advance notice of cyclical recovery from recessions). However, it is also highly volatile with sharp reversals in direction, which limits its use for forecasting future recessions. During the recovery of 1991–93, the PMI has fluctuated around 50, the threshold of zero change in manufacturing activity, although it has been generally further above than below the threshold.

References from Primary Data Sources

Bretz, Robert J. 1990. "Behind the Economic Indicators of the NAPM Report on Business." *Business Economics*. July.

Bretz, Robert J. 1990. "Forecasting with the Report on Business." *NAPM Insights*. August.

Torda, Theodore S. 1985. "Purchasing Management Index Provides Early Clue on Turning Points." *Business America*. June 24.

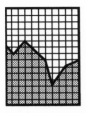

**45
RETAIL SALES**

Retail sales represent the dollar receipts of retail establishments for goods and services sold to households, businesses, and governments. Retail establishments cover stores, mail order houses, vending machines, and house-to-house canvass. Retailing includes a wide range of kinds of businesses, such as food, drug, liquor, department, variety, apparel, building material, hardware, furniture, sporting goods, book, jewelry, camera, and optical goods stores, automotive dealers, gasoline stations, restaurants, bars, and florists.

Where and When Available

Retail sales measures are provided monthly by the Bureau of the Census in the U. S. Department of Commerce. They are published in *Monthly Retail Trade* and in less detail in *Advance Retail Trade*. Secondary sources include *Economic Indicators* and the *Survey of Current Business.*

Advance data are available nine working days after the month to which they refer; the advance data are not as detailed by kind of business as the subsequent revised estimates in the preliminary and final figures. Preliminary data in the full report are available six weeks after the reference month, and final data are published one month later. Annual revisions are made every March.

Content

Retail sales are the dollar value of receipts of retail establishments after deductions for refunds, allowances for merchandise returned by customers, and rebates by the retailer. Sales reflect the full price of the item whether sold for cash or on credit, but they exclude receipts from interest and other credit charges to the customer. Receipts exclude sales and excise taxes collected directly from the customer, but include gasoline, liquor, tobacco, and other excise taxes collected by the manufacturer or wholesaler and passed along to the customer. Retailers mainly sell merchandise, although their receipts are also derived from delivery, installation, repair, and other services associated with the merchandise. Merchandise is composed of nondurable goods such as food and clothing that last less than three years and durable goods such as cars and furniture that last more than three years.

The retail sales data are seasonally adjusted.

Methodology

The retail sales data are obtained from monthly surveys of retailers. The survey sample of retailers is updated quarterly to account for new firms that start in business (births) and existing firms that go out of business (deaths). In order to reduce the reporting burden, the largest firms are surveyed every month while other firms are assigned to panels of respondents that report quarterly. (Inventory data are also obtained on these surveys; see *Inventory–*Sales Ratios.)

The monthly sales figures are estimated from two components: (1) the actual survey data for the month are weighted 25 percent for the preliminary and 20 percent for the revised estimates, and (2) the month-to-month change in the survey data between the current month and the previous month is weighted 75 percent in the preliminary and 80 percent in the revised estimates. Imputations of about 20 percent of sales are made for nonrespondents, late reporters, and suspect data that fail edits. The monthly data are further revised in the following year to reflect more complete and accurate annual information in the bench-mark *Annual Retail Trade Survey*. They are subsequently revised for the last time every five years based on data in the *Census of Retail Trade*.

Accuracy

The sampling error for retail sales in nine of ten cases is plus or minus 0.8 percent in the preliminary and plus or minus 0.7 per-cent in the final *level* of sales, and plus or minus 0.4 percentage point in the *percentage change* in sales between the preliminary and final estimates for two consecutive months. Revisions of retail sales levels from the advance to the preliminary estimate range from minus 0.9 to plus 1.5 percent and from the prelimi-nary to the final estimate from minus 0.3 to plus 0.5 percent.

Relevance

Retail sales are a key indicator of the strength of consumer spend-ing. Consumer spending accounts for 65 percent of the *gross do-mestic product,* and retail sales of durable and nondurable goods account for 45 percent of consumer spending. In addition to being an economic indicator in their own right, retail sales are a major data source used in preparing the consumer expenditures component of the gross domestic product. Because the ultimate purpose of economic production is to provide for the well-being of people, consumer spending is a bedrock of the economy. Through its impact on economic output, consumer spending is also an underlying factor affecting *plant and equipment expenditures.*

Recent Trends

Monthly retail sales rose from $80 billion in 1980 to $161 billion in 1992 (Table 45.1). The average annual increase over this twelve-

Table 45.1

Retail Sales

	Billions of dollars (monthly average)	Percent change
1980	79.8	6.7%
1981	86.6	8.5
1982	89.1	2.9
1983	97.5	9.5
1984	107.2	10.0
1985	114.6	6.8
1986	120.8	5.4
1987	128.4	6.3
1988	137.5	7.1
1989	145.6	5.8
1990	152.1	4.5
1991	153.6	0.9
1992	161.1	4.9

year period was $6.8 billion and 6.0 percent. Annual increases ranged from 1 percent in 1991 to 10 percent in 1983 and 1984. The large increases in 1983–84 following the depressed recession levels in 1982 contrast with the modest increase in 1992 following the 1991 recession.

Reference from Primary Data Source

Bureau of the Census, U. S. Department of Commerce. Annual. *Combined Annual and Revised Monthly Retail Trade.*

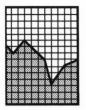

46
STOCK MARKET PRICE INDEXES
AND DIVIDEND YIELDS

Common stock is the ownership instrument of American corporations. Holders of common stock are risk-taking investors who share in the profits if dividends are paid. Rising and falling stock prices affect capital gains and losses to investors. The current rate of return on a share of common stock—also referred to as the dividend yield —is the percentage that annual cash dividends are of the market price.

Where and When Available

The six stock market price indexes covered here are provided daily by the New York Stock Exchange, Inc.; Nasdaq (National Association of Securities Dealers Automated Quotations); AMEX (American Stock Exchange); Standard & Poor's Corporation; Dow Jones & Co., Inc.; and Wilshire Associates. They are published in daily newspapers, *Barron's,* and Standard & Poors *Current Statistics.* Secondary sources include *Economic Indicators* and the *Survey of Current Business.*

The indexes are also disseminated electronically continuously during the trading day, except for the Wilshire index, which is available only for the closing at the end of the day.

Content

The indexes exclude the effect of changes in the capitalized financial structure of companies such as stock splits, mergers, and spinoffs so that price movements are not distorted by changes in the underlying value of a share of stock following a new capitalization of the company. Therefore, the index levels cannot be compared with an average of actual current market prices for the same companies because the latter would reflect the effect of new capitalizations on the price per share without adjusting for changes in the underlying value of each share.

The indexes exclude the payment in cash dividends in the value of the index, except for the American Stock Exchange Index, which includes cash dividends as being reinvested in the index. This conforms to the Securities and Exchange Commission regulations on corporate executive compensation that companies provide total-return information (price change plus cash dividends) for the past five years in their proxy statements to stockholders. The reinvested dividends only affect the AMEX index on the day companies are ex-dividend, and they are inconsequential in the index's overall movement.

The stock market price indexes are not seasonally adjusted.

New York Stock Exchange Composite Index

This index covers prices of all of the over 2,000 companies listed on the New York Stock Exchange. The index reflects the change in the price of an average share of stock of companies since December 31, 1965, when the average market value was approximately $50. Component indexes of the composite are provided for companies in the industrial, transportation, utility, and finance groups.

Nasdaq Composite Index

This index covers the prices of the over 4,000 companies traded on the Nasdaq market. The index reflects the change in the price of an average share of stock of the companies since February 1971. Component indexes of the composite are provided for companies classified as industrial, banking, insurance, other finance, transportation, and utilities.

AMEX Market Value Index

This index covers the prices of the approximately 850 companies and 950 stock issues (some companies have more than one issue) listed on the AMEX. The index reflects the change in the price of an average share of stock of the companies since July 1983 when the index was set at 50. Adjustments are made for cash dividends to include them in the value of the stock as if they are reinvested in the index; this offsets the ex-dividend deduction from the quoted price on the day the dividend is declared. Component indexes of the composite are provided for companies classified as high technology, capital goods, consumer goods, services, retail, financial, natural resources, and housing, construction, and land development.

Dow Jones Industrial Average

This index covers prices of thirty companies listed on the New York Stock Exchange. They are widely held large "blue chip" companies that are mainly in manufacturing industries, but also include mining, communications, finance, and retail firms. They account for approximately 25 percent of the market value of all companies on the New York Stock Exchange and 20 percent of the market value of the over 5,000 companies traded on all U.S. Stock exchanges in the early 1990s. The average reflects the price of an average share of stock based on the capitalized structure of companies when they were first incorporated in the index. Other Dow Jones indexes are provided for transportation and utility companies and for the composite index of sixty-five industrial, transportation, and utility companies.

Standard & Poor's 500 Composite Price Index

This index covers prices of 500 companies on the New York Stock Exchange, Nasdaq, and AMEX. Of the total index, companies on the New York Stock Exchange account for 92 percent of the market value, the Nasdaq for 7 percent, and the AMEX for 1 percent. They include large and medium-size companies, and account for 67 percent of the market value of over 5,000 publicly traded stocks in 1991. The index reflects the price of an average share of common stock based on the capitalized structure of companies during 1941–43, when the average market value was $10. Component indexes of the 500 composite are provided for companies in the industrial, transportation, utilities, and financial groups. Supplementary indexes based on different categories of products and stock are available for companies in the consumer and capital goods industries, high-grade common stocks, and low-priced common stocks.

Wilshire 5000 Equity Index

This index covers prices of over 6,000 companies including all New York Stock Exchange, Nasdaq, and AMEX companies. Canadian stocks are excluded beginning in 1993. The "5,000" in the title has become outdated, as the index has expanded to over 6,000 companies. The index reflects the market value based on capitalized structure of companies as of December 31, 1980, when the market value was $1,404.596 billion (the base index is 12/31/80 = 1,404.596). It is the most comprehensive measure of common stock values traded in major markets. Of the total index, companies on the New York Stock Exchange account for approximately 85 percent of the market value, the Nasdaq for 13 percent, and the AMEX for 2 percent.

Dividend Yields

The dividend yield is based on cash dividends only (stock dividends are excluded). Dividend yields are provided for four of the six stock market price indexes: New York Stock Exchange, Dow Jones, Standard & Poor's, and Wilshire.

Methodology

As noted above, the stock price indexes are adjusted to eliminate the price effect of changes in the capitalized financial structure of companies, such as stock splits, mergers, and spinoffs. This maintains the capitalized structure of each company as it was when the company was included in the index. The New York Stock Exchange, Nasdaq, AMEX, Standard & Poor's, and Wilshire indexes are weighted using the market value of the companies in the index as weights. The market value of a company is the number of its common stock shares outstanding multiplied by the price per share. The Dow Jones index is weighted using the price per share of the companies in the index as weights.

New York Stock Exchange Composite Index

The index indicates the percent change in the market value of all listed stocks on the New York Stock Exchange between the base period (December 31, 1965) and the current period. The ratio change in the market value from the base period to the current period multiplied by 50 gives the current index. The number 50 is close to the average price of all stocks in the base period. The stocks are averaged in proportion to the market value of each company, which gives price movements of firms with large market values more weight than those with small market values. New companies are added and old companies are deleted from the index as the companies are listed and delisted on the New York Stock Exchange.

Nasdaq Composite Index

The index indicates the percent change in the market value of all stocks traded on the Nasdaq stock market between the base period (February 5, 1971 = 100) and the current period. The ratio change in the market value from the base period to the current period multiplied by 100 gives the current index. The stocks are averaged in proportion to the market values of each company, which gives price movements of firms with large market values more weight than those with small market values. New companies are added and old companies are deleted from the index as the companies are incorporated in or removed from the Nasdaq system.

AMEX Market Value Index

The index indicates the percent change in the market value plus the reinvestment of dividends paid by all stocks listed on the AMEX between the base period (July 5, 1983 = 50) and the current period. This assumes the dividends are reinvested in the index, which results in a "total return" index. The ratio change in the market value and the reinvested dividends from the base period to the current period multiplied by 50 gives the current index. The number 50 represents the index level in the base period. The stocks are average proportionately to the market values of each company, which gives price movements of firms with large market values more weight than those with small market values. New companies are added and old companies are deleted from the index as the companies are listed and delisted on the AMEX.

Dow Jones Industrial Average

The index indicates the average price per share of thirty stocks on the New York Stock Exchange. The stocks are averaged arithmetically according to the price per share of each company, which gives more weight to price movements of companies with high prices per share than those with low prices per share. New companies are substituted for old companies mainly because of mergers, but also to update the index to better represent large widely held companies.

Standard & Poor's 500 Composite Price Index

The index represents the percent change in the market value of 500 stocks on the New York Stock Exchange, Nasdaq, and AMEX between the base period (1941—43) and the current period. The selection of companies for inclusion in the index is based on an assessment of the following factors: position in the industry, market value size, distribution of shares among shareholders, trading volume, emerging companies or industries and stock price movements. The ratio change in the market value from the base period to the current period multiplied by 10 gives the current index. The number 10 is the assigned market value for the base period. The stocks are averaged in proportion to the market values of each company, which gives price movements of firms with large market values more weight than those with small market values. New companies are substituted for old companies because of mergers and bankruptcies and to update the representation of stocks to more closely reflect the composition of companies in the industrial, transportation, utilities, and financial groupings of the New York Stock Exchange Composite Index.

Wilshire 500 Equity Index

The index indicates the percent change in the market value of all stocks listed on the New York Stock Exchange, Nasdaq and AMEX between the base period (December 31, 1980) and the current period. The ratio change in the market value from the base period to the current period multiplied by 1,404.596 gives the current index. The number 1,404.596 represents the market value in the base period. The stocks are averaged in proportion to the market values of each company, which gives price movements of firms with large market values more weight than those with small market values. New companies are added and old companies are deleted from the index as the companies are listed and delisted on the New York Stock Exchange, Nasdaq, and AMEX.

New York Stock Exchange Composite Dividend Yield

The annual dividend yield is the percentage that the accumulated dividend payments during the latest twelve months is of the closing price on the last Wednesday of March, June, September, and

December. The calendar-year dividend yield is the twelve months ending in December. The relative importance of the various companies is based on the number of their shares outstanding.

Dow Jones Industrial Average Dividend Yield

Dividends represent a moving average of annualized dividends of the most recent four quarters, and the dividend yield is the percentage this four-quarter average is of the current market value of the stocks at the end of the quarter. The annual dividend yield is the average of the four quarters.

Standard & Poor's 500 Composite Index Dividend Yield

The dividend yield is the percentage that the annualized quarterly cash dividends are of the current market value of the stocks at the end of the quarter. The annual dividend yield is the average of the four quarters.

Wilshire 5000 Equity Dividend Yield

The dividend yield is the percentage that the actual monthly cash dividends are of the current market value of the stocks at the end of each month. This is much lower than an annualized dividend yield. The annual dividend yield is the sum of the yields for the twelve calendar months.

Accuracy

There are no estimates of sampling or revision error for the stock market price indexes and dividend yields. The New York Stock Exchange Composite Index, Nasdaq Composite Index, AMEX Market Value Index, and the Wilshire 5000 Equity Index are based on the universe of firms, and thus are not subject to sampling error.

Relevance

Stock prices influence the course of future economic activity because they affect *retail sales, home sales,* and *plant and equip-*

ment expenditures. High or rising stock prices encourage consumer and investment spending because they promote optimism about the economy. Low or falling stock prices discourage such spending because of the pessimistic outlook they foster. Stock prices reflect changes in confidence in the economy, as do *consumer attitude indexes* and *business optimism indexes.* The Standard & Poor's 500 Composite Price Index is a component of the leading index of the *leading, coincident, and lagging indexes.*

Stock prices affect consumer spending because of the effect of stocks on personal wealth. Households feel richer and more willing to spend when the value of their paper stockholdings is high than when the value of their stockholdings is low. Stock prices also influence investment spending because high stock prices make it easier for businesses to finance new investment by selling new equity stock or by obtaining loans through new bond sales or other debt financing. The choice of equity or debt financing is determined by differences in the cost of raising funds (dividends on stock versus interest on bonds) and by the effect of selling new stock on the ownership control of the company. Generally, it is easier to sell new stock when stock prices are high or rising than when they are weak.

Dividend yields implicitly incorporate investor perceptions of future trends in stock prices. Low yields suggest expectations of large or long-term price increases, and high yields indicate anticipated small price increases or long-term price declines. Dividend yields also affect patterns of investment. Thus, low yields may drive investors out of stocks into bonds, real estate, or other opportunities that have an expected higher return, while high yields may entice investors into stocks, both because of the high return and the anticipation that the high yield will stimulate higher stock prices.

Recent Trends

Stock market prices rose in nine or ten years during the twelve-year 1980–92 period, depending on the particular stock market

Table 46.1

Stock Price Indexes and Dividend Yields

Price indexes

	New York Stock Exchange Composite Index (12/31/65 = 50)	Nasdaq Composite Index (2/5/71 = 100)	AMEX Market Value Index (7/5/83 = 50)	Dow Jones Industrial Average	Standard & Poor's 500 Composite Price Index (1941–43 = 10)	Wilshire 5000 Equity Index (12/31/80 = 1,404.596)
1980	68.10	170.28	152.38	891.41	118.78	1,229.610
1981	74.02	203.49	171.78	932.92	128.05	1,340.827
1982	68.93	190.67	142.63	884.36	119.71	1,239.631
1983	92.63	286.01	217.28	1,190.34	160.41	1,691.623
1984	92.46	246.91	206.99	1,178.48	160.46	1,640.776
1985	108.09	293.37	231.63	1,328.23	186.84	1,945.067
1986	136.00	369.42	266.40	1,792.76	236.34	2,441.717
1987	161.70	399.94	312.79	2,275.99	286.83	2,831.136
1988	149.91	376.45	297.04	2,060.82	265.79	2,656.656
1989	180.02	439.95	357.54	2,508.91	322.84	3,199.643
1990	183.46	403.77	336.21	2,678.94	334.59	3,162.567
1991	206.33	502.01	365.15	2,929.33	376.18	3,659.137
1992	229.01	603.93	392.46	3,284.29	415.74	4,057.938
			Annual percent change			
1980	16.8%	23.4%	52.9%	5.6%	15.3%	19.5%
1981	8.7	19.5	12.7	4.7	7.8	9.0
1982	-6.9	-6.3	-17.0	-5.2	-6.5	-7.5
1983	34.4	50.0	52.3	34.6	34.0	36.5
1984	-0.2	-13.7	-4.7	-1.0	0.0	-3.0
1985	16.9	18.8	11.9	12.7	16.4	18.5

Year						
1986	25.8	25.9	15.0	35.0	26.5	25.5
1987	18.9	8.3	17.4	27.0	21.4	15.9
1988	-7.3	-5.9	-5.0	-9.5	-7.3	-6.2
1989	20.1	16.9	20.4	21.7	21.5	20.4
1990	1.9	-8.2	-6.0	6.8	3.6	-1.2
1991	12.5	24.3	8.6	9.3	12.4	15.7
1992	11.0	20.3	7.5	12.1	10.5	10.9

Dividend yields
(percent)

Year	New York Stock Exchange Composite Index*	Dow Jones Industrial Average	Standard & Poor's 500 Composite Index	Wilshire 5000 Equity Index
1980	5.4%	5.6%	5.3%	4.8%
1981	6.7	6.4	5.2	5.0
1982	5.2	5.2	5.8	5.1
1983	4.4	4.5	4.4	4.0
1984	4.5	5.0	4.6	4.3
1985	3.6	4.0	4.3	4.2
1986	3.4	3.5	3.5	3.2
1987	3.4	3.7	3.1	3.0
1988	3.6	3.7	3.6	4.1
1989	3.2	3.7	3.5	3.4
1990	3.7	3.9	3.6	3.4
1991	2.4	3.0	3.2	3.0
1992	3.0	3.1	3.0	2.6

*Because of a change in methodology in 1985, the figures are not comparable to those of earlier years.
Note: Dividend yields are not available for the Nasdaq and AMEX indexes.

index (Table 46.1). Declines occurred in 1982 in all six indexes, in 1984 in five indexes (one index had no change), in 1988 in all six indexes, and in 1990 in three indexes. The Dow Jones had the largest increase (268 percent) and the AMEX the smallest increase (158 percent) from 1980 to 1992. The 1980—92 changes in the other indexes were much closer to the high growth of the Dow Jones than to the low growth of the AMEX.

Dividend yields generally declined during 1980—92. From levels of 5—6 percent in the early 1980s, they dropped to 3 percent in 1991—92.

References from Primary Data Sources

American Stock Exchange. Undated. "AMEX Market Value Index."

Dow Jones & Co., Inc. 1993. *How to Read Stock Market Quotations and the Dow Jones Averages: A Non-Professional's Guide*. Revised edition.

National Association of Securities Dealers Automated Quotations. Undated. "Nasdaq Composite Index Description."

New York Stock Exchange, Inc. 1993. *Fact Book for the year 1992*.

Standard & Poor's Corporation. 1992. *S & P 500: 1992 Directory*.

Wilshire Associates. Undated. "Wilshire 500 Notes."

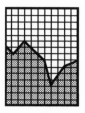

47
UNEMPLOYMENT

Unemployment counts the number of persons without jobs who are available for and actively seeking work. It covers all persons sixteen years and older who lost or quit previous jobs as well as school graduates, students, and others with no work experience or who re-enter the workplace. The unemployment rate is the percentage that unemployed persons are of the labor force, and the labor force is defined as the sum of the employed and unemployed. As a relative measure of additional workers available for employment, the unemployment rate reflects the slack or tightness in labor markets.

Where and When Available

Unemployment measures are provided monthly by the Bureau of Labor Statistics in the U.S. Department of Labor. The data are published in a press release and in two BLS monthly journals, the *Monthly Labor Review* and *Employment and Earnings.* Secondary sources include *Economic Indicators,* the *Survey of Current Business*, and the *Federal Reserve Bulletin*.

The figures are available on the third Friday after the week containing the twelfth of the month, which falls on the first or second Friday of the month following the month to which they refer. On the day the monthly numbers are released, the commissioner of labor statistics reports on recent unemployment and employment trends to the Joint Economic Committee of Congress. The monthly data are revised every January for the previous five years based on updated monthly seasonal factors.

Content

Unemployment figures measure the number of persons sixteen years and older who do not have jobs and are available for and actively seeking work. The labor force is defined as the sum of employed and unemployed persons living in the United States. Both citizens and foreigners are included. The unemployment rate is the percentage of persons in the labor force who are unemployed and is calculated by the following formula:

$$\text{Unemployment rate} = \frac{\text{Unemployed persons}}{\text{Employed + unemployed persons (labor force)}} \times 100.$$

Employed persons are defined as nonfarm and farm workers sixteen years and older who are not institutionalized. The definition includes full-time and part-time employees at paid jobs who work at least one hour a week, self-employed workers, and unpaid workers in family businesses who work at least fifteen hours a week. (These family workers are assumed to share in the profits of the business.) Because the employment measures count persons rather than jobs, individuals holding two or more jobs are counted only once—in the job they work the most hours during a week. Persons who are temporarily not working because of illness, vacation, strike, or lockout are included as employed whether or not they are paid while they are absent from work. (These definitions differ from an alternative measure discussed in *employment*; contrasts in the two measures are analyzed in that section.)

Unemployed persons are defined as those who have sought a job at least once in the previous four weeks through such actions as applying for work with an employer, answering a newspaper advertisement, visiting an employment agency, or checking with a friend or relative. They include individuals who collect unemployment insurance as well as those who are not eligible for unemployment insurance (for example, formerly employed workers who have exhausted their unemployment insurance or former students who have not accumulated job-related unemployment benefits). Students are counted as unemployed if they sought work and are available at least for part-time jobs.

Discouraged workers are not counted as unemployed. These are workers who say they want a job, but are not seeking work because they feel there are no jobs available in the local labor market or believe they do not qualify for the existing job vacancies. Persons are classified as discouraged only if they looked for a job at least once during the past twelve months.

There are two official national unemployment rates. One covers civilian workers and resident armed forces (stationed in the United States), while the other covers only civilian workers. Unemployment rates are also calculated for large states and metropolitan areas and by demographic components of workers such as age, race, gender, and marital status of adults in the household.

Table 47.1 shows the two official unemployment rate figures and six supplementary analytic measures. The official figures, referred to as U−5a and U−5b, differ only in that one covers the total of civilian workers and the U.S. armed forces stationed in the United States, while the other covers only civilian workers. The unemployment rate for the total is typically 0.1 percentage point lower than the civilian rate. The six supplementary measures calculate rates based on duration of unemployment, reason for unemployment, age of the unemployed, and full-time or part-time work status; rates including discouraged workers are also provided. These measures provide a range of unemployment rates significantly below and above the official rates.

The unemployment figures are seasonally adjusted.

Methodology

Unemployment figures are obtained from a survey of a sample of households conducted for the Bureau of Labor Statistics by the

Table 47.1

Unemployment: Alternative Definitions
(percent)

		1992:4Q[a]
U–1	Persons unemployed 15 weeks or longer as a percent of the civilian labor force	2.8
U–2	Job losers as a percent of the civilian labor force[a]	4.1
U–3	Unemployed persons 25 years and over as a percent of the civilian labor force	6.1
U–4	Unemployed full-time jobseekers as a percent of the full-time civilian labor force	7.0
U–5a*	Total unemployed (16 years and older) as a percent of the labor force, including the resident armed forces	7.2
U–5b*	Total unemployment (16 years and older) as a percent of the civilian labor force	7.3
U–6	Total full-time jobseekers plus 1/2 part-time jobseekers plus 1/2 total on part-time for economic reasons as a percent of the civilian labor force less 1/2 of the part-time labor force[c]	9.9
U–7	U–6 plus discouraged workers as a percent of the civilian labor force plus discouraged workers less 1/2 of the part-time labor force	10.7

* Official unemployment rates.
[a]Fourth quarter of 1992.
[b]Job losers are unemployed because they were laid off or fired.
[c]Part-time for economic reasons refers to persons who wish to work full-time but who are working less than 35 hours a week because of slack work, materials shortages, or other factors beyond their control.

Census Bureau. In 1992, of 96 million total American households, the survey sample included approximately 60,000 households. Census interviewers visit or telephone households during the calendar week that includes the nineteenth day of the month and ask respondents about their labor force activity during the week that includes the twelfth day of the month.

The sample is representative of the distribution of households in small and large metropolitan and rural areas. It undergoes major revision every ten years to reflect the decennial population census. The sample is based on the 1990 census of population beginning in 1994. The figures also are updated annually on a limited basis to reflect current changes in residential locations due to new construction. *Housing starts* data are used to make these revisions. Four to five percent of the sample households are not interviewed because the residents are not found at home after repeated calls or they refuse to participate in the survey.

In order to reduce the reporting burden on any group of households, the sample is divided into eight subsamples (panels) that are rotated over a sixteen-month period. Each subsample is surveyed for four consecutive months, is then dropped from the survey for eight months, and subsequently resurveyed for the following four months. At the end of the sixteen months, the subsample is eliminated from the sample and replaced with a new panel of households. The result of this procedure is that every month 25 percent of households in the sample are either new to the survey or are returning to it after an eight-month hiatus; correspondingly, 25 percent of the sample households drop out of the survey every month.

The unemployment rate is raised a few tenths of a percentage point due to new survey questions and interviewing techniques beginning in 1994. This is a one-time increase in the unemployment level arising from the new survey procedures. More generally, the new questionnaire and interviewing techniques result in a one-time rise in the absolute levels of both the civilian employment and unemployment components of the labor force because they identify more marginal workers.

Accuracy

In nine of ten cases, a monthly change in the unemployment rate of at least plus or minus 0.2 percentage point is regarded as statistically significant. Although a change of zero or plus or minus 0.1 percentage point is not statistically significant for one month, cumulative changes of 0.1 percentage point in the same direction for two or more consecutive months are statistically significant.

Relevance

The unemployment rate is a major indicator of the degree to which the economy provides jobs for those seeking work. It is a key consideration when the president, Congress, and Federal Reserve Board determine whether economic growth should be stimulated or restrained. In general, there is an inverse relationship between unemployment and the *gross domestic product*, which is referred to as Okun's Law. In the 1990s, this relationship functions roughly as follows: the yearly unemployment rate remains the same if annual real GDP increases by 2.5 percent, with every 1 percentage point growth in real GDP above 2.5 percent lowering the unemployment rate by 0.5 percentage point, and every 1 percentage point growth in real GDP below 2.5 percentage point raising unemployment by 0.5 percentage point. These figures reflect the relationship that averages out over the years but does not hold in every year.

The unemployment rate is also used to analyze trade-offs between unemployment and inflation. In an adaptation of the concept referred to as the Phillips Curve, the unemployment rate is contrasted with the *consumer price index* in an attempt to find a balance between lower unemployment and higher inflation. This kind of analysis is used to assess goals for minimum unemployment and inflation rates such as are included in the Full Employment and Balanced Growth Act of 1978 (Humphrey–Hawkins Act).

In addition, the unemployment rate determines when federally financed supplementary unemployment benefits go into effect for

Table 47.2

Unemployment Rates (percent)

	All workers: civilian and armed forces	Civilian workers
1980	7.0%	7.1%
1981	7.5	7.6
1982	9.5	9.7
1983	9.5	9.6
1984	7.4	7.5
1985	7.1	7.2
1986	6.9	7.0
1987	6.1	6.2
1988	5.4	5.5
1989	5.2	5.3
1990	5.4	5.5
1991	6.6	6.7
1992	7.3	7.4

particular localities when unemployment is persistently high. These benefits supplement regular state-provided unemployment benefits that have been exhausted and are triggered by a formula that includes both the national unemployment rate and state and metropolitan area unemployment rates.

Recent Trends

The unemployment rate fluctuated with a range of 4 percentage points during 1980–92 (Table 47.2). After rising to a peak of 9.5 percent in 1982–83 (all workers), it declined to a low of 5.2 percent in 1989, and then rose to 7.3 percent in 1992. The all worker rate was 0.1–0.2 percentage point lower than the civilian worker rate over the thirteen-year period.

References from Primary Data Source

Bowie, Chester E.; Lawrence S. Cahoon; and Elizabeth A. Martin. 1993. "Overhauling the Current Population Survey: Evaluating changes in the estimates." *Monthly Labor Review. September.*

Bregger, John E. 1984. "The Current Population Survey: A historical perspective and BLS' role." *Monthly Labor Review.* June.

Bregger, John E., and Cathryn S. Dippo. 1993. "Overhauling the Current Population Survey: Why is it necessary to change?" *Monthly Labor Review.* September.

Bureau of Labor Statistics, U.S. Department of Labor. 1992. *BLS Handbook of Methods.* Chapter 1. September.

Polivka, Anne E., and Jennifer M. Rothgeb. 1993. "Overhauling the Current Population Survey: Redesigning the questionnaire." *Monthly Labor Review.* September.

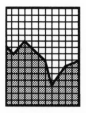

**48
UNIT LABOR COSTS**

Unit labor costs (ULC) represent the relationship of labor costs per hour to *productivity*. When employee compensation per hour increases more (or declines less) than productivity, ULC increases. Similarly, when compensation increases less (or declines more) than productivity, ULC declines. ULC may also be considered as compensation per unit of output, or the share that compensation is of output.

Where and When Available

The measure of unit labor costs (ULC) is provided on a quarterly basis by the Bureau of Labor Statistics in the U.S. Department of Labor. The data are published in a monthly press release and in two BLS monthly journals, the *Monthly Labor Review* and *Employment and Earnings*. Secondary sources include *Economic Indicators* and the *Survey of Current Business*.

Preliminary figures for the immediately preceding quarter are provided in the second month following the quarter (May for the first quarter, August for the second quarter, November for the third quarter, and February for the fourth quarter). The data are available at the same time as the *productivity* figures and follow soon after publication of the *gross domestic product* measures. The data are initially revised in the subsequent two months. Additional revisions are made annually every September, and still more comprehensive benchmark revisions are made about every six years.

Content

ULC are defined as the ratio of compensation per hour to *productivity*. This is equivalent to the ratio of compensation to output, because the per hour terms in the numerator and denominator cancel out algebraically as shown in the following formula:

$$\text{ULC} = \frac{\dfrac{\text{Compensation*}}{\text{Labor hours*}}}{\text{Productivity}} = \frac{\dfrac{\text{Compensation*}}{\text{Labor hours†}}}{\dfrac{\text{Real GDP‡}}{\text{Labor hours†}}} = \frac{\text{Compensation}}{\text{Real GDP}} = \frac{\text{Compensation}}{\text{per unit of output}}$$

   * Wages and fringe benefits and the wage component of self-employment income.
   † Paid employees, the self-employed, and unpaid family workers.
   ‡ Business sector or nonfarm business sector in the gross domestic product.

The employee compensation component of ULC covers wages and salaries, fringe benefits, and the wage element of income from self-employment (it excludes the profit component of self-employment). ULC are provided as an index.

Separate figures are developed for the business sector, the nonfarm business sector, and the total of all manufacturing industries. They are based on real *gross domestic product* data adjusted to eliminate those components of the GDP that would cause an inappropriate measure of productivity because (1) the output indicator used is also an input measure, or (2) the output and input data are inconsistent. The business sector includes for-profit enterprise and government enterprise; it excludes not-for-profit organizations, general government (general government is financed mainly by taxes while government enterprises are financed mainly by user fees), household employment, owner-occupied housing, and profit flows of American companies abroad into the United States. The nonfarm business sector figures also exclude farming.

The ULC indexes are currently based on 1982 = 100.

The ULC figures are seasonally adjusted.

Methodology

The compensation data are obtained from the income side of the *gross domestic product*, which in turn is based on *employment* payroll and household surveys, *average weekly hours*, and average hourly earnings. An additional estimate is made for the wage component of self-employment income based on data on hours worked by proprietors from the household survey of *employment*; the estimate assumes that proprietors work for the same hourly earnings as employees in the industry. Productivity is based on figures for the *gross domestic product, employment,* and *average weekly hours* as described in *productivity*.

Accuracy

There are no estimates of sampling or revision error for the ULC figures. However, because the ULC are closely linked to the *productivity* measures, ULC revision error is assumed to mirror that of productivity. In ninteen of twenty cases, the second quarterly revision (two months after the preliminary figure) of labor hour productivity differs from the preliminary index by plus or minus two index points.

Relevance

ULC figures indicate inflationary cost pressures. When ULC rise significantly, businesses may raise prices to maintain profit margins. Analogously, when ULC rise slightly or decline, profit margins can be maintained with little or no price increases or even price declines. There is a two-way street between ULC and prices,

Table 48.1

Unit Labor Costs (annual percent change)

	Business sector	Nonfarm business sector	Manufacturing
1980	11.7%	11.6%	14.3%
1981	8.0	8.6	6.1
1982	7.4	7.4	5.2
1983	1.5	1.5	0.4
1984	1.9	1.9	2.0
1985	3.0	3.3	1.8
1986	2.8	3.0	1.4
1987	2.6	2.5	− 4.0
1988	3.3	3.3	1.5
1989	4.3	4.3	3.5
1990	5.0	5.1	4.1
1991	3.8	3.9	3.6
1992	1.7	2.0	0.1

however, because ULC are affected by cost-of-living wage increases made to compensate for inflation. Moreover, in addition to ULC, prices reflect demand for goods and services, production costs other than ULC such as purchased materials prices, interest rates, the impact of weather on food, and the effect on energy prices of actions taken by the Organization of Petroleum Exporting Countries to control oil production. Thus, ULC are an important, but not necessarily determining, factor of price movements and *inflation*. As in the case of *productivity*, quarterly changes in ULC reflect short-term movements in output associated with changes in economic activity over the business cycle, and consequently ULC movements over several quarters should be observed to determine more basic trends.

Recent Trends

Unit labor costs showed three overall patterns during 1980–92 (Table 48.1). There was a sharp fall in the annual rate of increase in the early 1980s, declining from 12 percent in 1980 to 2 percent in

1984 in the business sector. This was followed by an upward trend that peaked at 5 percent in 1990, which then declined to 2 percent in 1992. Similar although not identical movements occurred in manufacturing industries.

Reference from Primary Data Source

Bureau of Labor Statistics, U.S. Department of Labor. 1992. *BLS Handbook of Methods*. Chapter 10. September.

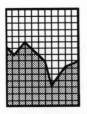

49
VALUE OF THE DOLLAR

The value of the dollar represents the foreign exchange price of the U.S. dollar in relation to other nations' currencies. If the dollar rises in value (and offsetting changes in the prices of exported and imported goods and services are not made), U.S. exports become more expensive to foreigners and imports become less expensive to Americans. If the dollar falls in value (and offsetting changes in the price of exported and imported goods and services are not made), U.S. exports become less expensive to foreigners and imports become more expensive to Americans. Various measures of the value of the dollar show different movements because they include different countries and are based on different concepts and methodologies. The data are provided in nominal values (market exchange rates) and in real values (purchasing power corrected for inflation).

Where and When Available

Monthly indexes of the value of the dollar are provided by the Federal Reserve Board, Morgan Guaranty Trust Company of New York, and Federal Reserve Bank of Dallas. The FRB index is published in a press release and in the monthly *Federal Reserve Bulletin*; the Morgan index is published in the bimonthly *World Financial Markets*; and the FR Dallas index is published monthly in *Trade-Weighted Value of the Dollar*.

The FRB figures are available weekly, for the previous week, and monthly, two days after the month to which they refer. The Morgan index is available daily. The IMF and FR Dallas figures are available thirty days after the month to which they refer. Measures of the real value of the dollar are published along with the nominal figures by Morgan and the FR Dallas; real values for the FRB index are available annually in the *Economic Report of the President*.

The Federal Reserve Board and Morgan indexes are not routinely revised, except for the Morgan real effective exchange rate, which is revised on an ongoing basis as additional price data become available. The FR Dallas indexes are revised for the previous five months, and the index weights are revised every year.

Content

The value of the dollar represents the combined average foreign exchange price of the currencies of a group of nations in relation to the U.S. dollar. In contrast to the nominal values, which focus on the exchange value of the currencies, the real values measure the rate of exchange in terms of the constant-dollar cost of U.S. exports and imports adjusted for *inflation* at home and abroad. The FRB and Morgan indexes include ten and fifteen industrial nations, respectively, and the FR Dallas index includes all of the 131 industrial and industrializing nations that trade with the United States (Table 49.1). Industrial nations have production technologies similar to those in the United States, while industrializing nations have less advanced technologies. The main difference among the indexes is the much more comprehensive coverage of the FR Dallas index. (Additional indexes developed by Morgan include some industrializing nations.)

Real value of the dollar measures are also provided for the Federal Reserve Board, Morgan, and FR Dallas indexes. The base periods of the value of the dollar indexes currently are: Federal Reserve Board (March 1973 = 100); Morgan Guaranty

Table 49.1

Value-of-the-Dollar Indexes: Country Coverage

Federal Reserve Board	Morgan Guaranty Trust Co. of New York	Federal Reserve Bank of Dallas
(10 nations)	(18 nations)	(131 nations. All U.S. trading partners with market economies.)
—	Australia	
—	Austria	
Belgium	Belgium	
Canada	Canada	
—	Denmark	
—	Finland	
France	France	
Germany	Germany	
—	Greece	
Italy	Italy	
Japan	Japan	
Netherlands	Netherlands	
—	Norway	
—	Portugal	
—		
—	Spain	
Sweden	Sweden	
Switzerland	Switzerland	
United Kingdom	United Kingdom	

(1990 = 100); and FR Dallas (1985 first quarter = 100).

The value of the dollar indexes are not seasonally adjusted.

Methodology

The three value-of-the-dollar indexes all use geometric averaging to calculate the percent change in each nation's currency between the base period and the current period. Geometric averaging (as opposed to arithmetic averaging) ensures that currencies having large changes in foreign exchange values do not influence the index more than currencies having small changes. (Technically, geometric averaging is done by taking the nth root of n numbers, and arithmetic averaging is the sum of n numbers divided by n.)

The indexes differ in the weights used to combine the foreign currencies into an index (see "Index Numbers" in the Introduction). In the definition of weights, "global" trade refers to a nation's trade with all other nations, and "bilateral" trade refers to a nation's trade with one other nation. There are also differences in the price indexes used to estimate the real value of the dollar.

The FRB weights are each nation's global export and import trade in manufactured, mineral, and agricultural goods in the 1972–76 period, valued in dollars. The real value of the dollar is based on differential movements in the *consumer price index* in the United States and other nations.

The *Morgan* weights are bilateral export and import trade between the United States and other nations for manufactured goods in 1990, valued in dollars, beginning in 1987. Prior to 1987, the weights are 1980 trade volumes. The real value of the dollar is based on differential price movements of *producer price indexes* for intermediate and finished manufactured goods (except food and fuel) in the United States and other nations; for some nations, intermediate goods prices are used because finished goods prices are not available.

The *FR Dallas* weights are the bilateral export and import trade between the United States and each nation in manufactured, mineral, and agricultural goods on a current basis, valued in dollars. The weights are changed every year based on moving averages of the trade in the most recent three years, in contrast to the other indexes, where weights are fixed for a single period. The real value of the dollar is based on differential movements of the *consumer price index* in the United States and other nations.

Accuracy

There are no estimates of sampling or revision error for the value-of-the-dollar indexes.

Relevance

The value of the dollar affects the U.S. economy through several avenues. It determines the competitive position of U.S. goods in export markets and domestically, and also affects inflation and Federal Reserve Board monetary policies.

A "low dollar" tends to boost production and inflation at home while a "high" dollar tends to lower production and inflation, although changes in the dollar are not transmitted to prices in a one-to-one relationship. Part or all of the dollar changes may be offset by opposing changes in export and import prices as American and foreign exporters try to maintain market shares and profit margins. Thus, a fall in the dollar may be followed by some increase in U.S. export prices and in import prices, while a rise in the dollar may be followed by some decrease in export prices and in import prices. The extent of these "pass throughs" of price changes that partly or fully offset changes in the value of the dollar can be calculated in relation to *import and export price indexes*.

The value of the dollar also affects the monetary policies by which the Federal Reserve Board influences the economy. For example, large deficits in the *balance of trade* are financed, in part, by foreigners who invest funds in the Untied States. If the dollar declines or is expected to decline in the future, this funding may be cut back. In this situation, the Federal Reserve is faced with the dilemma of accelerating growth in the *money supply*, which may heat up *inflation*, or allowing a slower growth in the money supply, which may raise *interest rates* and bring on a recession. For the Federal Reserve Board, this international dimension complicates the development of appropriate policies for the domestic economy.

Recent Trends

The Federal Reserve Board and Morgan Guaranty indexes moved in similar although not identical patterns, while the Federal Reserve Bank of Dallas index moved very differently during 1980–92 (Table 49.2). These distinctions were more evident in the nominal than in the real indexes. The FRB index had the largest changes in the year-to-year movements and the FRB Dallas index the smallest, with the Morgan index midway but closer to the FRB index.

Table 49.2

Value-of-the-Dollar Indexes: Nominal and Real
(annual percent change)

Nominal	Federal Reserve Board	Morgan Guaranty Trust Co. of New York	Federal Reserve Bank of Dallas
1980	−0.8	−0.2	2.0
1981	18.3	9.9	8.1
1982	12.8	10.2	13.5
1983	7.5	4.0	13.2
1984	10.3	7.1	14.9
1985	3.5	3.8	12.4
1986	−21.5	−16.6	−2.1
1987	−13.6	−11.2	−0.3
1988	−4.3	−6.7	1.4
1989	6.4	3.9	9.8
1990	−9.6	−4.6	8.6
1991	0.8	−1.5	6.8
1992	−3.6	−1.5	6.0
Real			
1988	−3.0	−6.6	−7.4
1989	7.0	5.5	1.7
1990	−8.9	−2.2	−1.7
1991	0.6	−1.2	−0.4
1992	−3.7	0.1	−0.3

References from Primary Data Sources

Board of Governors of the Federal Reserve System. 1978. "Index of Weighted-Average Exchange Value of the U.S. Dollar: Revision." *Federal Reserve Bulletin*. August.

Cox, W. Michael. 1986. "A New Alternative Trade-Weighted Dollar Exchange Rate Index." *Economic Review*. Federal Reserve Bank of Dallas. September.

Cox, W. Michael. 1987. "A Comprehensive New Real Dollar Exchange Rate Index." *Economic Review*. Federal Reserve Bank of Dallas. March.

Morgan Guaranty Trust Company of New York. 1993. "Effective exchange rates: OECD Currencies." *Economic Research Note*. December 30.

Pauls, B. Dianne. 1987. "Measuring the Foreign-Exchange Value of the Dollar." *Federal Reserve Bulletin*. June.

INDEX

About the Author

Norman Frumkin is an economic consultant in Washington, D.C. He is also the author of *Tracking America's Economy*.